New Political Economy

T0270754

Edited by
Richard McIntyre
University of Rhode Island

A Routledge Series

New Political Economy

Richard McIntyre, *General Editor*

MARKET SENSE
Toward a New Economics of
Markets and Society

Philip Kozel

Routledge
New York & London

Published in 2006 by
Routledge
Taylor & Francis Group
270 Madison Ave,
New York NY 10016

Published in Great Britain by
Routledge
Taylor & Francis Group
2 Park Square,
Milton Park, Abingdon,
Oxon, OX14 4RN

© 2006 by Taylor & Francis Group, LLC
Routledge is an imprint of Taylor & Francis Group

Transferred to Digital Printing 2010

International Standard Book Number-10: 0-415-97799-1 (Hardcover)
International Standard Book Number-13: 978-0-415-97799-9 (Hardcover)
Library of Congress Card Number 2005025831

Library of Congress Cataloging-in-Publication Data

Kozel, Philip.
　　Market sense : toward a new economics of markets and society / Philip Kozel.
　　　　p. cm. -- (New political economy)
　　Includes bibliographical references and index.
　　ISBN 0-415-97799-1
　　1. Free enterprise. 2. Commodity exchanges. 3. Globalization. I. Title. II. Series.

HB95.K69 2006
381--dc22　　　　　　　　　　　　　　　　　　　　　　　　　　　　　　2005025831

ISBN10: 0-415-97799-1 (hbk)
ISBN10: 0-415-88408-X (pbk)

ISBN13: 978-0-415-97799-9 (hbk)
ISBN13: 978-0-415-88408-2 (pbk)

Taylor & Francis Group
is the Academic Division of Informa plc.

Visit the Taylor & Francis Web site at
http://www.taylorandfrancis.com

and the Routledge Web site at
http://www.routledge-ny.com

Contents

Acknowledgments

I am grateful to all the people that contributed to this book. Erik Olsen and Yahya Madra proved invaluable in the early stages of writing, and Ceren Özselçuk, Kenan Ercel, Marian Aguiar and Esra Erden all read earlier drafts of various chapters and provided encouragement and thoughtful comments. Ric McIntyre gave numerous helpful suggestions on the manuscript. I appreciated Necia Warner's editing skills, thoughtful comments and good cheer. Ben Holtzman at Routledge was a pleasure to work with.

The members of AESA, the Association for Economic and Social Analysis, provided a great deal of intellectual support. George DeMartino in particular deserves special thanks, however, for he provided invaluable feedback throughout the writing process. It is difficult to express my gratitude for Stephen Resnick and Richard Wolff. As teachers, both Rick and Steve consistently provided a fertile ground for intellectual inquiry and the stimulus to begin digging for myself. As mentors, both exuded a degree of patience truly noteworthy and supplied a supportive intellectual environment. As radicals and philosophers, their energy and intellectual curiosity provided consistent inspiration for my own developments.

Chapter One
Markets and Market Sense.

Among the more compelling metaphors for society is the market. States are viewed as bartering protection and justice for tax revenues, social interactions are termed exchanges, society is considered a social compact, and even such intimate institutions as marriage are deemed contractual. Perhaps the popularity of this metaphor is due to the impressive reach of markets into daily life.

—Samuel Bowles and Herbert Gintis, *Democracy and Capitalism*

Under the market system, people act voluntarily and primarily for financial gain or personal satisfaction. Firms buy factors and produce outputs, selecting inputs and outputs in order to maximize their profits. Consumers supply factors and buy consumer goods to maximize their satisfactions. Agreements on production and consumption are made voluntarily and with the use of money, at prices determined in free markets, and on the basis of arrangements between buyers and sellers.

—Paul Samuelson and William Nordhaus, *Microeconomics*

Everyone recognizes the buying and selling of commodities as market activity, but the same people who enjoy shopping for commodities "online," hunting through tag sales, or nosing around farmer's markets may fear and dread looking for a job or buying a car. Going down to your favorite café to buy a coffee may call to mind feelings of comfort and comradery. Taking your car in for repairs may conversely inspire feelings of unease about the potential cost as well as worries about getting swindled. While each example here involves market activity, they also expose some of the deeper, conflicting meanings people associate with it.

Students in introductory economics classes know market activity when they see it and most possess extensive market experience. Their notions of the market provide the space, or rather the foot in the door, for

1

introducing a meaning specific to mainstream economic discourse. Almost every mainstream economic textbook opens by discussing how some people and businesses supply commodities while others demand them. The market in a textbook becomes thinly defined, and perhaps redefined for the students, as a space where the suppliers and demanders of commodities meet. Paul Samuelson, whose classic textbook on economics has been used extensively in Economics 101 for decades, defines markets as "an arrangement by which buyers and sellers of a commodity interact to determine its price and quantity" (Samuelson and Norhaus1989, 39). Instructors almost invariably search for exemplars to illustrate market activity and eBay provides a great example of a Samuelsonian marketplace.[1] Many students possess some familiarity with the site and understand how it brings together millions of buyers and sellers, interacting in cyberspace, to determine the price and quantity of thousands of items every minute of every day.

Philip Mirowski (2001) compellingly argues that most economists typically define market activity in terms of a single, generic market like eBay, and therefore fail to account for the myriad forms of actual and potential market activity and how they differ. Nobel Laureate Ronald Coase (1988) provides a similar argument in his reflections upon the discipline of economics, noting that notwithstanding the centrality of the marketplace in economic theory, explicit discussions of the marketplace itself have entirely disappeared from economic literature. Mirowski and Coase point out the peculiar tendency of modern economic theorists to neglect any deep reflection upon marketplace and to consider all types of market activity as simply particular examples of a universal market type. Economists therefore flatten the market landscape and, in effect, presume all market activity to be basically the same. This theoretical hustle allows instructors to explain how "laws of supply and demand" apply uniformly to markets as diverse as labor, steel and rents on apartments.

When I ask students to provide examples of markets, they usually bring up many other types of buying and selling activity that do not fit cleanly into Samuelson's definition. Walking down to the corner store to buy the daily newspaper or a soda surely constitutes market activity, but one of a different kind than eBay. You do not walk into the store and place a bid, or interact with other potential buyers and sellers to determine the price—you either pay the posted price or go somewhere else. The corner store offers something called a posted offer contract: no haggling over the price takes place and you as a buyer either accept the contract (pay the posted price) or reject it. In the United States, almost all purchases assume a posted offer form (although buying real estate or a car still constitute some important exceptions).

Although some people on the job market have leeway to negotiate wages and benefits, most face a similar situation here as at a grocery store. Suppose I walk into a café and ask for a job application. I might ask about the wage (the price of my commodity—i.e., my labor-power or my capacity to work) and working conditions; the proprietor will probably ask about my experience pulling espressos and lattes. Supposing I possess adequate barrista skills, they might make me an offer, say eight dollars an hour for twenty hours of work a week. They might offer me the job on the other hand only if I am willing to work 40 hours a week during the morning shift. I can then either choose to accept the wage and hours offered, or pound the streets looking for something else.

The intense debates surrounding the WTO and other trade agreements demonstrate people understand international market activity to mean something different than, say, a farmer's market on Saturday mornings. The critics of trade conducted under the auspices of the WTO place it in a different category from eBay or farmer's markets altogether, associating it with corporate power and the destruction of jobs and livelihoods. Champions of the WTO, however, treat international trade like any other type of market, extolling how it expands consumer choice and efficiency on an global scale.

Some economists do, however, consider the characteristics of *specific* markets and differentiate them. Fredric Mishkin (1997) provides an overview of how and why financial markets are different from more "standard" commodity markets like the ones for shoes or TVs, noting the asymmetric information that exists among the buyers and sellers of financial assets. George Akerlof made his reputation on this, illustrating how asymmetric information plays a role in the used car market.[2] Yet, asymmetric information in the end gets reduced by economists to something called a market imperfection, the very naming of which suggests that these markets would operate *like all other markets* if only the people had symmetric information.

Given that folding all market activity under the rubric of a generic market with universal laws masks how people often differentiate types of markets and associate different meanings with each, can we still find a commonality between all types of market activity? Trying to answer this question poses numerous difficulties; to see why, think about trying to express the commonalities of something less abstract than market activity, say, a tomato. We all have some idea of what a tomato is, but if asked to define the shared features of a tomato, what would we come up with? Tomatoes vary dramatically in size and even color. Tomatoes do not all taste the same either—think about one from a grocery store versus one from your garden or a farmer's market. While tomatoes grow on vines, so do lots of other fruits and vegetables. Tomatoes are usually roundish, but so are lots of other things. What, therefore, constitutes the essence of a tomato?[3]

Having a discussion about market activity at first pass seems quite unnecessary. Even as far back as the mid 19th century no less a thinker than Karl Marx noted the very normality of market exchange made it, like a commodity, "appear at first sight an extremely obvious, trivial thing" (Marx 1990, 163). Yet, exactly the same problems lurk whether we are trying to define a tomato or the common feature behind all market activity; not everyone shares the same understanding of the marketplace, something compounded when we consider markets in diverse historical and cultural settings.

Another thought exercise helps illustrate the irreducibility of commodity exchange to any essential feature. Putting aside for the time being Samuelson's definition, consider another one; market activity concerns voluntarily trading privately owned commodities for money—e.g., *quid pro quo* exchange. Several thorny issues arise even in this seemingly innocuous definition. What exactly does privately owned mean? Do private property rights consist of only state recognized individual or collective legal title, or do usufruct rights and common law count as well? What exactly is a commodity? Early theorists such as Aristotle defined market activity as involving only physical or material goods produced by other people, while modern theorists typically consider labor, land and services as commodities as well. If we cannot even agree upon what constitutes a "real" commodity, how can we discern the essence of commodity trade? Similarly, what exactly does money mean—actual specie like dollar bills or gold coins or do socially recognized units of value like cows or cowrie shells count?

Moving on to the voluntary nature of market activity, a quality commonly used to differentiate it from theft or piracy, think about the labor market. If you do not *need* a job, than looking for work may indeed be voluntary, but often people find themselves *compelled* to find or job or be out on the streets. In this light, what about other "forced" sales, like when farmers need to sell their crops to purchase other things they desperately need? Finally, consider the case when someone makes you "an offer you cannot refuse": suppose the local mob offers you "protection" for a payment each month. Each of these transactions involves payment for a commodity, but few would argue they constitute a voluntary transaction.

MAKING SENSE OF MARKETS.

Michael Walzer in *Thick and Thin* (1994) struggled with how to make sense of moral terms that were bandied about during the collapse of the

USSR. When he saw television footage in 1989 of marchers in Prague carrying placards demanding justice, he "knew immediately what the signs meant—and so did everyone else who saw the same picture" (1). Yet, he reflected that although everyone seeing the footage and marching along understood what justice meant, his own specific notion of justice (he being a moral philosopher) probably differed quite dramatically from theirs. Building on this thought, Walzer speculated that the people marching in Prague probably possessed a different idea of justice than the millions of people around the world watching them on TV. In fact, even the marchers themselves probably did not all share the exact idea of justice mobilizing them to take to the streets. Yet, everyone could still relate to the demand for justice motivating the marchers.

Walzer introduced the concepts of "thick" and "thin" to capture how people all recognize the term justice, but beneath this thin veneer of recognition, how each person embraces distinct, and perhaps radically different, ideas of what justice means for them. Borrowing loosely from Walzer, I see markets as possessing a thin (or minimum) and a thick (or maximal) level of meaning. A thin understanding of the market captures its very basics, the bare minimum of what market activity consists of. Like justice, most people immediately know a market when they see it. People use thin precepts of markets to recognize and discuss them, yet a little probing uncovers a much richer, thick level of meaning of what markets mean for them. The thick meaning of commodity exchange refers to the broader, maximal meanings of commodity exchange people associate with the marketplace.

I considered a range of thin definitions of market activity and looked at how people differentiated market activity from things like theft and piracy, but came up with inconsistent and at times even contradictory essential features. I decided in the end to use the phrase "commodity exchange" to represent and categorize market activity on a thin level in *Market Sense* because I saw a certain family resemblance among the notions of markets I encountered. Wittgenstein introduced the concept of family resemblance to express the difficulties in trying to define and explain even simple things, like a broom, a leaf, or in the following quote, a game:

> Consider for example the proceedings that we call "games." I mean board-games, card-games, ball-games, Olympic games and so on. What is common to them all?—Don't say: "There *must* be something in common, or they would not be called 'games' "—but *look* and *see* whether there is anything common to all.—For if you look at them you will not see something that is common to *all,* but similarities, relationships, and a whole series of them at that. To repeat: don't think, but look!—Look

for example at board-games with their multifarious relationships. Now
pass to card-games; here you find many correspondences with the first
group, but many common features drop out, and others appear. When
we pass next to ball-games, much that is common is retained, but much
is lost.—Are they all 'amusing'? Compare chess with noughts and
crosses. Or is there always winning and losing, or competition between
players? Think of patience. In ball games there is winning and losing;
but when a child throws his ball at the wall and catches it again, this
feature has disappeared. Look at the parts played by skill and luck; and
at the differences between skill in chess and skill in tennis. Think now
of games like ring-a-ring-a-roses; here is the element of amusement, but
how many other characteristic features have disappeared! And we can
go through the many, many other groups of games in the same way;
can see how similarities crop up and disappear.

And the result of this examination is: we see a complicated network
of similarities overlapping and criss-crossing: sometimes overall similarities, sometimes similarities of detail. I can think of no better expression to characterize these similarities than "family resemblances"' for
the various resemblances between members of a family: build, features,
colour of eyes, gait, temperament, etc. etc. overlap and criss-cross in
the same way.—And I shall say: 'games' form a family. (1958, 66–67)

Taking a page from Wittenstein, I assigned to the same "family," i.e.,
commodity exchange, social activities ranging from eBay bidding to job
hunting to trading goods internationally. Commodity exchange does not
have one unique, fundamental or essential feature: the common property
underpinning the familial association "is the *result* of their being assigned
to the same class, not the *cause*" (Bloor 1983, 31).[4] The familial traits of
commodity exchange include aspects of the thin definitions already presented; over the course of *Market Sense* I present several more, and use various authors' definitions, descriptions and explanations of commodity
exchange to populate its family tree.

On a thin level, defining commodity exchange as a family facilitates
making sense of the marketplace given the antediluvian, but varied, nature
of its existence in society. Separating the thick from the thin often proved
difficult, if not impossible, for even thin notions of commodity exchange
often slide into thick ones. Consider for instance the idea that an essential
feature of exchange involves participants' freedom of choice to buy or sell
what they wish. Scholars like Milton Friedman (1962) link this freedom
with people's desire to choose political representation—give people the
freedom to choose in the marketplace and they will soon be demanding a

choice in the political arena (and other aspects of society) as well. Hence, an essential feature of exchange for Friedman on a thin level possesses thicker implications for society at large. Although the distinction between thick and thin helps us specify different aspects of the meaning surrounding commodity exchange, a very blurry line often separates them. Although I recognize this problem, thick and thin provide useful analytical categories and I use them to guide the presentation of the theoretical material considered in *Market Sense*.

INTO THE THICK OF THINGS.

Thick understandings of commodity exchange concern its *significance*—what people think market activity entails for individuals and society at large. In the thick of things we find a vast array of connections drawn or assumed between commodity exchange and political, cultural and economic aspects of society, not to mention beliefs associated with particular markets. People often refer to particular political, cultural and economic things as part and parcel of market activity. The specific packages of things people associate with the market place informs their *market sense.* An individual's market sense guides how they perceive commodity exchange in its various manifestations, from international trade to eBay to the privatization of state owned assets.

Foucault's theoretical work provides a method for wading through the morass of meanings that cling to commodity exchange on a thick level. Deeply troubled by the rationalist tendency to produce histories of thought that focused solely on the origins and important breakthroughs in the evolution of ideas, Foucault developed instead what he called an archaeological description. Foucault employed his archaeology to uncover "the *regularity* of statements" (1972, 144) characterizing/defining the subjects he considered. Facing the plenitude of exchange entailments, I develop in *Market Sense* an archaeological description of certain clusters of exchange entailments which surround contemporary globalization and occur with regularity in historic philosophical and economic literature.

The first regularity I found concerns how people envision the relationship between commodity exchange and self-centered, greedy behavior. Some authors like Adam Smith, and much of contemporary economics, envision avarice as a natural behavioral trait and see commodity exchange undertaken for individual gain as a natural manifestation the human essence. Others like Aristotle and critics of contemporary globalization ruminate upon how commodity exchange *induces* greed and self-centered activity. People with either market vision associate greed and commodity exchange, but their *interpretation* of the linkage—what it means for society—varies dramatically. People who see greed and commodity exchange as natural tend to link market activity with social harmony. Those who see greed and commodity exchange as unnatural, or at least social products, associate markets with social conflict and decay. Hence, another regularity I found—i.e., envisioning commodity exchange as entailing social harmony/cohesion or its opposite, social breakdown/decay—relates to the first one and highlights the package nature of entailments.

Persistent linkages between commodity exchange and individual freedom and liberty also emerged in contemporary and historic discourse, as did their opposite—unfreedom and coercion. President G.W. Bush, in promoting China's admission to the WTO, remarked that "The case for trade is not just monetary, but moral. Economic freedom creates habits of liberty" (Kettle 2001, 7). Economic freedom here means the ability to engage in trade, which Bush envisions will *create* habits of liberty. Trade freely with China, Bush added, and political rights will follow; the connection between exchange and freedom and political rights would be familiar to any student of Hobbes, Locke, or more recently, Milton Friedman. Others today maintain trade will *undermine* freedom and liberty by eroding national sovereignty.[5]

I focus in *Market Sense* upon the clusters or packages of regularities found in the thick meanings of commodity exchange, for they underpin particular market senses. Whether or not people view contemporary market-based globalization as a good thing or not largely rests upon their understanding of what commodity exchange entails, which depends in turn upon their market sense. People who believe commodity exchange entails democracy, freedom and liberty tend to support a movement toward a world linked through market activity. Others condemn it because they see such activity as entailing greed, anti-social behavior and social conflict.

I see the extra-economic associations of markets, e.g., the thick meaning of commodity exchange, as crucial because they embody the primary persuasive arguments behind economic specific policy prescriptions and grand policy proposals. Consider in this light a recent statement by the US Trade Representative in support of the World Trade Organization (WTO):

> Trade is about more than economic efficiency; it reflects a system of values: openness, peaceful exchange, opportunity, inclusiveness and integration, mutual gains through interchange, freedom of choice, appreciation of differences, governance though agreed rules, and a hope for betterment of all peoples and lands. (Zoellick 2001)

Neoliberals like Zoellick seek to deepen and broaden market organization nationally and internationally with the goal being a global economy tightly integrated through the marketplace. Neoliberals rely upon neoclassical economic theory to argue that markets efficiently allocate resources nationally and globally, but sell their neoliberal economic policies to the public by citing a range of rather complex but positive things like freedom, liberty and democracy that markets supposedly entail. At first, I found it surprising how neoliberals and others simply assert such things as common (market) sense given the importance of such statements in their public pronouncements, but found that, in fact, extra-economic associations of markets are seldom defended with any rigor. Deirdre McCloskey avers rather than argues something similar to Zoellick for instance in her recent statement that "a market society is alert, flexible, innovative, bubbling up, democratic, unintended, creative" (2000, 27) and such assertions constitute the norm rather than the exception.

The *particular* economic, political and cultural aspects of society Zoellick, McCloskey and others associate with the marketplace I call entailments. Anderson and Belnap (1975) denote entailments as if/then statements: if X (e.g., market) then Y and Z (democracy and freedom). Entailments of the marketplace refer to the specific social relations, individual feelings, beliefs, and other things people envision as part and parcel of the marketplace. Zoellick and McCloskey evoke a series of positive entailments and Colin MacLeod (1998) provides a concise summary of a traditional left-wing view of the marketplace, inculpating it with exploitation, alienation, a hostility to genuine freedom and a corrosion of social bonds.

Positive and negative exchange entailments haunt discussions of the marketplace and exert a profound role in how people make sense of modern market society and contemporary globalization. Packages of entailments comprise people's visions of what the market entails for society and fundamentally influence how they make sense of the world around them and the world they seek to create. Neoliberals cast a favorable eye toward the broadening and deepening of global market interaction, primarily due to the extra-economic things they believe it entails, like hope, freedom and democracy. Critics on the other hand counter by bemoaning the extra-economic things they believe the market entails, like the subversion of democracy, freedom and the public interest.

A helpful way of representing the exchange entailments comprising a market sense involves constructing a chain of equivalence among them.[6] The following chain illustrates a set of common entailments associated with commodity exchange and a liberal market sense: commodity exchange = democracy = freedom = liberty. Finding people who evoke various chains requires little effort, and many such chains will be demonstrated over the course of *Market Sense*. Just to cite a specific example, take the recent statement by Don Evans, the former US secretary of trade, who averred: "Trade brings prosperity. Prosperity brings civilization. Civilization brings democracy. Democracy and trade are the pillars of a peaceful world" (2001). Here we find a chain, commodity exchange = prosperity = civilization = democracy, that underpins his market sense.

Watkins (1998) astutely points out that such generalizations appear suspect even in their generality, or perhaps because of their generality, and points toward the complex and very different networks of social relations enmeshing various instances of commodity exchange in modern and historical societies. Although I completely agree with Watkins, I think it is also important to note that these types of statements often serve as the primary public justification for economic policy that impacts billions of people. The public relations spin propagated to support the normalization of trade relations between the USA and China in 2000 relied largely upon a chain informing a liberal market sense, to wit, that commodity exchange will facilitate the transition of China to a democratic society. Liberal pundits also used their particular market sense to dismiss arguments regarding human rights, representing all opposition as simply incapable of grasping the basic fact that commodity exchange is a *foundational requirement* of democracy and human rights. If you view the world through this lens, the best way to promote human rights in China involves more, not less, commodity exchange. Further, placing restrictions on trade with China until its human rights record improves is at best counterproductive.

Exchange entailments often emerge as something akin to a ghost in a machine. People often insinuate or imply them when mentioning exchange, and they serve as a referent, coming to mind with others mention market activity. Once certain chains take root and become accepted as common market sense, people no longer have to justify or explain them for they can simply be evoked to defend or to critique economic policy and even contemporary society. Competing visions represent different thick understandings of what commodity exchange entails, but insofar as one chain dominates the others or assumes hegemonic status, other contesting, alternative chains become displaced or marginalized. Certain associations of commodity exchange constitute a common (market) sense today and hence packages of supposedly fundamentally related things are treated as accepted wisdom. Dominant chains serve as important tools to rationalize certain economic policy since they require no rigorous theoretical defense—they are simply asserted as facts.

VISION AND MARKET SENSE.

Robert Heilbroner and William Milberg write about the role of vision in social analysis in their text *The Crisis of Vision in Modern Economic*

Thought (1995). They define vision as "The political hopes and fears, social stereotypes, and value judgements—all usually unarticulated—that infuse all social thought . . . as psychological, perhaps existential necessities" (1995, 4). Vision for them refers to the presuppositions that underpin all social analysis, what "sets the stage and peoples the case for all social inquiry" (4). Heilbroner and Milberg wrote their book to criticize neoclassical economic theorists, who they see today as being too caught up in the tools of the trade to recognize the vision they themselves employ; an omission they attribute to an "extraordinary combination of arrogance and innocence" (6).

On the other hand, I see neoliberal visionaries, the people advocating certain "market orientated" economic policy, consistently making grand claims about what markets entail that go far beyond what the discipline of economics warrants. George DeMartino argues, in the context of debates over economic policy, that particular visions lay behind certain policy positions and involve a "complex of complementary economic, political and cultural arguments, the wisdom of which is generally taken as given and even self-evident" (2000, 36). DeMartino uses vision in the same way I use market sense, i.e., to identify the complementary things people see as part and parcel of commodity exchange.

I originally intended *Market Sense* to highlight the role market sense plays in informing how people understand and represent contemporary globalization, and the last few chapters do address this important phenomena. Yet, the more I researched the matter, I discovered a range of different and often contradictory market senses in the literature, and quickly realized that particular visions of what markets entail for society play a profound role in social inquiry. Celebrants of contemporary globalization draw heavily from the associations of the marketplace found in Adam Smith's classic *The Wealth of Nations* (1981), and critics, often unwittingly, evoke negative associations of the marketplace with roots dating back to Ancient Greece. Accordingly, I devote several chapters of *Market Sense* to tease out, via close reading, the specific market vision found within these important, if often underappreciated, texts to highlight the role they still play in contemporary analyses of society.

Particular visions of the marketplace play a powerful—perhaps too powerful—role in shaping how we understand the world around us. In my research, I discovered that people reduce multifaceted aspects of society simply to products of market activity. Consider the following statement by Don Evans, the former Secretary of Commerce for the USA: "As President Bush has said, trade is not just about economics; it's a moral imperative. Free and open trade is a foundation for economic development, democracy, social freedom and political stability" (2001). Markets (trade) constitute for Evans a *foundational requirement* of democracy and so forth, implying that without them, tyranny, economic stagnation, social unfreedom and political instability will abound.

I do not believe such equations are very useful, and I believe they do more harm than good. I envision market activity as potentially *promoting and/or undermining* economic development, social freedom, and political stability depending on the social context where it takes place. Markets are always complex ensembles of economic, political and cultural practices, and what they entail in any given situation depends upon all the social relations imbricating it. A partial list of the social relations animating exchange activity includes: all of the beliefs motivating exchange activity, whether or not prices are set or bargained, whether or not money mediates the exchanges, the specific constitution of the property rights involved, the scope of exchange (e.g., what may or may not be sold), the scale or pervasiveness of exchange, and so on (and on).

All too often, people use their market sense to defend or attack economic policy like trade agreements, effectively precluding any exploration into how such policy may entail a wide, and even contradictory, range of political, cultural and economic practices at any given point in time and place. I see a real need to move beyond the uncritical acceptance of market common sense to engender a more meaningful discussion about the role of the market in promoting and/or undermining certain economic, political and cultural outcomes we collectively desire or abhor. Given the multiple existing and potential forms of market activity, each replete with often contradictory impacts on society, simply advocating or denouncing market activity in terms of what it supposedly entails constitutes an empty platitude, one we need to move beyond. We need a new economics of markets and society, and I see *Market Sense* as contributing to this objective.

MARKET SENSE AS A FRAMING DEVICE.

Liberals used popular exchange entailments to frame the debate over expanding US trade relations with China. By evoking democracy and human rights as immanent with commodity exchange, they managed to portray their opponents as hypocritical, self-interested or simply ignorant. Using market sense to frame debates over economic policy occurs with some regularity and has at least since the time of Adam Smith. A popular framing gambit implicit in the debate over trade relations with China involves broadly dividing societies into two types—ones with "free" commodity exchange and ones without. People attribute to societies with free commodity exchange a familiar list of things like democracy, freedom and efficiency. Conversely, societies without free commodity exchange get characterized by totalitarianism, subjugation and inefficiency.

Although neoliberals today use positive entailments of exchange to defend trade and capitalist society, even critics of capitalism often employ them. John Maynard Keynes, in his concluding notes to *The General Theory*, constructed a frame based upon liberal market sense to champion the new economic policy he prescribed to his audience. Keynes recognized the instability of the existing economic order, but averred "it may be possible by a right analysis of the problem to cure the disease whilst preserving efficiency and freedom" (1973, 380–1). Keynes claimed that people in capitalist society faced a choice: follow his advice and therefore maintain the capitalistic individualism, efficiency and freedom associated with markets or welcome in Comrade Lenin and the Bolsheviks. No middle ground existed for Keynes: you either maintained "existing economic forms" via his policy prescriptions and therefore his positive chain of exchange entailments, or faced new, presumingly red economics forms (e.g., central planning) with exactly the opposite implications.

The rampant use of market sense to frame policy debates points toward the larger issue of how people often equate commodity exchange with capitalism. Neoliberals and even Keynesians tend to present commodity exchange as the essence of capitalism and, ironically, critics of capitalism often do so as well. The difference between their reduction of capitalism to commodity exchange lies in the market vision embraced by each: whereas champions of capitalism see commodity exchange and *ipso facto* capitalist society as entailing liberty, freedom and democracy, critics counter by representing commodity exchange, and thus capitalist society, as entailing (among other things) alienation, exploitation, and social disharmony.

I believe both of these market visions need to be challenged to facilitate the consideration of the constellation of social relations imbricating exchange. Despite the popular market visions animating the debate on contemporary globalization, commodity exchange does not possess any inherent features or attributes outside of the constellation of social relations enmeshing it. The controversy over globalization should not revolve around the pros and cons of commodity exchange because trade may assume an infinite array of particular forms. No universal ideal informs all types of commodity exchange: what may or may not be traded, the rules governing transactions, the understandings of property and property rights, and the scope and scale of exchange all play crucial and consequential roles in the significance of exchange at any particular conjuncture. To their credit, many involved in the "anti-globalization" struggle do argue that the main issue is not "the market" *per se,* but the social relations and other consequences they see as arising from specific international trade agreements, multinational corporate activity, and so forth. International trade involves market activity, and often corporations buy and sell commodities, but critics challenge the rules and norms situating it rather than the practice itself. The same people protesting the WTO likely have little qualms about shopping in a farmer's market, indicating a complex, thick understanding of market activity.

The controversy over global integration needs to be severed from the sterile controversy over the essential significance of "the market" as a singular universal type. This will allow space for a more productive discussion on types of markets and potential forms of economic integration. Commodity exchange always exists as a complex ensemble of economic, political and cultural practices that lack an innate, internal logic and, consequently, any necessary entailments. Contrary to a liberal market sense, many people see something different between "free trade" and fair trade, between the job market and shopping for shoes, and between buying a used car from a friend or from a used car lot. I explore in *Market Sense* some of the reasons why people make such distinctions and how it helps us make sense of the debates surrounding globalization.

CONCLUSION.

I developed in this chapter a number of concepts that play an important role in *Market Sense.* Commodity exchange refers to a thin definition of market activity. The thick meaning of commodity exchange refers to the different understandings people have of what commodity exchange means for them. The specific cultural, political and economic associations found within the thick meaning of exchange I call exchange entailments. Finally, people's thick meaning of commodity exchange shapes how they interpret the impact of commodity exchange, and I call this a market sense. I use these concepts to read what economists and philosophers have to say about commodity exchange and its thick meaning for society; by reading, I mean exploring how people and theorists define commodity exchange embrace thick meanings. Marx for instance spends some time comparing how Smith's vision of commodity exchange differs from his, but Smith in turn consistently juxtaposes his thick understanding of commodity exchange to mercantile and other economic thinking. I concentrate in *Market Sense* how each theorist defined and redefined exchange, as well as how they linked it to various aspects of society.

My reading of Aristotle's sophisticated notion of how commodity exchange may either support or undermine social cohesion and positively or negatively impact the population at large comprises the next chapter. The imputed significance of exchange for Aristotle depends first and foremost upon the specific beliefs and practices animating market activity. Aristotle's understanding of exchange proved profoundly influential, with echoes of his ideas clearly reflected in early Christian scholarly work by Thomas Aquinas, as well as the debate on the global economy today.

Chapter Three, *Adam Smith's Market Sense,* primarily examines his analysis of exchange in his *Wealth of Nations.* Smith explicitly linked commodity exchange with individual liberty, freedom and prosperity—exchange entailments often evoked by neoliberals and other celebrants of the current economic order. Smith's theoretical statements regarding exchange also relate to the two regularities within the debate over what exchange entails. Smith sees commodity exchange as naturally fostering harmony unless impaired by social rules and regulations. Smith also argues avarice constitutes the essence of human behavior and via commodity exchange actually promotes social harmony and prosperity.

Chapter Four, *A Critique of the Market Mystique,* evaluates Smith's market sense on two levels. On the one hand, I present an immanent critique inspired by the works of Marx, demonstrating how the same understanding of commodity exchange Smith developed entails freedom, liberty and expanding wealth, but also unfreedom, tyranny, and social crisis. On the other hand, I provide a reading of Marx and Karl Polanyi's critique of the naturalism Smith builds his analysis of exchange upon. As part of this latter, "external" critique, Marx developed the concept of commodity fetishism and Polanyi "fictitious" commodities and the impossibility of a pure market system.

In the fifth chapter, *Simple Exchange, Merchant Capital and Augmented Circulation,* I present various types of exchange as distinguished by non-liberal scholars and explore the thick layers of meaning surrounding them. Here I will distinguish "simple" commodity exchange from "merchant capital" and explore the relationship between production and exchange. The labor market also receives consideration as does the interaction between merchants and producers in historical and contemporary society.

The last two chapters, *Liberals and Contemporary Globalization* and *The Market Sense of Contemporary Globalization's Critics,* consider the current debate over globalization. The globalization debate largely mirrors the debate over exchange, not only in the significance awarded to trade, but in the rhetorical tropes employed in the controversy. Commodity exchange often serves as a stand in or proxy for a certain understanding of capitalist society, and globalization today performs essentially the same role. Globalization entails in liberal market sense an expansion of wealth, individual freedom and liberty—a positive chain of exchange entailments since the time of Smith. How liberals use their market sense to frame the debate over trade agreements receives particular attention, as does the role it plays in justifying a range of public policy. The detractors of globalization by no means possess a united front, but a group I call "neosmithians" stands out today due to their popularity and prominence. After a careful examination of the neosmithian market sense, I move on to consider critiques based upon alternative market senses that point the way to a new economics of markets and society.

Chapter Two

Aristotle's Discourse on Commodity Exchange.

Whenever Aristotle touched on a question of the economy he aimed at developing its relationship to society as a whole. The frame of reference was the community as such, which exists at different levels within all functioning human groups.

—Karl Polanyi, *Aristotle Discovers the Economy.*

Aristotle's economic writing was an attempt to harness and discipline the exchange process; it was an attempt to solve the problem of using the exchange process without being dominated by it. The problem remains.

—Thomas Lewis, *Acquisition and Anxiety: Aristotle's Case Against the Market.*

Hammurapi's Code from the nineteenth century B.C. demarcating official exchange prices (Gordon 1965) demonstrates how long markets have played a role in human society. Aristotle's classical examination of commodity exchange, something he considered an element of distribution distinct from, say plunder and gift-giving, built upon prior understandings of exchange developed over the millennia and a half following the erection of the Code. Aristotle's analysis of market activity constituted an act of creation as well, for although he did discuss the proper ratios for exchanging goods, his primary focus concerned the role exchange may play in building or undermining community and individual virtue. Although historically and materially situated in the slave societies of the Ancients, Aristotle's vision and analysis of what commodity exchange entails for society continues to shape perceptions of the global capitalist economy.

Aristotle's writings on the economy were not voluminous; book one of *The Politics* and chapter five of the *Nicomachean Ethics* contain most of his writings on the subject. Aristotle explicated in detail nonetheless how commodity exchange may support and/or undermine social cohesion and individual virtue; whether or not exchange builds community or tears it apart, promotes individual virtue or vice, depended upon the socially instituted function of exchange and the motivations of people partaking in the process. The striking originality of Aristotle's position today becomes apparent when juxtaposed to theorists who envision all market participants as uniform in motivation (e.g., maximizing utility or profit) and/or impute a uniform and singular implication of exchange upon society and its members (e.g., entailing efficiency, exploitation, or cultural imperialism).[1]

Aristotle's vision and analysis of exchange proved very influential for many early political economists, who both grappled with and actively transformed it (Meek 1956; Roll 1946). Adam Smith's analysis of exchange in *The Wealth of Nations* (1981) bears traces of Aristotle where he explicitly reworked negative exchange entailments with roots in the Ancient philosopher's writings (Sims 2002). The nuanced writings of Karl Marx on exchange, particularly in volume one of *Capital* (1990) and the *Grundrisse* (1993), interrogate Aristotle's ideas on exchange directly. What is perhaps most influential about Aristotle's work is how he linked commodity exchange (motivated by avarice) and the destabilization of society. Aristotle's market sense echoes within popular or "ersatz" economics today, along with certain literature on globalization that focuses upon issues ranging from the social and political impact of multinational corporations to fair-trade initiatives.[2]

Exploring Aristotle's market sense provides insights to contemporary visions of the marketplace and highlights some of their limitations. Aristotle placed the blame of social and political decay upon avarice, but he did not reduce society's ills solely to individuals corrupted by greed. In his quest to identify the causes of greed he fingered commodity exchange, more specifically, a type of commodity exchange guided by profits he linked with foreign merchants. Hence, his analysis did not stop by identifying greed as the problem, for he sought to discern the cause of such individual corruption. Popular critics of the contemporary economy the other hand often reduce a range of problems—from corporate scandals to financial crises—simply to individuals contaminated by greed, missing the richness of Aristotle's social analysis of the phenomena. Before proceeding, let us first consider Aristotle's discourse on commodity exchange.

ARISTOTELIAN AND PLATONIC IDEAL FORMS OF SOCIETY.

Like others writing about economic activity before the physiocrats, Aristotle did not conceive of the market operating within its own, distinct sphere of society. Aristotle discussed commodity exchange in *The Politics* as a supplementary way to provision society's needs outside of direct production and appropriation; by society, Aristotle meant both households, i.e., the slave plantations that comprised Ancient Greece, and the *polis* [the ancient Greek city state, which included its political and economic aspects]. In contrast, *Nicomachean Ethics* is a broad analysis of moral behavior and virtue, and a consideration of how commodity exchange might promote or undermine these aspects of humanity. One rationale for Aristotle's exploration of the social implications of social relations like commodity exchange concerns the intellectual legacy bequeathed to him by Plato. Both Plato's and Aristotle's work featured an ontological quest for an optimal social arrangement—a cohesive *polis* embodying justice and virtue. Plato's *The Republic* and Aristotle's *The Politics* explicate an idealized form of the *polis* (i.e., a platonic Ideal Form) and use this Form as a yardstick to evaluate societies.[3]

Plato's formative years coincided with the 30-year Peloponnesian War, a period of great political and economic upheaval in Athens, and it influenced his thought to no small degree. Plato witnessed first hand the vaunted democratic reforms instituted by Solon become corrupted as Athens moved from democracy to demagoguery to tyranny. These political changes resulted in the Athenian quest for empire and with it, the humiliating defeat of Athens by Sparta in the Peloponnesian War. Economically, the war financially exhausted the Athenian treasury and laid waste to the countryside—the location of the slave-plantations of the elite and the primary source of wealth in Ancient Greece (de Ste. Croix 1981). Thucydides (1982), in his famous contemporary history of the era, argued that during and after the Peloponnesian War, *arete* [the aggregate of qualities such as valor and virtue that make up good character] and proper statesmanship—key components for both Plato and Aristotle in any just *polis*—became increasingly contaminated by greed and *hubris* [excessive pride or self-confidence], with disastrous social consequences. Plato turned his intellectual prowess toward uncovering what social institutions or practices promoted greed, which he believed lay at the root of the degeneration of the Athenian *polis*.

Although his Ideal *polis* differed from Plato, Aristotle also argued that greed thwarted the emergence of a just society. Two related questions guided Plato's and Aristotle's analyses: what exactly were the outside influences inducing greed amongst the population and what can be done to eradicate it? Plato argued that private property was the contagion that fostered greed and avarice, and was the root cause of war as well as that of "most evil, individual and social" (*The Republic* 374e). The pursuit of private property for Plato not only bred selfishness, but lay behind the Athenian quest for empire.

Plato devoted the entire second book of *The Republic* to the second question of how to suppress avarice in order to facilitate progress toward his Ideal. Since Plato's vision of society entailed that the elites of society assume full responsibility for political decisions and the defense of the *polis,* private property would have to be abolished among this stratum of society due its corrosive moral implications. The property ban would not apply to the lower classes, i.e., slaves or citizens without estates, only because they ideally would not possess any influence upon political or military institutions. Although Plato thought commodity exchange could exist to (re)distribute private property among the lower classes, the only people suited to be merchants would be those "least fit physically, and unsuitable for other work" (*The Republic* 371e) culled from the lowest strata of the population. If abolishing private property was one means of controlling the spread of greed, Plato's account of the dialogue *Protagoras* by Socrates suggests another. In the *Protagoras,* Plato demonstrated the teachablity of wisdom and, therefore, that a proper education in the moral virtues may also help eradicate the evils of avarice. Finally, Plato also placed some faith in the sentiments of compassion and concern for the weak to counter divisiveness induced by unequal property accumulation. Aristotle's *Nicomachean Ethics* (X, chapter 14) and Adam Smith's discussion of sympathy found in *The Theory of Moral Sentiments* (2000) demonstrates that they also supported such an idea.

Even though Plato and Aristotle shared the idea that avariciousness constituted the outside, corrupting influence at the root of the problem of social conflict, they traced the cause of such perverse behavior to different aspects of society. Unlike Plato, Aristotle condoned and championed private property and argued that the spread of avarice arose from foreign merchants engaging in profit-driven exchange (Lowry 1987a; Pack 1985). Aristotle differentiated two types of exchange—a natural form, which helped build the bonds of community through the distribution of private property, and an unnatural form, which promoted greed and social conflict. The following section explores how Aristotle differentiated these two forms of exchange and examines his proposals to separate greed from commodity exchange.

ARISTOTLE'S MARKET SENSE.

Josef Soudek notes "one of Aristotle's most challenging contributions to the development of economic thought is his theory of exchange" (1952, 45).

Aristotle's writings on exchange have been debated in some detail (Finley 1970; Kauder 1953; Lowry, 1987a, 1987b; Pack 1985), in part because he discussed commodity exchange in two different contexts. In *The Politics,* Aristotle contemplates commodity exchange as a means of provisioning the household, i.e., as a *techne* [craft or art], and its implications for *oikonomia* [household-management] within the larger community. In the *Nicomachean Ethics,* Aristotle considered exchange in light of his theory of ethics; more specifically, how it may promote or undermine *arete,* social cohesion, and distributive justice (Finley 1970; Lowry 1987a, 1987b).

In both contexts Aristotle presented commodity exchange as involving material use-values either directly bartered or mediated via coinage. Karl Polanyi's notion of genuine exchange captures this usage of exchange, for he argued trade naturally consisted of material use-values produced by human hands; the commodity status of land, labor and money he saw as entirely fictitious (1968b). In a manner akin to Marx's distinction between exchange-value and use-value, Aristotle argued that any piece of property has a double use: usefulness in exchange as well as its "proper use," consumption (Lowry 1974). Aristotle considered all property to possess exchange value and maintained that money came into existence specifically to facilitate the exchange process: "This is why all items for exchange must be comparable in some way. Currency came along to do exactly this" (*Nicomachean Ethics:* 1133a20).

Economists tend to focus on Aristotle's discussion of prices in the *Nicomachean Ethics,* and much of the debate surrounding Aristotle's economics concerns the value-form supposedly determining prices. The controversy initiated by Joseph Schumpeter over whether or not Aristotle or other Ancient Greeks such as Xenophon in his *Ways and Means* produced a systemic analysis of economic activity (i.e., a theory of prices) or simply dispensed "pompous common sense" (Schumpeter 1954, 57) also has its roots in this debate. Marginalist theorists (Kauder 1953; Soudek 1952) read Aristotle as expressing a nascent version of a subjective theory of value. Soudek also sees hints of formalism in Aristotle, maintaining that he presented a "kind of mathematical model, thus setting a precedent to what has become, among mathematically oriented economics, a generally accepted principle" (1952, 45). Marx argued Aristotle was the "first to analyze the value-form, like so many other forms of thought, society, and nature" (1990, 151), but thought he was groping toward a labor theory of value, even though the prevalence of slave-based production in Ancient Greece undermined his efforts.[4] Aristotle's theory of prices is, however, tangential to his primary rationale for exploring exchange in the first place, namely, how and why market activity may support or undermine social cohesion and thwart the emergence of his Ideal.

Aristotle explicated his Ideal in *The Politics,* and in the introductory note on *oikonomia* [household management] therein, he states: "Since every *polis* consists of households, it is essential to begin with household-management" (1253b). Aristotle's households consisted primarily of estates characterized by large scale slave agricultural production (de Ste. Croix 1981; Lewis 1978) and he divided households into four parts: master/slave, husband/wife, father/children and finally, *chrematistike* [the acquisition of goods or wealth]. The final component concerns us here and received special attention from Aristotle as well because "some people regard [*chrematistike*] as covering the whole of household-management, others as its most important part" (*The Politics* 1253b). Aristotle's expressed concerns about the pursuit of property becoming transformed into an end in itself and undermining social cohesion by subverting a just distribution of property.

Aristotle began his economic analysis through a Socratic probing of his own initial statement (above), asking the following: "Is the acquisition of goods the same as household-management, or a part of it, or a subsidiary to it? And if it is subsidiary, is it so in the same way as shuttle-making is subsidiary to weaving, or as bronze-founding is to the making of statues?" (*The Politics* 1256a). Aristotle argued household management cannot be simply equated with the acquisition of goods, "because it is the task of the one [*chrematistike*] to provide, the other [*oikonomia*] to use" (*The Politics* 1256a). Aristotle then considered whether or not the acquisition of goods via exchange still constituted part of household management at all. He answered his query by stating that acquiring property for its use-value constituted a natural part of household management while pursuing exchange simply to garner profits did not (*The Politics* 1256b). Supplementing household provisioning with exchange served to re-establish "nature's own equilibrium of self-sufficiency" (*The Politics* 1257a): because households differ in their resources, some commodity exchange serves the natural purpose of rectifying the imbalances of nature. If one household finds itself with an excess of wine and another of grain, then they should exchange their surpluses to ensure both have the necessities of life (Lowry 1987a, 191; 197).

Several parallels emerge between Aristotle's notion of natural exchange and the peasant mode of production literature inspired by A.V. Chayanov's *The Theory of Peasant Economy* (1966), and by other more Marxian accounts of peasant production (de Janvry 1981; Schejtman 1988). All of these scholars attribute self-subsistence as the paramount motivation amongst agrarian societies, with only the extra use-values produced, e.g., those useful objects surplus to subsistence needs, finding their way to market. Lowry (1987a) argues compellingly that a similar line of thought underpins Aristotle's analysis. This market vision stands in marked contrast to liberals like Sol Tax (1953) who saw Guatemalan peasants as "penny capitalists," undertaking careful cost/benefit calculations based upon market signals concerning what to produce. Samuel Popkin (1979) and Theodore Schultz (1964) also represent peasants as rational maximizers, producing primarily for pecuniary gain. Aristotelian and liberal theorists begin with competing notions of why peasants go to the marketplace and derive different conclusions about peasant production accordingly.

Another important characteristic of natural exchange comes from the *Nicomachean Ethics* and involves the proper ratio of exchanging property. Aristotle contended property must be exchanged proportionally for exchange to be considered just: "What is just, then, is what is proportionate, and what is unjust is counter-proportionate" (1131a30). Proportionate exchanges build community, for "reciprocity that is proportionate rather than equal, holds people together; for a city is maintained by proportionate reciprocity" (1132b30). The correct proportionality depended upon both the status relations between exchanging agents and the object's customary price, but interpretations of this passage proliferate.[5]

Regardless of the specific, proper proportionality Aristotle prescribed, he argued social conflict arose when one party in the exchange felt cheated. In *Nicomachean Ethics,* profits originate in exchange, derived from an unequal, or more properly, a disproportionate, exchange. Making a profit in exchange implies someone received more than their proportional share from the transaction and, *ipso facto,* someone less. Exchange emerges in Aristotle's writings as a zero sum game, an idea quite pervasive prior to David Hume and Adam Smith (Hirschman 1977; 1986). Consider the following in this regard:

> In fact, however, these names 'loss' and 'profit' are derived from voluntary exchange. For having more than one's own share is called making a profit, and having less than what one had in the beginning is called suffering a loss, i.e., in buying and selling and in other transactions permitted by law. And when people get neither more nor less, but precisely what belongs to them, they say they have their own share, and make neither a loss nor a profit. (*Nicomachean Ethics* 1132b)

The profits and losses incurred by individuals in exchange produce social tension since any gains in exchange come at the expense of others in the community. Far from promoting bonds of reciprocity, seeking profits in exchange entails mistrust and social conflict: "Indeed, whenever equals receive unequal shares, or unequals equal shares, in a distribution, that is the source of quarrels and accusations" (1131a). Aristotle traced the origins of such behavior to the development of foreign trade, where merchants undertook exchange simply for profit (Lowry 1987a, 225). Aristotle considered it natural for people to engage in trade to acquire the use-value or materiality of property, but unnatural when avarice motivates the exchange process. Aristotle's distinction between the two forms of exchange parallels the distinction Marx made in *Capital* between simple exchange and merchant capital as demonstrated in chapter 5, *Simple Exchange, Merchant Capital and Augmented Circulation*.

Although Aristotle condemned profit as a motivation for trade, he realized the difficulty in distinguishing natural from unnatural exchange since they both involve the same process of trading goods for money. To clarify the difference and to provide an understanding behind their conflation Aristotle brought forth his notion of the "good life" and the limits of wealth. Leading the good life entails pursuing all the activities one engages in with a clear goal or discrete end (*telos*) that coincides with their virtuous accomplishment. All human pursuits for Aristotle ideally serve only as a means toward *teleios* [the ultimate end, e.g., the good life] not an end in itself; the *techne* of doctoring concerns health, that of military leadership, victory. The good life requires health and a enough wealth to live free from need, but people may pursue any *techne* beyond its (limited) end, even though such action violates its express purpose—namely, the facilitation of the pursuit of the good life and happiness. Someone who pursues health "to the point where well-being is not furthered, perhaps even diminished, [would] violate the virtue of the art" (Lewis 1978, 74). The following quote exemplifies Aristotle's logic:

> The art of healing aims at producing unlimited health, and every other skill aims at its own end without limit, wishing to secure that to the highest possible degree; on the other hand the *means* toward the end are not unlimited, the end itself setting the limit in each case. (*The Politics* 1257b25)

Aristotle maintained that the good life is the ultimate goal of human happiness, and "[t]he kind of life needed for perfect happiness is something fixed and given, being somehow dictated by men's very nature" (Saunders 1981, 37). Living the good life implies the pursuit of many activities, with the end goal or complete end (*teleios*) being the happiness obtained from fulfilling them (Staveren 1999, 66–68). For Aristotle, happiness (*eudaimonia*) does not arise from hedonistic pleasure, but from the ability to pursue a range of *techne* virtuously (Staveren 1999). The good life requires a certain amount of wealth or property "for neither life itself nor the good life is possible without a certain minimum supply of the necessities" (*The Politics* 1253b23). Yet, in the unnatural form of exchange "the end provides no limit, because the end is wealth in that form, i.e., the possession of goods. The kind which is household-management, on the other hand, does have a limit . . ." (*The Politics* 1257b25).

Aristotle felt that people's unlimited desire for life occasionally led to the desire for unlimited wealth, and exchange motivated by limitless individual gain would result in disastrous social consequences (Lowry 1987a). Profit-driven exchange channeled an individual's energy at the expense of aspects of individual interests and communal values, perverting the people involved. Property obtained via exchange in excess of need also violates virtuous behavior in the craft or art of household provisioning for a variety of reasons. Obtaining an excess of goods implies property cannot be put to its proper use: *praktikon* [practice or use]. Individual accumulation wastes social wealth, for when one member of society amasses property above what he needs, others in the community become deprived from the use-values they lack. An excess of wealth for one implies for Aristotle a deficiency of wealth for another.[6] The lust for lucre undermines both individual virtue and communal cohesion by breeding mistrust and a 'disproportionate' distribution of wealth.

Aristotle also argued that pursuing gain in trade bred political decay—a pivotal facet of communal life. Vivienne Brown notes "In Aristotle's *The Politics*, it is inconceivable that the state could be divorced from questions concerning virtuous activity and political participation for its citizens as the state is necessary for the sake of a perfect and self-sufficing life" (1994, 210). Whereas people leading a good life participate in social and political activities, those obsessed with amassing wealth for 'pleasures of the body' forsake them in their pursuit of gain. A simple logic rests behind this argument as T.J. Lewis highlights: "Acquisition beyond the necessary amount is a diversion of the citizen's capacities from the sphere of *polis* life" (1978, 73).

THWARTING UNNATURAL EXCHANGE.

Plato indicted greed and avariciousness as the contagion behind the breakdown of the *polis;* since he linked such deviant behavior to private property, he argued accordingly for its abolition, at least among all citizens that mattered. Aristotle associated the same destabilizing beliefs with commodity exchange undertaken for gain. He believed the singular focus upon lucre and individual enrichment in exchange led to forsaking political obligations and a systemic and divisive swindling of members of the *polis,* thereby undermining communal solidarity. Unlike Plato's concrete proposal to abolish private property to stem greed in society, Aristotle surprisingly stopped short of proposing a systemic program to keep such unnatural behavior in check (Lowry 1987a). One rationale for the lack resides in the complexity of Aristotle's explanation for avarice. Unlike Plato's essential connection between private property and greed, Aristotle thought commodity exchange "naturally" played a valuable role in Athenian society. I see Aristotle's vision of the marketplace producing a conundrum: how to preserve commodity exchange and the good things it entailed while simultaneously ridding the process of avarice. Not all Aristotelian scholars interpret the relationship between avarice and exchange in the same way however.

William Kern (1983) argues the absence of a concrete proposal to eradicate unnatural exchange results from it being simply a manifestation of people's unlimited desire for pleasure. The root problem in Kern's reading of Aristotle becomes this unlimited desire for pleasure, and he suggests Aristotle appealed to reason and education in the moral virtues to address how passion dominates the intellect. Lewis (1978) largely concurs with Kern's interpretation, but reads Aristotle as supplementing education with an unreasonable ethical mandate governing the exchange process. For Lewis, undertaking exchange in the manner suggested by Aristotle "requires the application of standards of behavior to exchange which are so demanding that we, like most of Aristotle's contemporaries, refuse to be confined to a form of exchange requiring the imposition of such standards" (1978, 88).

Kern and Lewis argue that compellingly both Plato and Aristotle saw a role for educating the population in the moral virtues to help combat self-centered greed, or what Aristotle called a "type of wickedness" (*Nicomachean Ethics* 1130a25). Yet, their analyses reduce avarice to simply an individual flaw or perversion and by doing so miss how Plato's and Aristotle's focus on the social relations that promote such behavior. Spencer Pack (1985) maintained that Aristotle did not reduce avarice to an individual vice but understood it as related to social interaction. On a similar note, Lowry argues that for Aristotle, "hedonic self-interest was not explicable solely as a problem of the inner soul; he sought an explanation in terms of interactions *between* individuals" (1987a, 214).

I concur with Pack's and Lowry's reading, for it makes more sense given the logical structure of Aristotle's argument in *Politics*, i.e., his detailed discussion distinguishing natural from unnatural exchange and his association of the latter with foreign trade—an activity not bound by communal ties of reciprocity (Lowry 1987a, 225). It also helps make sense of the actions Plato and Aristotle proposed to shape social relations and mitigate the influence of avarice. Although Aristotle did not propose something as concrete as Plato's abolition of private property, Lowry argues he did embrace an "administrative authority" to help ensure profits would not come at the expense of need and to arbitrate the proper exchange proportions to avoid disputes (1987a, 196). Lowry also claims that the pervasive system of price controls governing most uniform (imported) commodities such as grain and wine in ancient Athens found intellectual justification in Aristotle's market sense. The Athenian state "resort[ed] to public regulation to assure reasonable prices and profits while protecting flows of stables, such as corn (grain), upon which the people depended" (1987a, 236). The administrative authority preserved commodity exchange but kept profiteering in check "so as not to impinge deleteriously upon the proper functioning of the *oikonomia* of the household and state" (Lowry 1987a, 238). Promoting education in the moral virtues comprised one line of attack for excising greed from the marketplace, but Aristotle also thought more direct action was necessary; doing otherwise would be treating the symptom rather than the disease.

ARISTOTELIAN MARKET SENSE IN PRACTICE AND THEORY.

Aristotle's vision and analysis of commodity exchange proved very influential and underpinned a wide range of actions undertaken over the ages to keep the unnatural form of exchange from tearing society apart. Concerning Aristotle's market sense, Tawney argued that philosophers in the middle ages "All insist[ed] that Christianity has no more deadly foe than the *appetitus divitiarum infinitus,* the unbridled indulgence of the acquisitive appetite" (1954, 4), and viewed commodity exchange (with its perceived connection to avarice) with suspicion. Roll notes how the "Canonists accepted Aristotle's distinction between the natural economy of the household [*oikonomia*] and the unnatural from of the science of supply [*chrematistike*], the art of money making" (1946, 38). Aquinas provides an explicit statement in this regard:

> The first [form of exchange] may be called natural and necessary; and obtains when exchange is made either of goods against goods, or goods against money, to meet the necessities of life . . . The other form of exchange, either of money against money or of any sort of goods against money, is carried on not for the necessary business of life, but for the sake of profit. (Qu. 77, Art. 4)

Commodity exchange played an important role in society for Aristotle and Aquinas as long as it rectified imbalances of resources and wealth as either nature or divine will intended. Aquinas lauded the praiseworthy character of commodity exchange in household provisioning, but condemned profiteering in exchange as sordid, "for of itself it serves only the desire for gain, which knows no bounds but spreads always further" (ibid).

Cannon Law, the economic and moral strictures of the Middle Ages, essentially combined "the teachings of the Gospels and of the early Christian Fathers with those of Aristotle, the philosopher who had tempered his realistic views of the economic process with ethical postulates" (Roll 1946, 37). Cannon Law's "just prices" constituted an explicit attempt to govern commodity transactions in order to promote bonds of reciprocity and social cohesion rather than greed and social decay. The teachings of the Gospels, which condemned the pursuit of profits in exchange as sinful behavior, attempted to instill moral virtues to keep greed in check while directly enforcing just prices. The administrative enforcement of just prices and the condemnation of avarice in the Gospels paralleled the Aristotelian market sense solutions to unnatural exchange and existed as common sense until well after the Reformation.

Liberals have spent over 200 years relentlessly dismissing Aristotle's vision of the marketplace, but the connection between profit-driven exchange and social conflict refuses to go away. Many so-called developing nations attempted to administer commodity exchange to promote the common weal and stymie profiteering by instituting price controls. The rhetoric surrounding the implementation of such policy reads like a script from Aristotle, with the blame for social ills being firmly assigned to people who use commodity exchange to enrich themselves. Consider the following statement by Eduardo Frei, the elected president of Chile in 1964, in which he defended "Christian Democrat" economic policies:

> It [the state] ought to be strong enough to prevent the creation beyond its regulatory authority of economic powers which can oppress and control the market for products and for work. It cannot be the impotent witness of what goes on in the market, because it would mean the end of liberty if each citizen were left to act according to his interest and his influence. (1969, 387)

Early political economists also grappled with Aristotle's market vision and analysis (Lowry 1979; Meek 1956; Roll 1946). Lowry (1987a, 1987b) and Kimberley Sims (2002) note how an Aristotelian market sense constitute the "other" in Adam Smith's vision of exchange in *The Wealth of*

Nations (1981). In the next chapter I examine in detail how Smith linked exchange motivated by self-interest with a host of positive entailments. Karl Marx, particularly in volume one of *Capital* (1990) and the *Grundrisse* (1993), also grapples with an Aristotelian market sense, as does Karl Polanyi in *The Great Transformation* (2001). Both theorists are considered in detail in forthcoming chapters.

Today, a considerable portion of the more academic literature critical of globalization sounds very Aristotelian in its objection to existing international trade agreements, on the grounds that greedy corporations enrich themselves in the global marketplace at the expense of needy individuals. Scholars operating within fair trade frameworks see benefits to international trade, but condemn contemporary trade agreements which allow for socially harmful profiteering upon weak labor or environmental regulation (DeMartino 2000; O'Brien 2004). The proliferation of fair trade coffee and other commodities such as cocoa today highlights, in least in principle, an Aristotelian market sense among those who seek to ensure the actual producers of such products receive a just price (Waridel 2002). Aristotle's distinction between exchange based upon distribution and need and exchange predicated upon profit and gain, and the implications of each form, helps us make sense of the seeming cacophony of dissenting voices on globalization today, something I present in detail in the final chapters of *Market Sense*. I also demonstrate how liberal proponents of trade agreements like Paul Krugman (2003) and Jagdish Bhagwati (1993; 2004) today dismiss alternatives to their market sense as nonsense—e.g., ignorant understandings of what exchange undertaken for gain "really" entails.

CONCLUSION.

Aristotle and Plato saw greed and avariciousness as destabilizing for the *polis,* promoting social conflict and thwarting the obtainment of Ideal society. Both scholar's probings of avarice arose in response to widespread social decay and conflict. Aristotle's quest to discern society's deviation from his Ideal led him to single out and condemn exchange motivated by avarice as the fly in the ointment. Aristotle's vision and analysis of commodity exchange produced a common market sense that extended well beyond the context of Ancient Greece, including 21st century economic discourse.

On a thin level, Aristotle defined commodity exchange as the transaction of physically produced goods for money, and he saw the activity as a natural part of Greek life. On a thicker level, Aristotle divided commodity exchange into two types predicated upon how people employed the process and he associated a distinct set of meanings, i.e., entailments, with each. He lauded the use of exchange as nature intended as promoting individual virtue, social cohesion and political engagement; on the other hand, he equated unnatural pursuit of profits in exchange with a corruption of virtue and withdrawal from social and political life. Other associations of the unnatural form of exchange included a maldistribution of property, for it led some people to acquire excess wealth while others lacked the necessities of a good life.

Aristotle's analysis of exchange led him to a conundrum: how to preserve commodity exchange and the good things it entailed while simultaneously ridding the process of avarice. A similar problem haunts much of critical contemporary globalization literature. Many see the global marketplace as potentially beneficial for everyone, but worry about its corruption by greedy CEO's, rapacious merchants and a rouge's gallery of international bankers scouring markets for profit. Some people also blame the recent rash of corporate scandals rocking the American corporate landscape on a few bad, avaricious apples manipulating markets for personal gain. Aristotle's market sense helps us make sense of these arguments, but it also points out its limitations.

Singling out greed as the problem behind today's social, economic and political woes resonates today in many activist circles, but focusing solely on avaricious individuals leads to some deep philosophical and practical problems. Aristotle and Plato presented greed as a social rather than an individual problem. Plato's call for the abolition of private property and Aristotle's support for administrative authority to regulate prices constitute explicit attempts to change the social relations they indicted as inducing greed. Instilling virtue through education possessed benefits, but in end they saw this as akin to treating symptoms rather than the disease itself. Condemning individual greed as the root cause behind contemporary problems individuates and reduces social ills to the perverse behavior of a few bad apples and directs attention away from the institutional structure engendering such behavior. Ridding society of greedy merchants, purging corporate boards of directors of avaricious CEO's and so forth only treats the outward manifestation of a deeper, social problem, implying along the way a tacit acceptance of the *status quo*.

Chapter Three
Adam Smith's Market Sense.

Adam Smith's name has become a byword for free market economics.
The account of the benefits of free competitive markets found in An
Inquiry into the Nature and Causes of the Wealth of Nations *is*
regarded as the classic statement of the virtues of a laissez-faire capital-
ism in which economic agents contribute most effectively to the public
good by selfishly pursuing their own interests guided only by the profit
motive.

—Vivienne Brown, *Adam Smith's Discourse.*

Marx sardonically quipped over a century ago that celebrants of the market envision it as "the exclusive realm of Freedom, Equality, Property and
Bentham" (1990, 280). He also noted this understanding of the marketplace "provide[s] the 'free-trader *vulgaris*' with his views, his concepts and
the standard by which he judges the society of capital and wage labor"
(ibid). The sophisticated analysis of the market contained in Adam Smith's
Wealth of Nations (1981) played no small role in the production of the
market sense underpinning the defense of free-traders in the nineteenth century, as well as contemporary liberal globalization.[1] Smith's analysis of the
exchange process in his *Wealth of Nations* (1776) did not arise in a vac-
uum; several theoretical shifts occurred during the sixteenth and seventeenth centuries that laid the groundwork for his analysis.

By the middle of the eighteenth century, a new market sense began to
emerge that associated the pursuit of profits in commodity exchange with
freedom, liberty and expanding wealth. In this period, the gradual recasting
of greed, avarice, or "economic self-interest" from a vice or perversion into
an intrinsic and tolerated aspect of human nature stands out as a major
rethinking of individuality that directly challenged Aristotle's market sense.
Understanding all individuals as naturally self-interested led in turn to a profound retheorization of society, touching off a spate of new philosophical

inquiries by social contract theorists who attempted to reconcile social harmony with *homo economicus* (economic man). Finally, considering individuals as naturally endowed with innate human rights such as freedom and liberty influenced market sense as well, for such rights often rested upon particular understandings of commodity exchange and private property.

These radical theoretical transformations were of course related to the great material transformations occurring during this time. Commodity exchange exploded in scope during in the sixteenth and seventeenth centuries at roughly the same time as the breakdown of the feudal order. As the symbiotic feudal system imploded, so did certain understandings of society, such as the idea that "all human activities are treated as a part of a single system, the nature of which is determined by the spiritual destiny of humanity" (Colletti 1974, 201). It is no accident that commodity exchange, avarice and social conflict entered the theoretical spotlight during this transitional time given the dominant, classical market sense that linked them together.

Marxian and other radical scholars associated the rapid expansion of commodity exchange repeatedly to various disruptive effects in Western Europe.[2] Dobb summarizes the familiar story quite concisely:

> How the growth of trade carried in its wake the trader and the trading community, which nourished itself like an alien body within the pores of feudal society; how with exchange came an increasing percolation of money into the self-sufficiency of manorial economy; how the presence of the merchant encouraged a growing inclination to barter surplus products and produce for the market—all this, with much richness of detail, has been told many times. (1947, 37)

Commodity exchange served as the common thread uniting the stories, even though a lively debate took place over whether it was a cause or an effect of the breakdown of the feudal order. Regardless of who won the debate, it highlighted the diverse social and cultural changes occurring alongside the increasing prevalence of exchange during this unsettled time.

Smith argued, in direct contrast to an Aristotelian market sense, that allowing people to follow their "natural" inclinations for self enrichment promoted an expansion of wealth that, in turn, provided the foundation for social harmony. The linkage between commodity exchange and expanding wealth arrived in Smith's *Wealth of Nations* and was mediated by the division and specialization of a labor; however, commodity exchange served as the prime mover behind them. The analytical argument underpinning Smith's vision of the marketplace does not receive much attention, but his linkage between commodity exchange and expanding wealth comprises a crucial component of contemporary liberal market sense.

Smith's representation of society as a mass of individuals all indulging their own self-interest in the marketplace comprised a theoretical *a priori* in the *Wealth of Nations* and underpinned his analysis of commodity exchange. Discerning the key to expanding wealth *given a society composed of selfish individuals* animates the *Wealth of Nations* (Callari 1981, 102).[3] The beauty of Smith's argument resided in the idea that allowing people to buy and sell commodities according to their own best interests will naturally and harmoniously yield the maximum amount of wealth in society. Numerous theoretical tracts (Brown 1994; Hirschman 1986; Lux 1990) demonstrate compellingly that Smith never intended the *Wealth of Nations* as an apologia for the emerging umbrella of processes often grouped under modern capitalism, but it still serves as a poster child for exactly this.[4] After discussing the intellectual and material climate that gave birth to Smith, a close reading of his analysis of market activity unfolds below, ending with a detailed evaluation of the market sense he left in his wake.

SMITH'S INTELLECTUAL MILIEU.

The transmogrification of avaricious and self-centered individualism from a vice into an ineradicable trait of human nature began as far back as the sixteenth century (Roll 1946). By the eighteenth century, such an understanding of humanity was commonplace (although by no means universally accepted) in political, "economic" and philosophical circles.[5] Hirschman's tightly argued *The Passions and the Interests* provides a detailed examination (and (re)construction) of the intellectual climate in Europe over the time period ushering the change, and concluded that the naturalization of self-interest was "both the outcome of a long train of Western thought and an important ingredient of the intellectual climate of the seventeenth and eighteenth centuries" (1977, 69).[6] Regardless of the specifics behind the change in thought, it exerted numerous implications for what market activity means for society.

The common understanding of avarice as an intrinsic aspect of human nature facilitated the dissolution of Aristotle's classical distinction between the natural and unnatural form of commodity exchange. The basis of Aristotle's distinction between the two forms rested upon different motivations guiding the exchange process. Aristotle considered avarice to be an individual perversion potentially fostered in exchange, a behavior he in turn linked to social conflict and political decay. When people began to consider avarice as "naturally" the sole motivation behind buying and selling commodities, Aristotle's distinction between exchange motivated by avarice versus need fulfillment fell apart. Smith embraced and endorsed this new intellectual trend in the *Wealth of Nations,* claiming that people universally pursue their own self-interest, and that humanity has a natural propensity "to truck, barter and trade" (Smith 1981, 25). The contemporary acceptance by many economists of the pursuit of economic self-interest and market activity as "natural" helps explain why they often read Aristotle's theory of exchange as prescribing unrealistic moral constraints upon exchanging individuals. Aristotle's natural exchange becomes interpreted as placing artificial ethical compulsions or stipulations upon people in the marketplace, implying in turn that an authentic human nature being is constrained by Aristotle's demanding standards of behavior. Whereas Plato, Aristotle and early Christian philosophers denounced the pursuit of economic gain as unnatural and linked such activity to the influence of specific social institutions such as private property or commodity exchange, people who believe avarice constitutes a natural behavioral trait possess no use for discussions of the social institutions that promote or deter it. The emerging understanding of individuality and avarice stood classical and Christian philosophy on its head: rather than seeing avarice as a *product of* social and cultural institutions, it became increasingly understood as the *impetus behind* them.

Another implication of the sedimentation in philosophical discourse of self-interested behavior *qua* human nature involved placing economic activity guided by such an impulse outside of ethical and moral considerations—a striking rupture with prior philosophical inquiry. Aquinas for instance "never discussed economic subjects abstractly, but always in connection with larger problems of ethics or politics" (Monroe 1924, 52). Tawney makes a similar point in his introduction to *Religion and the Rise of Capitalism,* namely that all the major religious movements in Europe prior to and immediately after the restoration rested upon "the assumption that the institution of property, the transactions of the market-place, the whole fabric of society and the whole range of its activities, stand by no absolute title, but must justify themselves at the bar of religion" (1954, 4). Viewing avarice as human nature renders moral evaluation and debate philosophically moot. This should not suggest avarice and commodity exchange became completely divorced from ethical discussion, but scholars who accepted or at least tolerated avarice as part of human nature treated debates over the morality of this behavior as either futile or belonging to the realm of religion. According to Tawney, what emerged was "the doctrine that religion and economic interests form two separate and co-ordinate kingdoms, of which neither, without presumption, can encroach on the other" (1954, 4). Transactions in the market place (and the motivations behind them) for most enlightenment scholars became located outside of ethical considerations altogether, as evidenced in the popular maxim "trade is one thing, religion is another."

Obviously, the separation of economic activity from religious scrutiny seriously undermined Christian philosophy's ability to regulate economic life and, in fact, Roll notes that Canonist doctrine collapsed completely in this regard (1946, 47). Although many complicated issues contributed to the Reformation, I see it as at least partially engendered by the collapse of the Canonist doctrine regarding economic affairs. Kenneth Lux (1990) adds that the Reformation constituted not only a response to the breakdown of Canon law, but also to a decline in more traditional, heavy-handed guidance to temper self-interest. One of the central issues propelling the religious revolution involved a radical questioning of the notion that self-seeking, greedy behavior *necessarily* leads to hell and damnation. Calvinist doctrine no longer treated 'economic motivations' as "alien to the life of the spirit . . . and it is perhaps the first systematic body of religious teaching which can be said to recognize and applaud the economic virtues" (Tawney 1954, 93).

Calvinist doctrine recognized and applauded economic self-interest, but still called for some restraints on it, lest social conflict ensue. Rather than continuing the Canonist attempt at regulation of these new-found "virtues" via an administrative authority (e.g., just prices) or the public condemnation of excessive profiteering, the Reformation called for an *individuation* of moral and ethical obligations to mitigate the perceived negative social and individual consequences of avarice. The Puritan movement, a particular strand of Reformation thought very influential in Smith's Scotland, exemplified the individuation of moral obligations:

> In their emphasis on the moral duty of untiring activity, on work as an end in itself, on the evils of luxury and extravagance, on foresight and thrift, on moderation and self-discipline and rational calculation, they had created an ideal of Christian conduct, which canonized as an ethical principle the efficiency which economic theorists were preaching as a specific for social disorders. (Tawney 1954, 206)

Calvin and his followers did not abandon the notion that economic aspects of society must stand before ethical judgment, or the notion that such behavior needed to be regulated to ensure social harmony. Instead of attempting a perceived fruitless quest to (re)institute broader social regulations however, they proposed their own (very strict) code of *individual* conduct to mitigate the perceived socially divisive implications of avarice, private property and commodity exchange. The increasing tolerance of economic motivations found within reformist strains of Christian philosophy, and the plea for individual moderation and self-discipline to temper greed and avarice, profoundly impacted Smith, steeped as he was within the Scottish Protestant movement which gave birth to the Puritans.[7]

Given this backdrop, let us now turn to the more philosophical responses, e.g., the search for social institutions to maintain social harmony *given* humanity's presumed innate proclivity for self-enrichment. However much individual economic self-interest became accepted, recognized or tolerated as a fundamental part of human nature in this time period, many thinkers still considered such behavior to be *a,* if not *the,* primary source of social conflict. As a result, much of social and political theory written during this time, especially tracts written by social contract theorists such as Hobbes, emerged as competing solutions posed to the perceived conundrum of avarice and social harmony. The social contract theorists' concern with social cohesion reflected the material breakdown of the feudal regime, just as Aristotle's concerns regarding social harmony and political decay related to the collapse of the Athenian empire and its democratic project.

The ontological framework or problematic constituting the conundrum possess as much interest for making sense of Smith's analysis of commodity exchange as the solutions posed. The philosophical quest in the seventeenth century for the set of social institutions most compatible with an essentialized notion of individuality opened up a Pandora's box of speculation. A heated debate ensued concerning the specific nature of the human essence, for if society ideally consisted of institutions that would allow the human essence to flourish, it becomes of critical importance to deduce what exactly the human essence consists of. One of the leading claims made by luminaries such as Hobbes (and embraced *in toto* by Smith in his *Wealth of Nations*) maintained that individuals naturally sought to improve their material conditions and/or possess an innate desire for pecuniary gain. The struggle to find optimal social institutions to rectify self-interest and social harmony reflected a new understanding of science for society.

Even if philosophers had somehow reached an agreement upon the correct essence of humanity, it does not necessarily follow that they would agree upon the optimal social milieu for it to flourish. The tacit and formal acceptance of economic self-interest as an intrinsic trait of humanity in no way mitigated the link between the pursuit of self-interest and social conflict.[8] More contemporaneous to Smith, Hobbes theorized that the pursuit of self-interest would inherently lead to a war of all against all. Hobbes associated this behavior primarily with a quest for power rather than pecuniary gain: "I put for a generall inclination of all mankind, a perpetuall and restlesse desire of Power after power, that ceaseth onely in Death" (1986, 161). Given the belief that a state of never ending war would result from unchecked individual action, Hobbes theorized citizens would willingly surrender some of their personal liberties and freedoms to a Leviathan, a political entity charged with enforcing social law and preventing social conflict. Hobbes was not alone in calling for some sort of political institution or system of laws to ensure the restraint of self-interested behavior, but others like Giambattista Vico began thinking such behavior might actually promote the 'common weal.' Later Enlightenment thought began to think of greed alone as capable of counter-acting other vices and passions in society, and as Bock notes (1994), the notion that individual actions could result in unintended or unexpected social benefits actually became quite popular.

Vico's *The New Science*, originally published in 1725, offers a classic and representative example of such thinking and the ontology upon which its rests. Vico's text covered an immense philosophical range, but the most revolutionary idea it contained concerns his proclamation that the social world is the work of man. In Book Four of *The New Science,* Vico juxtaposes three forms of society: divine, heroic, and rational. In the one based upon reason, people recognize the social constructed nature of all social institutions and the possibility of reconstructing and improving them. Vico contrasted this rational understanding of society to the Divine, which accepted and defended the existing (presumably the old feudal) order as divine providence, regardless of whether or not the perceived natural propensities of humanity are promoted or thwarted.[9]

Vico embraced a rational conception of society and therefore interpreted every social process and institution as a product of man. He, like other enlightenment scholars, argued that the inner nature of man could be grasped via reason; however, he went further by proposing a new science that centered on a rational deduction of the best form of society, taking various presumptions about human nature as given. Vico's theoretical work aimed to create a science of human society that could do for the world of nations what scholars like Galileo and Newton had done for the world of nature (Fisch 1970, xxxxviii). Vico's *The New Science* was primarily concerned with the proper method of social analysis and hence differs from the more prescriptivist interventions of the social contract theorists like Hobbes. Nonetheless, Vico makes a striking claim in *The New Science,* namely that "the strength, riches and wisdom of commonwealth" emerged unwittingly from men living according to their "three great vices, ferocity, avarice and ambition and all pursuing them according to their own self-interest" (1970, 131–2).

Vico and Hobbes receive attention here not just because of the solutions they proposed to reconcile social harmony and individual self-interest, but also due to the theoretical implications of the perceived problem they addressed. By the eighteenth century, "While God could still be recognized as the author of human beings, the emphasis now was on humankind as a part of nature and, therefore, subject to the same kinds of comprehension and controls used in understanding and dealing with other natural phenomena" (Bock 1994, 31). Tawney notes a more specialized shift in economic thinking that reflected this change, to wit:

> The rise of Political Arithmetic after the Restoration, profoundly influenced, as it was, by the Cartesian philosophy and by the progress of natural science, stamped their spontaneous and doctrine less individualism with the seal of theoretical orthodoxy. . . . The exact analysis of natural conditions, the calculations of forces and strains, the reduction of the complex to the operation of simple, constant and measurable forces, was the natural bias of an age interested primarily in mathematics and physics. (1954, 208)

Reducing the individual to essentially a rational animal motivated by avarice simplified the human subject and made humanity in general comprehensible. "Enlightenment thinkers also undertook seriously to deny the operation of blind and unintelligible forces in human affairs" (Bock 1994, 45). The fear of unintelligibility led to various attempts to deduce some social laws of motion existing underneath the social complexity. Hirschman argues convincingly that although Smith is typically credited with the palatable representation of society whereby social harmony would naturally occur *not despite but because of* activity motivated by avarice, other scholars such as Vico already opened the theoretical door. Hirschman summarizes emerging theoretical trends nicely, arguing that scholars began to consider how "*one set of passions, hitherto known variously as greed, avarice, or love of lucre, could be usefully employed to oppose and bridle such other passions as ambition, lust for power, or sexual lust*" (1977, 41). What was unique about Smith's solution for social harmony is how he specifically made *commodity exchange* the arena for the interplay of these innate passions, resulting in a powerful new market sense.

Enlightenment thought touched commodity exchange primarily through its perceived associations with liberty, freedom and equality before the law. Even though liberty, like freedom, often emerged in liberal discourse in negative terms, e.g., through a discussion of specific *violations* of liberty and freedom, a positive theme throughout linked liberty and commodity exchange (and also, of course, private property). Locke and other liberal philosophers always associated liberty and private property (Colletti 1974); commodity exchange entered the scene as the optimal means of distributing private property without violating private property rights. Liberty and freedom became linked with private property and the untrammeled right of amassing and disposing it via market activity, influencing market sense in the process.

Liberty concerns the ability "each man hath, to use his own power, as he will himselfe, for the preservation of his own Nature; that is to say, of his own life; and consequently, of doing any thing, which in his own Judgement, and Reason, hee shall conceive to be the aptest means thereunto" (Hobbes 1986, 189). Hobbes defined liberty itself as "the absence of externall Impediments: which Impediments, may oft take away part of a mans power to do what hee would" (ibid). Hobbes makes amply clear in *Leviathan* that "what hee would" meant the pursuit of self-interest, power, and personal property.

Locke more explicitly discussed (and therefore related) the economic aspects of liberty and freedom. Liberty for Locke meant being:

> free from restraint and violence from others . . . *a liberty to dispose, and order, as he lists, his Person, Actions, Possessions, and his whole Property,* within the Allowance of those Laws under which he is; and therein not to be subject to the arbitrary Will of another, but freely to follow his own. (1960, 57, emphasis mine)

Hobbes and Locke evoke a maxim of individual rights predicated upon individual liberty derived from deductive reason rather than a preordained plan or design. Locke went further than Hobbes by presenting the concept of liberty (like that of property) as an innate and inalienable right, which as Colletti notes did not derive "from society and therefore from his historical relations with the species but from a direct transcendental investiture" (1974, 150).[10] Locke specified the connection between individual liberty and exchange by *defining* liberty (in part) as the ability to exchange property (and labor power) without restraint. Liberty became folded into market sense via the explicit linkage between liberty and commodity exchange by Locke and other contract theorists.

This brief investigation highlights some of the broad shifts in thinking with manifold implications for the meaning and significance of commodity exchange prior to Smith's *Wealth of Nations*. The transmogrification of avaricious and self-centered individualism from an individual corruption or vice into an innate and tolerated aspect of humanity eroded Aristotle's market sense. Infusing commodity exchange with notions of individual rights such as freedom and liberty contributed to the emergence of a new market sense as well. Both of these played a large role in defining the central problematic of Enlightenment discourse—the deduction of optimal social controls or institutions allowing the human essence to flourish while maintaining social cohesion or harmony. In the course of struggling within this problematic, Enlightenment philosophers encountered a contradiction that would haunt social theory for centuries, namely that the social institutions proposed as necessary to maintain social harmony all, to some degree, infringed upon individual freedom and liberty. The broad philosophical quest for social and individual controls to prevent greed from leading to social conflict constituted an important component of the theoretical backdrop for the *Wealth of Nations*.

The next section, *Smith and the System of Natural Liberty*, demonstrates how Adam Smith severed the Gordian knot binding individual self-interest and social conflict. Smith's system adroitly reconciled social harmony with self-centered individualism by celebrating market activity motivated by avarice. Smith's solution also resolved a similar problem within mercantile economic thought: "Most of what is considered political economy rested upon the assumption that without a large state presence to promote various sectors of the economy, and to regulate economic life, the state and society would fall apart" (Brown 1994, 157).[11] Both contract theory and mercantile economic thought envisioned various rules and regulations implemented by the state as necessary to maintain order and stability, even though they also infringed upon the rights of citizens and the freedom and liberty of exchanging subjects. Smith in contrast argued that unleashing self-interested exchange from its "artificial" constraints (e.g., state rules and regulations) would promote social harmony *and* solve the economic balances mercantilism worried about. Smith's major rupture with established philosophy rested with his vision and analysis of market activity as naturally promoting social harmony. Further, he recast social conflict as arising from political interventions that thwarted individuals from freely engaging in market activity.

SMITH AND THE SYSTEM OF NATURAL LIBERTY.

Celebrants of the current social order often equate the marketplace with individual freedom and liberty. As the discussion of Hobbes, Locke and the Reformation elucidated, these exchange entailments arose in part because of philosophical inquiries preceding Adam Smith.[12] Smith did play a foundational role in solidifying these associations with commodity exchange and added the crucial component of social harmony. The central argument elucidated in his *Wealth of Nations* revolved around how exchanging subjects, if and when given the liberty and freedom to engage in commodity exchange for personal gain, provide a foundation for social harmony and the expansion of wealth rather than social conflict and a perpetual state of war.[13] Smith's analytical case for his vision of the marketplace rested with his system of natural liberty.

Coming to grips with Smith's system of natural liberty is essential for making sense of his intervention in the *Wealth of Nations*. A close reading of the *Wealth of Nations* brings out three distinct aspects of the system. First, it functions as an *a priori* conceptualization of social evolution, a logico-deductive model of the laws of motion that guide the development of society. Second, the system connotes an ideal or optimal economic situation, a vision of what society would be like without infringements on the liberty and freedom to exchange commodities. Third, Smith employs it as an economic contract similar to a Hobbesian social contract to govern the realm of commodity exchange.

The first step in making sense of this system involves considering its foundations, for it rests upon a very specific representation of the individual and society. In marked contrast to Smith's expansive notion of individuality in *The Theory of Moral Sentiments* (2000), he reduced individuals in the *Wealth of Nations* to simply buyers and sellers of commodities who are intrinsically motivated by economic gain. Smith portrayed society as "composed of individuals who are all like each other, who are all defined as individuals by the fact that they consume, and who therefore have the same set of concerns and interests" (Callari 1981, 104). Smith reduced commodity exchange to an innate human propensity and in doing so deftly sidestepped any discussion of the socio-historic temporality of this process. Such a treatment of commodity exchange characterizes most liberal notions of commercial society arising after Smith. The second step to understanding the system of natural liberty involves its rhetorical function in the *Wealth of Nations,* for Smith employed it a hypothetical construct akin to Aristotle's and Plato's Ideal to judge the societies around him. Smith's system of natural liberty emerges in this light as a counterfactual to the existing order.

The system of natural liberty is "that order of things which necessity imposes in general, though not in every particular country, is, in every particular country, promoted by the natural inclinations of man" (Smith 1981, 377). The evolutionary facet of the system also emerges in how Smith describes the path of social progression:

> According to the natural course of things . . . the greater part of the capital of every growing society is, first, directed to agriculture, afterwards

to manufactures, and last of all to foreign commerce. This order of
things is so very natural, that in every society that had any territory, it
has always, I believe, been in some degree observed. (1981, 380)

Smith deems the system natural because he argued that if only humans
were allowed to follow their innate proclivities unimpeded, the system of
natural liberty would emerge spontaneously.

The system of natural liberty also refers to an idealist vision of society
Smith deduced from his representation of human nature. Smith repeatedly
argues that if only certain economic actors would quit infringing upon the
natural order of things, expanding wealth and individual happiness would
ensue for everyone in society. The importance of this idea rests in how Smith
theorized infringements as being, first and foremost, rules and regulations that
constrained or distorted people's natural freedom and liberty to exchange
commodities. Smith makes his economic utopia easily attainable, for achiev-
ing it simply requires the removal of such constraints or distortions—an imag-
inary not lost on celebrants of the current social order. Scholars who focus
upon the utopian aspect of the system often represent Smith as an apostle of
individualistic, unbridled greed in economic affairs, although a bevy of scholars contest this reading (Brown, 1994; Evensky, 1992; Lux, 1990). Brown
argues for instance that people have subsequently turned this idea into "an
argument in favour of *laissez-faire* commercial capitalism, and a prescient ideological statement for a new economic age waiting in the wings" (1994, 165).

Another facet of Smith's system of natural liberty involves its hypothetical contract nature. Whereas Hobbes and Locke explicate a political or
social contract, Smith outlines (albeit sporadically) the system of natural
liberty as an economic contract. Like contract theorists in general, Smith
grounds his system upon supposed natural human propensities and produces a knowledge of society where certain actions are justified in everyone's best interest. Unlike Hobbes, Smith sees no inherent reason for social
conflict and hence no need to cede rights such as individual freedom and
liberty to some state entity to prevent it. Smith's economic contract involves
simply the mutual assurance among the members of society of their right to
buy and sell commodities without infringement. This means for Smith in
particular that economic actors have a social obligation *not* to use state
policy to skew the exchange game in their favor.

THE NATURAL PATH OF SOCIAL PROGRESSION.

According to Smith, all societies naturally progress through well defined
stages, each characterized by greater wealth and opulence, though various

artificial social constraints may slow or hamper this accumulation process.[14] Agriculture represents the first stage of social evolution, where society as a whole begins to engage in sedentary farming communities. Before towns are able to be populated by craftsmen, artisans, merchants and other specialists, or even to exist severed from the agricultural sector, there needs to be a surfeit of food stuffs to feed the non-agrarian population. Due to agricultural advancement induced by technical change (driven by the innate desire of humanity to better its lot), a surplus of agricultural commodities eventually emerges. Smith claims the surplus becomes available *in the form of commodities* to support craftsmen and so forth living in cities and in turn, the specialized craftsmen in the city *produce goods in order to exchange* for agrarian products. Even in this early stage of society, Smith claims all useful objects take the form of commodities, a bold claim which is predicated upon the naturalness of commodity exchange and ignores a vast array of other potentially pervasive distributional processes.

Smith maintains the manufacturing and merchant sectors in towns developed in response to the effective demand from the agrarian sector for specialized tools and so forth. The net result is that the countryside is supplied with manufactured goods like plows and specialized agrarian technology. The infusion of new technology in the countryside facilitates a division of agrarian labor, which, in turn, increases the production of excess food. The new agrarian surplus allows the expansion of specialized craftsmen in towns and cities and hence ever more, better agrarian technology. As the wealth in the countryside expanded, the agrarian population purchased more manufactured goods from the towns and vice versa, setting in motion a cycle of expanding wealth in both town and country. Once the agrarian sector became sated with manufactured goods, the excess supply of manufactured or agrarian commodities began to be traded internationally for various luxuries, exotic commodities and so forth, and society entered its final stage: commercial society.[15]

The commodities involved—i.e., the use-values being bought, sold, and haggled over in all of Smith's stages of development—include labor power, land and capital alongside more traditional commodities such as food and manufactured goods. Owners of labor power in every stage desire the highest price for their commodity and move to whatever sector pays the best wages. Likewise, owners of capital advance their stock in whatever sector yields the highest reward in the form of profit. Smith argued, not incidentally, the most profitable sectors for both labor and capital change hand in hand with the path of social progression he elucidated.[16] The movement of capital and labor by the buyers and sellers of these commodities results in competition or struggle amongst them, ultimately inducing not only a division of labor, but technological change. Unlike the modern marginalist understanding of competition, for Smith "competition secures the greatest annual revenue, not by promoting market equilibrium, but by means of facilitating the proper course of sectoral development which underlies the natural progress of opulence" (Brown 1994, 183).

Smith explains the division as being ultimately due to the struggle amongst individuals in the realm of commodity exchange pursuing their own self-interest, or in other words, by sellers looking to get the most money for their respective commodities and buyers looking for the best deal:

> This division of labor, from which so many advantages are derived, is not originally the effect of any human wisdom, which foresees and intends that general opulence to which it gives occasion. It is necessary, though very slow and gradual consequence of a certain propensity in human nature which has in view no such extensive utility; the propensity to truck, barter and exchange one thing for another. (Smith 1981, 25)

Smith's assertion of an innate human proclivity to exchange commodities, coupled with the claim that people possess a universal desire to better their lot, constitutes the driving force behind social progression. Even though the human motivations behind the increase in the annual product in each stage of development remain identical, more and more social wealth characterizes each stage of social evolution. People undertaking commodity exchange with only their self-interest in mind, whether it be the selling of agricultural goods, labor power, or manufactured goods to foreign nations, has the unintentional consequence of promoting opulence for society as a whole like an invisible hand.

> By preferring the support of domestick to that of foreign industry, he [the merchant] intends only his own security; and by directing that industry in such a manner as its produce may be of the greatest value, he intends only his own gain, and he is in this, as in many other cases, led by an invisible hand to promote an end which was no part of his intention. Nor is it always the worse for the society that it was no part of it. By pursuing his own interest he frequently promotes that of the society more effectually than when he really intends to promote it. I have never known much good done by those who affected to trade for the publick good. (Smith 1981, 456)

Smith differentiates each stage of his teleological theory of social progress by the sectorial allocation of production and the total amount of social wealth. The final stage, commercial society, denotes a state of affairs where the division of labor has so thoroughly advanced that everyone becomes a specialized producer. Hence, even though people's motivations behind exchange remain constant, society still assumes a different form because specialization has left everyone dependent upon exchange for their means of subsistence. With everyone needing to sell what they produce in order to obtain the means to purchase their means of subsistence, "Every man thus lives by exchanging, or becomes in some measure a merchant, and the society itself grows to be what is properly a commercial society" (Smith 1981, 37).[17]

Smith represents all social formations as aggregates of exchanging agents motivated by their own personal interests, a view explicated in his *Theory of Moral Sentiments:*

> Society may subsist among different men, as among different merchants, from a sense of its utility, without any mutual love of affection; and though no man in it should owe any obligation, or be bound in gratitude to any other, it may still be upheld by a mercenary exchange of good offices according to an agreed valuation. (Smith 2000, 124)

Smith's representation of society constitutes an important part of contemporary market sense: it became the basic premise of neoclassical and liberal economic thinking and facilitated an understanding of modern society as simply individuals linked via their mutual dependence upon commodity exchange for survival (and of course individual gain).

By locating infringements upon the system of natural liberty as the primary source of social conflict, e.g., misguided state economic policy favoring some groups' ability to exchange their commodities over others, Smith shifted conflict *away* from private property, commodity exchange, and of course production processes. Smith did not turn a blind eye to the social tensions all around him, such as the grinding poverty side by side the explosion of merchant and industrial wealth, but he did maintain that the resolution of such problems simply entailed the removal of the misguided economic policies ultimately behind them.

Vico speculated the desire for economic gain might be able to promote social riches, but he never articulated an explicit linkage. Smith on the other hand firmly linked commodity exchange motivated by economic self-interest with individual liberty, freedom, riches *and* social harmony. Hobbes envisioned a conflict between the pursuit of self-interest and social cohesion, leading him to argue that citizens possess an obligation to relinquish some of their freedoms to the state to preserve society: only a

Leviathan would be able to establish social harmony given the innate propensities of humanity. Smith's system of natural liberty rebutted the idea of an innate conflict between avarice and social harmony.

MERCANTILE POLICY AND THE SMITHIAN ECONOMIC CONTRACT.

Rhetorically, Smith consistently presents his system of natural liberty as a response to political economy, an obvious and common sense alternative to the directing hand of the statesman or legislator "to oversee economic development" (Brown 1994, 156). Smith used a wide range of literary devices to defend it in this role, including numerous illustrative examples and innuendos. Brown illustrates this by comparing and contrasting the language Smith utilized in his juxtaposition of his system of natural liberty with mercantile economic policy; Smith represented his system of natural liberty as natural and reasonable in contrast to mercantile sophistry and prejudice.[18] The policies that received the brunt of his criticism—merchant monopolies, charters, trade guilds and so forth—he presented as the outcome of rapacious merchant and industrial capitalists unjustly influencing commodity exchange via state policy for their own ends. Smith consistently placed the selfish interests of merchants and manufacturers as contra society at large, and chastised them for breaking his perceived economic contract through their general propensity to deceive, cheat and even oppress the public in order to glean the most profits as possible for themselves.

The following quotes are symptomatic of Smith's usage of the system of natural liberty to critique the specific mercantile policies and practices that undermined the expansion of wealth and induced social conflict:

> The uniform, constant, and uninterrupted effort of every man to better his condition, the principle from which publick and national, as well as private opulence is originally derived, is frequently powerful enough to maintain the natural progress of things toward improvement, in spite both of the extravagance of government and the greatest errors of administration. (1981, 343)
>
> But though the profusion of government must, undoubtedly, have retarded the natural progress of England toward wealth and improvement, it has not been able to stop it. . . . In the midst of all the exactions of government, this capital has been silently and gradually accumulated by the private frugality and good conduct of individuals, by their universal, continual, and uninterrupted effort to better their own condition. It is this effort, protected by law and allowed by liberty to exert

itself in the manner that is most advantageous [by buying and selling their commodities], which has maintained the progress of England toward opulence and improvement in almost all former times, and which, it is to be hoped, will do so in all future times. (1981, 345)

The profusion of governmental laws enacted on behalf of merchants and manufacturers exists as a fly in the ointment for the system of natural liberty, and Smith directed his full wrath at the ability and desire of certain individuals to skew the exchange game in their favor. Smith bemoaned for instance how linen manufactures and merchants managed to enact duties on linen to raise the price of their product, thus raising the price of linen for consumers and, through the encouragement of the importation of foreign linen yarn, suppressing the wages in the linen industry—i.e., the weavers' commodity.[19]

The rapacious pursuit of profits, manifested in everyone seeking the highest price possible for their commodities, benefits society through the promotion of a division and specialization of labor and moves society along its natural path of progression. Smith used caution when presenting this thesis however, for he also envisioned the desire for profit as potentially slowing down the expansion of wealth if and when some group of exchanging agents manages to co-opt the state into enacting policy to favor them. Merchants who violate the economic contract have an unfair advantage in the realm of exchange and thereby reduce the rate at which wealth expands for society as a whole, induce a skewed distribution of the social product, and promote social unrest. Yet, Smith did not see an *inherent* problem in pursuing profits in exchange: the real danger lies with policy makers and social theorists who, due to their false consciousness, keep enacting policies that hamper the natural progression of society by restricting exchange for their own self-enrichment. Callari also notes how Smith reduces conflict to political rather than economic sources, for social unrest arises due to state economic policy rather than the "given nature of the class structure" (1981, 107).

The charm of the *Wealth of Nations* rests not only in how Smith represented the origins of social conflict, but also with how he cached the entire argument behind the system of natural liberty in terms of society in general—from the meanest laborer to the wealthiest capitalist. Laborers comprised the majority of the population in commercial society and Smith argued that "their prosperity is necessary to the stability of society" (Callari 1981, 109). If merchant and industrial capitalists refused to recognize this and insisted upon enacting state policy to favor themselves, not only would social conflict ensue, but these capitalists would be, in the long run, digging their own graves, for their interests and those of the meaner classes are fundamentally imbricated. Smith took exceptional pains to point out to the intellectual and wealthier strata of society (presumably his audience) that it is not only just, but their *duty* to insure everyone benefits from the expansion of wealth:

> Is this improvement in the circumstances of the lower ranks of the people to be regarded as an advantage or as an inconveniency to the society? The answer seems at first sight abundantly plain. Servants, laboureres and workmen of different kinds, make up the far greater part of every great political society. But what improves the circumstances of the greater part can never be regarded as an inconveniency to the whole. No society can surely be flourishing and happy, of which the far greater part of the members are poor and miserable. It is but equity, besides, that they who feed, cloath and lodge the whole body of the people, should have such a share of the produce of their own labor as to be themselves tolerably well fed, cloathed and lodged. (1981, 96)

Fortunately, the only duty the social and economic elite needed to perform was to simply allow everyone, including the poorest, to exchange commodities freely.[20]

Smith's intervention in the *Wealth of Nations* appealed to many for a number of reasons. First, his system of natural liberty "postulates a natural order of development, entirely undirected by politics or state intervention, which perfectly mirrors the ideal sequence of development" (Brown 1994, 176). Secondly, since Smith's system of natural liberty rests upon assumed innate human proclivities, it requires no change in human behavior, no complicated social institutions, and no guiding hand of statesmen to bring it about.[21] The system of natural liberty emerges from the pages of the *Wealth of Nations* as the natural course of affairs, or what emerges in any society unless some social/economic actors hold it at bay.

Another attraction involved how the system of natural liberty addressed the central problem of prior social contract theory. Smith disagreed with Hobbes that greedy, self-serving individuals present a problem for social cohesion. If large merchants and manufacturers manage to restrain themselves from exerting political influence and tampering with the rules surrounding the exchange process, (a omnipresent danger given their own selfish interests), then social harmony will reign, being secured through expanding wealth for everyone. As a consequence, Smith rejected the premise that a state would have to impinge upon liberty and freedom to ensure social harmony. If only the system of natural liberty were allowed to flourish, social harmony would naturally ensue without the need to restrict individual freedoms and liberty.

Smith dealt with the central problem of mercantile economic policy in a similar manner. Prior to Smith, mercantile economic theory structured its analysis upon the presence of a strong state, not to maintain social cohesion through law *per se,* but to guide the expansion of wealth by enacting policy to promote a positive balance of trade, favoring certain industries, and ensuring the provisioning of the state itself, including its armies. The natural order of progress discussed under the rubric of the system of natural liberty unfolds without any guidance, since it occurs naturally as an outgrowth of human nature. Employing the state to direct the process of wealth expansion or the stages of economic development actually hinders the expansion of wealth by infringing upon the system rather than letting it flourish.

Smith agreed with the Physiocratic critique of mercantilism and Callari notes that the system of natural liberty is "similar to the physiocrat's concept of *laissez-faire*" (1981, 152). In fact, Smith employed Quensay's *laissez-faire, laissez aller* to further buttress his critique of mercantile policy guiding the accumulation of public and private wealth.[22] The accumulation of wealth ensures social harmony because even in a society characterized by rampant income inequality, an expanding economic pie mitigates the social tensions of inequity. As Myrdal points out, a central tenet of liberalism today is quite similar, in that "whenever someone increases his income, all benefit. For he can only succeed by offering to his fellows better and cheaper services than his rival" (1953, 44–5).[23]

Via his system of natural liberty, Smith provided an analysis of how individual self-seeking behavior could be harnessed and, in fact, promote social harmony if and when society allowed commodity exchange to flourish. As Meek (1956) has pointed out, the *Wealth of Nations* did not attract much attention for its abstract discussions of value or money: its charm to Smith's contemporaries lay in its focus on the idea of a harmoniously working social order.[24] Further, Smith solved the problems posed by both contract theory and mercantile economic policy by turning them on their head: social cohesion and wealth expansion arguably ensues in the *absence* of a strong state. Smith presents state economic policy, even if undertaken with the best intentions, as inevitably slowing down the natural accumulation of wealth by interrupting the natural progress of social evolution that the system of natural liberty arguably represents.

Smith's analysis of commodity exchange framed debates on its significance in a radically new way. The system of natural liberty emerged as a yardstick to compare/contrast with existing societies, just as Plato and Aristotle employed their Ideals to evaluate Ancient Greek society. In place of the classical natural/unnatural form of exchange, Smith juxtaposed the system of natural liberty with state-sponsored restrictions upon the exchange process. Smith associated the system of natural liberty with wealth, social harmony, liberty and freedom; in contrast, restricted exchange meant growing poverty, social discord, and a violation of individual rights.

All of this stated, Smith never set out to provide an apologia for the status quo and, in fact, the *Wealth of Nations* provides numerous, forceful critiques of the emerging social order. The invisible hand constitutes Smith's most famous legacy, but he introduced it rhetorically in opposition to the state-sanctioned trade monopolies such as the East India Company and colonial economic policy in general. In Smith's opinion, such economic policy benefited primarily the wealthy at the expense of the poor: just the opposite of what proper policy should do. Nevertheless, the invisible hand serves today for many as a justification for just the sort of economic policy Smith decried—economy policy favoring large merchants and manufactures at the expense of the meaner strata of society. It is with some irony therefore that practically every modern day celebrant of the current social order makes use of Smith's market sense, which developed as a critique of the emerging order, to defend a *status quo* predicated upon economic policies he would have opposed. Another irony involves how many critics of today's liberal globalization employ a very Smithian argument to denounce its celebrants. Let us now relate Smith's intervention explicitly to how it shaped the thick meaning of commodity exchange and produced a new market sense in the process.

CREATING A NEW MARKET SENSE.

Aristotle, like much economic writing which proceeded Smith, situated commodity exchange within two distinct constellations of social processes and individual beliefs. Commodity exchange undertaken for profit and motivated by avarice entailed social conflict and individual corrosion. On the other hand, exchange undertaken to provision the household, and approached without the desire for individual gain or profit, promoted individual virtue and social harmony. Aristotle's negative connotations of undertaking exchange for profit—greed, avarice and social conflict—clung resiliently to market activity. Early Christian philosophy embraced this market sense and much of Cannon economic law (e.g., just prices) became enacted to mitigate the unnatural exchange. Smith produced in his *Wealth of Nations* a new market sense that directly challenged the ugly associations of profit-orientated market activity.

Smith built upon the philosophical thought preceding him, recasting the act of exchanging for profit as an innate behavioral traits rather than a corruption or perversion of the individual, effectually naturalizing the very greed and avarice Aristotle condemned. The gradual recasting of greed, avarice, or economic self-interest into an intrinsic aspect of human nature, along with the championing of individual freedom and liberty as innate human rights, occurred before Smith. Prior Enlightenment thought, including its quest to deduce the correct human essence, made palatable Smith's notion of individuals motivated by economic self interest. Such an understanding of subjectivity nonetheless played a very important role in the argument Smith put forth in the *Wealth of Nations,* for it facilitated the exorcism of the notion that self-interested behavior was unnatural, a form of perversion, and ultimately imbricated with specific social/cultural influences such as commodity exchange or private property. Although representing individuals as being born to shop did not break any new theoretical ground, placing self-interest and avarice as the driving impetus behind social evolution did constitute a novel theoretical claim.

Smith also argued that exchange undertaken for personal gain constitutes an embodiment of individual rights such as freedom and liberty, thereby equating any attempt to constrain or regulate commodity exchange with human rights violations. Smith eloquently enunciated the linkage between commodity exchange and individual liberty and freedom while simultaneously reducing these rights to the marketplace. Hobbes and Locke discussed a much richer notion of freedom and liberty, not only pertaining to economic aspects of society, but also to political process such as the freedom of arbitrary subjection and rule. In other words, whereas Hobbes and Locke mentioned commodity exchange *as one facet* of liberty and freedom, Smith *subsumed them entirely* to the exchange process: individual freedom becomes simply economic freedom, or the liberty to buy and sell commodities. Smith did not discuss or relate freedom from arbitrary rule directly to commodity exchange, but latter day market celebrants have had no difficulty enriching his analysis; today, democracy also informs the positive market sense behind contemporary global policy regimes.[25]

Smith defined liberty in the negative, i.e., through his repeated entreaties against the economic policy of Europe for violating the (economic) liberty of exchanging subjects. He presented mercantile economic policy as restraining the competition in some employments (e.g., international trade) to a smaller number than would otherwise be disposed to enter into them, while at the same time increasing employments in others beyond what it naturally would be. According to Smith, existing economic policy also obstructed the free circulation of labor and stock, both from employment to employment and from place to place. Smith evokes liberty, like freedom, in this context as the ability to exchange commodities without regulations or restrictions. Such 'perfect liberty' should hold for any commodity, including labor power: "Perfect liberty [is] where he may change his trade as often as he pleases" (1981, 73). Smith discussed the restrictions on freedom and liberty primarily as a critique of mercantile policy, guilds, and state subsidized industry or occupations distorting commodity exchange, but the linkage between liberty and exchange has lived far longer than the economic doctrines it was directed against.

Rather than considering exchange undertaken for profit as leading to social decay, Smith presented it as the driving force behind social evolution. Self-interested exchange constitutes for Smith the power behind the expansion of wealth, inducing the division and specialization of labor and allowing for ever greater numbers of commodities (wealth). The importance of this argument resides in how increases in social wealth serve to placate social unrest. For Smith, social disharmony first and foremost results from state economic policy infringing upon the system of natural liberty, which in practice involves the imposition of artificial constraints upon exchange. Mercantile economic policy places restraints upon certain buyers and sellers of commodities and therefore, slows down the expansion of wealth, impoverishes sectors of the population, and leads to a widening gap between the rich and poor. Smith's solution to social inequality and conflict involves simply letting exchange occur unhindered. In fact, Smith's representation of commercial society as innately harmonious comes about by identifying policies which distort exchange as the *primary* source of social conflict in the first place. Smith assumed away conflict from private property, profit motivated exchange, and production processes that characterize commercial society via his analysis of commodity exchange. In doing so, he banished the need for complicated social institutions, state welfare policies, or radical changes in the class structure to accomplish social harmony.

Smith's thick meaning of commodity exchange underpins later economic writers such as Bastiat. Similar to Smith, Bastiat's *Economic Harmonies* (1964) maintained that commercial society results from natural laws in line with human nature, and that all social classes (differentiated like Smith by the commodities they possess, e.g., land, labor and capital) work in harmony in the production of wealth. Bastiat argued that infringements upon the natural order (e.g., Smith's system of natural liberty) create social tension and conflict. Bastiat directed the tract specifically against socialists who, foreshadowing twentieth-century debates, were represented as desiring various restrictions upon exchange and private property in order to produce a better society.

Smith's vision and analysis of commodity exchange theoretically countered the negative social exchange entailments that haunted it for centuries. Aristotle forcefully argued that commodity exchange undertaken for profit serves as the primary source of social conflict, an association resulting in part from his understanding that all profits derive from unequal exchange. Smith's *Wealth of Nations* countered Aristotle's argument in two ways. First, Smith linked exchange undertaken for profit with the expansion of wealth, which together placate social unrest. Secondly, Smith built upon the theoretical work of Quensay, who rebutted the notion that profits result solely from unequal exchange.

Although Quensay maintained that profits may occur from unequal exchange, such an event constitutes an abnormality induced by state restrictions of market activity, including state sanctioned merchant monopolies, tariffs and so forth. For Smith, as for Quensay, ideal commodity exchange is free from interference and involves an exchange of equivalents, even if profit and avarice are the motivations behind it, for profit naturally arises outside exchange. This is crucial, for as Marx notes, "Before the Physiocrats, surplus-value—that is, profit in the form of profit—was explained purely from *exchange,* the sale of the commodity above its value" (Marx 1969, 41). By locating the source of profits (pecuniary gain) outside of commodity exchange, the notion that profit comes at the expense of others in the community dissipates, as does the linkage between exchange undertaken for profit and social conflict.

Some important differences separate Quensay and Smith, however. While Quensay maintained surplus—the net product—lies at the root of wealth, he argued that it is a "gift of nature" that comes from laboring activity in agriculture. On the other hand, Smith expanded the notion of surplus production (and hence wealth creation) to laboring activity in general; as a result, Smith located productive labor not only in agriculture, but wherever human labor physically transforms raw material.[26] This relocation of the source of profits would come back to haunt Smith's discourse, but he definitely broke the linkage (theoretically) between commodity exchange and profits.[27]

The analytics of commodity exchange contained in the *Wealth of Nations* produced two distinct chains of equivalence. Commodity exchange, when undertaken with self-interest in mind and if not distorted by mercantile policy, entails: the division and specialization of labor; increasing wealth; social harmony; individual rights; and individual fulfillment. Self-interested commodity exchange for Smith is not only a natural inclination of humanity, it is the very foundation of the natural order of things represented by the system of natural liberty. Smith also produced a knowledge of what impaired exchange entails: poverty; increasing disparity between rich and poor; social conflict; restricted freedom and liberty; and individual frustration and despair. These two sides of Smith's market sense play an important discursive role, for they reduce all social formations into one of two social types: those with free commodity exchange and those without.

Defendants of the current liberal status quo make heavy use of Smith's market sense. Although the specifics have varied over the years, a constant theme in such rhetoric involves linking unhindered exchange and a Panglossian vision of the existing economic order. Another persistent motif involves blaming social conflict, inequality and so forth upon hindered commodity exchange, making the cure for these social ills the provision of people with the freedom and liberty to engage in buying and selling commodities. Commodity exchange has become part and parcel of celebratory accounts of commercial society for at least two reasons. For one, the promulgation of Smith's bifurcation of societies into free and hindered exchange societies, and the chains of equivalence with each, constructed a lens for viewing all social formations. Theorists who ascribe to such a position do not turn a blind eye to social problems, but simply prescribe more exchange (free trade) as a cure for social strife. An entire range of social ills becomes reduced in the process to restricted exchange.

Second, Smith represents commercial society as a sphere of commodity exchange populated by homogenous individuals who pursue their self-interest; this representation underpins a certain theoretical maneuver that celebrants of commercial society consistently evoke. The first step involves reducing society to a sea of exchanging agents, while the second involves representing commodity exchange in a purely positive light by reiterating its positive associations such as individual liberty, freedom and wealth. In this instance, simply by de-facto equation, commodity exchange, and therefore commercial society, emerges as a bastion of human rights, liberty and social harmony. Celebrants of the current social order use such a representation of exchange to justify existing society and dismiss any alternatives to it as violations of the natural right to exchange commodities. One powerful defense of global liberalism involves the argument that commodity exchange on a global scale is a necessary requirement of any democratic and free society; Smith's arguments in the *Wealth of Nations* helped facilitate this mantra.

In conclusion, in the few centuries prior to Smith, avarice became increasingly seen as an innate human proclivity. As a result, such behavior no longer was presented as being a product of private property (Plato) or commodity exchange (Aristotle, early Christian philosophy).[28] Smith furthered this transition by arguing that private property and exchange, far from unwanted byproducts of avarice and greed, *result from* these innate human proclivities. Such an argument implicitly mitigated the negative associations of profit-driven exchange that were enunciated by Aristotle. We also saw how contract theorists presented liberty and freedom as innate human rights interwoven with the ability to amass and exchange private property. Smith built upon this foundation and discussed freedom and liberty solely in terms of the ability to buy and sell commodities.

Sinisi (1992) demonstrated how part of Smith's political project involved explicating how commodity exchange undertaken under the auspices of self-interest would bring about social harmony. The allure of Smith's *Wealth of Nations* is his harmonious representation of society, and that this harmony comes about by everyone doing just what they have a natural inclination to do, namely to barter, truck and exchange one thing for another. As long as private property rights are respected in these exchanges, innate human rights such as liberty and freedom are promoted and commodity exchange becomes equated with "natural liberty" and individual freedom (Hardt and Negri 2000, 86). Finally, in the process of producing such a knowledge of commercial society, Smith transformed various ugly entailments of commodity exchange (markets make people greedy and self-centered, markets produce social disharmony, markets encourage swindling) into beautiful ones, including social harmony, expansion of wealth, and individual liberty. Smith also divided societies into two camps—those with and without free markets—and ascribed a host of thick meanings to each. Contemporary liberals still make heavy use of Smith's vision and analysis of markets.

Chapter Four
A Critique of the Market Mystique.

No less a thinker than Adam Smith suggested that the division of labor in society was dependent upon the existence of markets, or, as he put it, man's "propensity to barter, truck and exchange one thing for another." This phrase was later to yield the concept of Economic Man. In retrospect it can be said that no reading of the past ever proved more prophetic of the future.

—Karl Polanyi, *The Great Transformation.*

In this society of free competition, the individual appears detached from the natural bonds etc. which in earlier historical periods make him the accessory of a definite and limited human conglomerate. Smith and Ricardo still stand with both feet on the shoulders of the eighteenth-century prophets, in whose imaginations this eighteenth-century individual . . . appears as an ideal, whose existence they project into the past. Not as a historic result but as history's point of departure. As the Natural Individual appropriate to their notion of human nature, not arising historically, but posited by nature.

—Karl Marx, *Grundrisse.*

Karl Marx and Karl Polanyi challenged Smith's market sense on a number of levels. Their arguments sound remarkably fresh today given that much of the contemporary celebratory market sense surrounding globalization has roots in Smith's market sense. Marx provided a stinging "internal" or "immanent" critique of Smith's analysis of what the marketplace entails, demonstrating the contradictions *within* Smith's analysis. Marx, along with Polanyi, also undertook a detailed "external" or "transcendent" critique, confronting Smith's analysis with arguments based upon their own understanding of markets and society.

In Smith's commercial society, commodity exchange mediates the social metabolism by linking individuals in the marketplace—every act of exchange becomes simply a moment in a vast interconnected network of buying and selling. Smith, Marx and Polanyi explore the meaning of commodity exchange in such a context, though they used different terms for it in their work; Marx referred to a developed system of commodity exchange as "circulation" while Polanyi called it a "pure market economy." Marx and Polanyi also presented dramatically different visions and analyses of what commodity exchange within such a social context entails: Smith represented the impersonal social interaction of the marketplace as the hallmark of individual liberty and freedom; Marx demonstrated how it also entailed just its opposite, e.g., dependence and subjugation; Polanyi argued that it constituted a dystopia.

Marx and Polanyi both rejected the liberal "flattening" of the market landscape and saw something unique about the role of the marketplace in commercial society. Secondly, they both saw the marketplace as an "instituted" rather than natural process, and portrayed the naturalism underpinning Smith's market sense as an apologia for existing market forms. In this chapter, I draw on the work of Marx and Polanyi to provide an internal and external critique of Smith's market sense. The following chapter explores their alternative visions and analyses of market activity in more detail.

AN IMMANENT CRITIQUE OF SMITH'S ANALYSIS OF EXCHANGE.

We need to take a brief philosophical journey before proceeding to an immanent critique of Smith. To arrive at a thick level of commodity exchange, e.g., what it entails for society, we must first embrace some thin idea of what commodity exchange is. Philosophers call the starting point of such an analysis an "abstraction" or "entry point." After specifying one or more entry points, people produce statements connecting these points to a range of other things in society. The initial presuppositions Smith used to define commodity exchange, together with how he connected it to things like wealth and social harmony, comprise his analysis of what the marketplace entails. Smith averred two presuppositions (or entry points) about human nature which served to thinly define commodity exchange: people innately possess the ability to truck, barter and trade commodities and individual gain naturally motivates all exchange activity. After specifying these entry points, Smith deduced how commodity exchange naturally entails freedom, wealth and social harmony. An immanent critique accepts the entry points and the logic of an analysis, but demonstrates its internal contradictions.

The immanent critique presented here has its roots in my reading of Marx, in particular his *Grundrisse* and *Capital,* where he investigated in detail Smith's *telos* of social development—i.e., his fully developed system of exchange in commercial society. In this system, commodity exchange mediates the social metabolism by connecting the individuals in society as buyers and sellers. It also induces everyone to become "to some measure a merchant" (Smith 1981, 37), buying and selling commodities on a regular basis. Marx referred to commodity exchange in the context of Smith's commercial society as "circulation" and defined it as follows:

> An essential characteristic of circulation is that it circulates exchange values (products of labor), and, in particular, exchange values in the form of *prices*. Thus, not every form of commodity exchange, e.g., barter, payment in kind, feudal services, etc., constitute circulation. To get circulation, two things are required above all. Firstly: the precondition that commodities are prices. Secondly: not isolated acts of exchange, but a circle of exchange, a totality of the same, in constant flux, proceeding more or less over the entire surface of society; as a system of acts of exchange. (1993, 188)

The system of acts of exchange defining circulation refers to the scale of commodity exchange in commercial society, something Marx, Polanyi and Smith used to differentiate modern from historical societies. Marx and Polanyi both provide very different analyses of how commercial society arose, but we will leave this aside until the following chapter. For now we will concentrate on circulation, the developed system of exchange Smith used to define commercial society, and the positive entailments he ascribed to it.

Although Marx did not reject how Smith linked freedom, wealth and other positive entailments to circulation, he did argue that the following negative entailments also flowed directly from Smith's analysis: unfreedom, poverty, social conflict, and tyranny. Marx's deduction of negative entailments from the circulation process did not presume the incorrectness of Smith's positive entailments; in fact, Marx actually elaborated on Smith's arguments. In contrast to Smith's "one-sided" positive assessment of a developed system of exchange, Marx produced a complex and contradictory vision of what this system means for society. Marx began by mordantly and concisely summarizing Smith's exchange entailments:

> The sphere of circulation or commodity exchange, within whose boundaries the sale and purchase of labour-power goes on, is in fact the very Eden of the innate rights of man. It is the exclusive realm of Freedom,

Equality, Property, and Bentham. Freedom, because both buyer and seller
of a commodity, let us say of labour-power, are determined by their own
free will. Their contract is the final result in which their joint will finds a
common legal expression. Equality, because each enters into relation
with the other, as with a simple owner of commodities, and they
exchange equivalent for equivalent. Property, because each disposes only
of what is his own. And Bentham, because each looks only to his own
advantage. The only force bringing them together, and putting them into
relation with each other, is the selfishness, the gain and the private interest of each. Each pays heed to himself only, and no one worries about the
others. And precisely for that reason, either in accordance with the pre-
established harmony of things, or under the auspices of an omniscient
providence, they all work together to their mutual advantage, for the
common weal, and in the common interest. (1990, 280)

Using this statement as an entry point, Marx explored how circulation
entails freedom *and* unfreedom, liberty *and* tyranny, and wealth *and* economic crisis.

Let us first consider the mutual recognition of private ownership,
which serves as a condition of possibility for circulation. Well defined property rights are a hallmark of circulation, and ensure that all property
exchanged passes from one owner to another. Property rights, coupled with
the desire to improve one's lot, also facilitate an understanding of commodity exchange as a strictly voluntary activity. Leaving aside state appropria-
tions (something liberals typically decry), property rights ensure that no
one can legally take your possessions without your consent. If you decide to
dispose or acquire property, you voluntarily do so under your own free
will. The vision of commodity exchange as embodying freedom depends
upon its supposed voluntary nature, for it implies non-compulsory activity
and therefore choice. In Marx's words:

Although individual A feels a need for the commodity of individual B,
he does not appropriate it by force, nor vice versa, but rather they recognize one another reciprocally as proprietors, as persons whose will
penetrates their commodities. Accordingly, the juridical moment of the
Person enters here, as well as that of freedom, in so far as it is contained in the former. No one seized hold of another's property by force.
Each divests himself of his property voluntarily. (1993, 243)

Modern liberals like Milton Friedman make heavy use of the voluntary
nature of exchange when asserting a fundamental link between "capitalism"

(e.g., a "system of markets") and freedom. Friedman, in his classic *Capitalism and Freedom* (1962), breaks societies into two types—those with and without free, voluntary commodity exchange—and then considers how each achieves the production and distribution of goods and services. A capitalist "free market exchange economy" works via the voluntary cooperation of individuals in the marketplace, while the other involves "central direction involving the use of coercion—the technique of the army and the modern totalitarian state" (1962, 13). The voluntary nature of commodity exchange constitutes the very essence of economic freedom in his account and serves as his primary defense and celebration of capitalism contra all (perceived) alternatives. Circulation presupposes the private exchange of all products of labor, all activities, and all wealth; for Friedman, this stands in antithesis to a political subordination of individuals in society.

Besides giving individuals the freedom to buy whatever they desire, circulation promotes a form of equality and assumes that everyone engaged in exchange possesses the same legal rights and privileges: "a worker who buys commodities with 3 shillings is equal to the king that does the same thing. As long as money appears as a general contract, all distinctions between the contracting parties is extinguished" (Marx 1993, 246). The formal, legal equality does not belie the very real differences in power, rank, and social status that exist in society, but in the "pure economic form" of circulation, money and exchange erase distinctions between exchanging agents. Everyone freely enters "into relations with each other on a footing of equality as owners of commodities, with the sole difference that one is a buyer, the other a seller; both are therefore equal in the eyes of the law" (Marx 1990, 271).

The individual independence afforded by circulation informs another rationale connecting commodity exchange and freedom; when people can legally own property and participate in exchange, and the extent of exchange reaches the scope of circulation, people can survive via marketplace rather than depend on familial ties or communal bonds. People can produce and sell commodities independently of prior social support networks, and can use the proceeds they receive to purchase what they wish, thereby eradicating the need for "onerous" personal ties and the dependence upon them for survival. In other words, circulation implies the freedom from social networks of dependence, kinship duties, communal loyalties, corporative solidarities, religious rituals, a hierarchical stratification of life and so forth.[1] Circulation therefore provides a critical condition of existence for individual independence, enables the freedom and liberty of people to exit oppressive social situations, and creates the conditions of possibility for representing those *without* property rights and the ability to exchange as economically oppressed.

> In the developed system of exchange (and this semblance seduces the democrats), the ties of personal dependence, of distinctions of blood, education, etc. are in fact exploded, ripped up (at least, personal ties all appear as *personal* relations); and individuals *seem* independent (this independence which is at bottom merely an illusion, and it is more correctly called indifference), free to collide with one another and engage in exchange with this freedom. (Marx 1993, 161)

The dissolution of "traditional" society into an amalgamation of individuals exchanging commodities did not arouse much sympathy in the nineteenth century, for common (market) sense celebrated replacing "oppressive" kinship roles with the marketplace's freedom, liberty, and economic prosperity. Such market sense constituted the foundation of economic development literature in the 1950's and underpins the celebration of the global marketplace today. Marx viewed the emergence of circulation as revolutionary precisely for this reason—the dissolution of all fixed personal (historic) relations of dependence enable the possibility for radical social restructuring and a conscious transformation of society.[2] Marx qualified his assessment by carefully pointing out the extensive pain and dislocation such a restructuring may entail, but still embraced its potential.[3]

A recurrent theme in Marx's work is the dialectic between the revolutionary aspects of circulation and its pitfalls. This dialectic underpins his approach to the ascribed entailments of exchange. Marx used the same method in his early works to discuss free trade (1973) and weigh its potential negative impact on jobs and wages against its potential benefits for society. In his words, free trade "breaks up old nationalities and pushes the antagonism of the proletariat and the bourgeoisie to the extreme point. In a word, the free trade system hastens the social revolution. It is in this revolutionary sense alone, gentlemen, that I vote in favour of free trade" (1973, 195).[4] Marx teased out the negative aspects of circulation alongside its positives, and argued that the role of circulation in promoting freedom, equality and independence among the population in no way mitigates its other, more nefarious social implications like dependence, unfreedom and tyranny.

This vision of commercial society—i.e., one comprised of individuals who produce and exchange commodities *voluntarily*—constitutes a core principle in Smith's and latter liberals' market sense. The *formal* freedom to participate in exchange possesses social implications, such as the ability to exchange distinguished Roman citizens from mere residents. However, the positive connection between freedom and commodity exchange really depends upon *substantive* freedom to participate in the process, such as whether or not people have property to sell or the means to purchase commodities. The substantive freedom associated with exchange rests first and foremost on people's material ability to engage in the buying and selling of commodities. Smith assumed that people obtained the means to purchase commodities by selling what they themselves produced, why Etienne Balibar (1995) aptly characterizes individuals in the liberal vision of society as "producer-exchangers." People all produce commodities to sell and purchase what they desire, making both production and consumption dependent upon the discretion of all involved.

Milton Friedman takes this argument one step further, claiming that if people see no individual advantage in producing commodities for exchange, they can always provide for themselves. "Since the household always has the alternative of producing for itself, it need not enter into any exchange unless it benefits from it. Hence, no exchange will take place unless both parties do benefit from it" (1962, 13). Friedman's critical assumption here is that individuals can "opt-out" of the exchange process anytime they wish, making any and all transactions strictly voluntary and mutually beneficial. The optionality of exchange in commercial society relates to his vision of it as "a collection of Robinson Crusoes" (1962, 13) all capable of supporting themselves independently outside of the marketplace.

Friedman's assumption lends support to the vision of the marketplace as completely voluntary, but it contains some problems. First, it begs the question of how possible it really is to refuse participation in exchange in modern society. At the very least, everyone would need enough land to support themselves (e.g., forty acres and a mule) and all the skills of "homesteading" families. Secondly, it runs counter to Smith's vision of commercial society—an amalgamation of specialized commodity producers/artisans. Self-sufficient peasant households belonged to a prior stage of social progress that Smith explicitly *differentiated* commercial society from. In commercial society, the complete specialization of labor forces everyone to become "to some measure a merchant" by producing and selling commodities. Smith championed the specialized production induced by commodity exchange as the driving force behind the expansion of wealth; once people develop their talents in a complex division of labor, they no longer possess the skills or the desire to produce everything for themselves.

The dissolution of society into a vast network of independent commodity producers highlights another side to the freedom and liberty of circulation that Friedman attempted to sidestep: the all around dependence of everyone in commercial society upon circulation. Individuals who exercise their freedom to produce and exchange commodities by exiting *direct* social networks of dependence become *indirectly* dependent upon the very circulation process that liberates them from other social ties. In other words, if everyone becomes a merchant, the marketplace replaces social bonds and exchange value becomes the "all-sided mediation" (Marx 1993, 156) linking individuals.[5] This reciprocal dependence upon circulation underpins Marx's claim that the independence and freedom of individuals within circulation "has as its counterpart and supplement a system of all-round material dependence" (1990, 203).

> The dissolution of all products and activities into exchange values presupposes the dissolution of all fixed personal (historic) relations of dependence in production, as well as the all-sided dependence of the producers on one another. Each individual's production is dependent on the production of all others; and the transformation of his product into the necessaries of his own life is dependent on the consumption of all others." (Marx 1993, 156)

The pursuit of individual self-interest, expressed through producing and buying what you like, only becomes possible when people become dependent upon circulation.[6] Individual producer-exchangers may be independent; however, they are also dependent upon commodity exchange for both their material subsistence proper and the means to acquire this subsistence. The price tag of circulation's freedom and independence becomes a general dependence upon exchange.[7]

Consumer sovereignty further circumscribes the individual freedom and liberty that circulation affords. Samuelson defines consumer sovereignty as "the outcome of a pure market or price system in which consumers are the ultimate dictators of the kind and quantity of commodities to be produced" (Samuelson and Nordhaus 1989, 623). It implies that the more freedom people have to purchase commodities, the less freedom is enjoyed by producers, since they must cater to the will of consumers. Yet, Smith represented people in commercial society as *individual* producers (artisans) and consumers, i.e., producer-exchangers. The more freedom producer-exchangers have in the realm of consumption, the less they have in the production sphere. Even consumer sovereignty implies therefore both individual freedom and unfreedom.

Other sides to the positive exchange entailments Smith elucidated may be teased out in a similar manner. Consider the linkage between commodity exchange and wealth. Smith considered wealth as the total sum of commodities a society produced. In circulation people produce and sell commodities according to their self-interest, and in order to capture profitable opportunities, develop their talents and become specialized producers. Exchange promotes the division of labor and yields increasing wealth via a virtuous dynamic: the expansion of commodity exchange facilitates an increasingly specialized and productive society which in turn produces more commodities. The positive entailment of wealth and commodity exchange underpins modern liberal thinking and resonates within the literature on economic development. Early development economists (Lewis 1954; Myint 1954; Nurske 1953) especially echoed Smith's exchange-infused understanding of productivity and specialization, and maintained that the lack of markets constituted the primary reason behind economic "backwardness."

Marx concurred with some of the basic premises of Smith's argument, noting how "the need for exchange and for the transformation of the product into pure exchange value progresses in step with the division of labor, i.e., with the increasingly social character of production" (1993, 146). Nonetheless, the more that society becomes populated by specialized commodity producers, the greater the chances for general social and economic crises. With everyone dependent upon the sale of commodities for a livelihood, a potential gap always exists between production and consumption. More specifically, commodity producers always face the possibility of failing to realize the exchange value of what they make, i.e., they cannot sell what they produce. Whenever commodity producers fail to find buyers, they are left with what seem to be useless commodities and have no means to purchase the things they need. The gap between production and consumption may arise from a vast array of occurrences and lies at the heart of many Marxian crisis theories concerned with underconsumption, overproduction, and sectorial imbalances, or what Richard Wolff calls "recurring disjunctures between supplies and demands known as recessions, depressions, inflations, and so on" (1995, 397).[8]

Specialized commodity production also supposedly mitigates social conflict by increasing wealth. Although this serves to cast exchange in a favorable light, "One could just as well deduce [given Smith's assumptions about human nature] . . . that each individual reciprocally blocks the assertion of the other's interests, so that, instead of a general affirmation, this war of all against all produces a general negation" (Marx 1993, 156). Marx employed the same theoretical presuppositions regarding exchanging agents and commodity exchange to deduce that the expansion of wealth and (hence) social harmony can just as easily be used to deduce the opposite: social conflict. In other words, what ensures that everyone will obey the economic contract? Even Smith worried about this, as demonstrated by his repeated entreaties in the *Wealth of Nations* for people not to skew the exchange game in their favor.

The essentialist way Smith linked the division of labor with commodity exchange poses some other problems as well. First, a systemic division of labor is quite possible without use-values taking the form of commodities. Plato argued the specialization of labor yields better and more plentiful use-values for all the individuals or households concerned, but he did not include commodity exchange as a prerequisite for, or even a necessary component of, the specialization and division of labor. Marx notes something similar:

> Though it is correct to say that individual exchange presupposes division of labour, it is wrong to maintain that division of labor presupposes individual exchange. For example, division of labour had reached an exceptionally high degree of development among the Peruvians, although no individual exchange, no exchange of products in the form of commodities, took place. (1970, 60)

In effect, Smith committed a fundamental error by taking a *historical prerequisite* of any commodity exchange—specialized use-value production in society—as being induced by exchange itself. By casting exchange as the prime mover behind the division of labor, Smith ignored how specialization occurs even without exchange. Just to cite one example, familial production such as meals and cleaning, often involves a pronounced division of labor even though the goods and services produced do not assume the form of commodities.

Another problem emerges in the specific way Smith linked the division and specialization of labor with commodity exchange, for specialization *within manufacture* occurs due to the organization/coordination of the production process and is entirely outside of the exchange rubric. Smith provided his most compelling case of the specialization and division of labor with his famous pin factory exemplar. Instead of making pins from start to finish, people became specialized, with one drawing the wire, one honing the point, one putting on the cap and so forth. Smith compellingly argued that the total pin production from the specialized workplace far exceeded the combined total if everyone made each pin by themselves. Yet, the specialization in the pin factory did not involve individual pin-makers *exchanging commodities,* but an association of workers performing minute, specialized tasks *within one manufacturing process.* The gains in the labor productivity of pin-making possess no direct relationship to commodity exchange, and instead depend upon the organization of production. Smith seemed to be aware of this, maintaining that the increases in work quantity resulted from an increase in dexterity, time savings, and machines. Yet, at the same time, he consistently asserted a link between increases in labor productivity and commodity exchange.

The problem comes down to this: whenever Smith discussed how the division of labor leads to greater social wealth, he used exemplars like the pin factory, yet whenever he discussed freedom and liberty, he evoked *individual, autonomous* craftsmen, artisans and so forth. Smith's pin factory exemplar described individuals cooperating in production—not the championed artisans populating other parts of his text. In fact, all the concrete examples Smith produces regarding the division of labor concern not individual producers, but people employed as common laborers, miners, furnace builders and tenders, lumberjacks, brick-makers and layers, mill-wrights, forgers, smiths and so forth. It is true that any productive arrangement involving more than one person requires some degree of cooperation, but the specific forms of cooperation vary tremendously.

Turning once again to Smith's pin factory, let us consider the implications of some of the myriad ways of organizing the cooperation and/or coordination necessary to produce pins. In a true co-op, the pin makers decide amongst themselves the details of the production process and allocate tasks accordingly. Perhaps this is what Smith had in mind: an association of independent artisans where everyone voluntarily contributes to production and receives an appropriate share of the collective fruits of their labor. Alternatively, one person or a group of individuals directs the actual production in a hierarchical manner, inducing cooperation by fiat—consider slaves producing pins, where a master/owner compels slaves to perform certain duties by force. Even in "free" wage labor contracts, a manager and/or owner induces the workers to perform their assigned duties by threat of dismissal.[9] In either case, despotism rather than freedom characterizes the division of labor within the site, with the actual pin workers enjoying little if any freedom and liberty in what and how much they produce. The freedom that workers possess in the realm of exchange stops at the (pin) factory gate.

If the production of commodities under circulation becomes characterized by manufacturing firms organized in totalitarian ways, then the growing piles of commodities induced by the increased specialization of labor corresponds with an expansion of tyranny and unfreedom. Interestingly enough, Smith's instructor in the eighteenth-century political economy, Adam Ferguson, became wary of manufacture for precisely this reason, fearing the erosion of freedom in emerging commercial society. Ferguson saw the increases in wealth from manufacturing, but exclaimed that in doing so, "we make a nation of Helots, and have no free citizens" (1767, 285).

The combination (and contradiction) of freedom in exchange and tyranny in production within modern society has long been a subject of debate outside of the Marxian tradition. For example, Bauman (1988) lucidly explores whether or not consumer freedom makes up for productive unfreedom within market society. Bauman splits economic freedom into two parts—consumptive and productive. Whereas consumptive freedom concerns the liberty to buy and sell commodities freely, productive freedom involves the right to share in the joint determination of what gets produced and how. However much circulation entails consumptive freedom, productive freedom depends upon the organization of the workplace, and the two spheres of economic life should not be conflated.[10] Further, given that, for many people, the only commodity they have to sell is their labor-power, individuals fell compelled to sell this commodity to secure the necessities of life, even if it means embracing tyranny in doing so.

We just considered a range of contradictions within Smith's vision and analysis of commercial society without going beyond the initial confines of his argument. The immanent critique of circulation demonstrated how the exchange entailments of freedom, liberty and the expansion of wealth arrive part and parcel with unfreedom, tyranny and economic crisis. We are left with a new, contradictory market sense in contrast to the one-sided, positive rendition so popular today. People who use their market sense to champion or denounce commodity exchange ignore its other, contradictory side in an ideological manner. We can celebrate the independence circulation offers us as consumers while simultaneously being aware of our dependence upon it for our means of livelihood. Accepting that exchange will always be plagued by contradictions opens up an entire new way of thinking about what it means for society and creates the space for a more productive discussion about its role in the global economy.

Besides challenging the dominant market sense with a more complex, contradictory vision, the immanent critique also brings to the fore an important ontological implication. That circulation entails numerous contradictory entailments should not induce despair, but it should raise awareness of the good, the bad and the ugly of the process. The contradictions of dependence/independence and freedom/unfreedom will always constitute an aspect of society anytime production becomes specialized. The ubiquitousness of dependence/independence and freedom/unfreedom in any specialized society, *regardless of how it distributes the social product,* implies that true freedom or independence requires the *recognition* of social ties that bind rather than turning a blind eye toward them.

Marx exemplified this way of thinking. He did not criticize circulation for entailing dependence *per se,* but did question how the specific form of dependence it entails goes largely unrecognized. Circulation presumes production in the form of commodities, which gives production relations both a private and social character. Private, free decisions govern actual production, but each private decision shapes the production and distribution of the social product, something all members of society depend upon. Marx played with the private/social sides of commodity production, arguing that the social aspect of production upon which society is dependent, i.e., the production of commodities distributed via exchange, exists independently of any direct control of society at all. As a consequence, the anarchy of production and distribution via circulation exposes society to repeated crises and disruptions. Marx takes umbrage not at the social dependence entailed by exchange, or that production may be determined by exchange, but with the fact that such dependence results in periodic and painful economic crises.

EXTERNAL/TRANSCENDENT CRITIQUES OF COMMERCIAL SOCIETY.

The rest of this chapter explores the external/transcendent critique of Smith's market sense found in Marx and Polanyi. An immanent critique involves teasing out the contradictions within an analysis and taking the presuppositions and logic of the theory as a given, while an external critique challenges them. Marx and Polanyi launched external, detailed critiques of the self-interested, exchanging individual Smith used as an entry point, and the naturalness of circulation he presupposed. Their critiques will be discussed in turn.

The *Grundrisse* provides a very explicit, condensed summary of Marx's argument against the individual at the heart of Smith's market sense in the section "Independent Individuals, Eighteenth-Century Ideas" (1993, 83–85). Marx juxtaposed his historical materialist approach toward understanding people's propensity to exchange with the essentialist formulations found in Smith, Hobbes, Locke and others. Nonetheless, Marx did not attempt to supplant Smith's understanding of human nature with a better or more correct notion of individuality, for he rejected the idea of an essential human nature and the theoretical project of deducing a notion of society predicated upon *any* such idea.[11] One reason behind Marx's objection concerns the consequences of deducing an optimal society predicated upon some assumed innate human behavior, for it bestows an aura of "naturalness" upon the deduced system. As Doug Henwood recently reflected: "It's usually dangerous to apply the word 'natural' to a social system; it's been used to justify everything from fascism to anarchism" (2002, 1).

Marx argues that Smith employed a notion of individual behavior derived from modern society, and then used it to explain its origins: a textbook example of circular reasoning. People who perform such a theoretical feat basically assert what needs to be explained in the first place, i.e., the *particular* notion of individuality essentialized in the analysis. Social contract theory, Smith's *Wealth of Nations,* the 'Robinsonades' produced in the eighteenth century, and even contemporary neoclassical economics all build their analyses upon an asserted universal notion of human nature, after which they deduce a knowledge of society "naturally" in accordance with it (e.g., the proper set of social institutions to allow their essence to flourish). Marx derided these approaches, arguing that the "naturally independent, autonomous subjects [brought] into relation and connection by contract" (1993, 83) in Smith's system of natural liberty only make sense in light of Smith's notion of commercial society itself. Marx notes that a notion of individuality predating society is "as much an absurdity as is the development of language without individuals living *together* and talking to each other" (1993, 84).

Marx dismissed the notion of an invariant human nature driving human history and averred "there is no point in dwelling on this any longer. The point could go entirely unmentioned if this twaddle, which has sense and reason for eighteenth-century characters, had not been earnestly pulled back into the center of the most modern economists by Bastiat, Carey, Prudhon, etc." (1993, 84). Such "twaddle" received attention in his work precisely because economists still employed specific notions about human essence to *justify* their particular vision of society and the role of exchange therein. Marx's anxieties regarding essentialist notions of human nature in accounts of circulation arose because of the political and cultural ramifications they engender, e.g., their *implications* for society.

Through the celebration of free commodity exchange as a natural outgrowth of the human essence, Smith implicitly relegated the alternatives to free markets as not only conflict-ridden and rife with violations of individual freedom and liberty, but contrary to human nature. Marx claimed that "the degree and universality of the development of wealth where *this* individuality becomes possible supposes production on the basis of exchange values as a prior condition" (1993, 162).[12] Yet, since Smith claimed exchange as a human essence, it makes his path of social progression applicable to all societies. The only thing separating different stages of development is the amount of exchange taking place and the consequent specialization of labor it entails. The idea that all societies naturally progress through the same stages of development, with commercial society as the natural *telos,* lends theoretical support to the claim that "there is no alternative" to market or commercial society. Viewing existing society as natural and an outcome of human nature supports the *status quo* entrenched in commercial society.

Marx criticized the supposed naturalness of circulation as being fetishistic. Marxian interpretations of commodity fetishism have produced rich discourses exploring the ideological implications of commodity exchange upon class processes (Althusser and Balibar 1979; Lefebvre 1991; Ollman 1971; Sweezy 1942), so-called *homo faber* (Avineri 1971; Lukács 1994), and even epistemology (Sohn-Rethel 1978).[13] The aspect of commodity fetishism explored here focuses solely upon the naturalistic representation of circulation. In nineteenth-century Europe, "fetishistic people" were those who worshipped and obeyed "false" idols. Their "falseness" arose from the notion that idols, once carved (or whatever), took on a life of their own, fundamentally influencing the behavior of their makers and shaping how they viewed the world around them. Marx saw something similar with commodity exchange; although circulation is a product of society, over time it became seen as natural and something that shaped the behavior and world views of its participants.

Circulation implies dependence on exchange by producer-exchangers because, as we have already seen, they must buy and sell commodities to secure their conditions of existence: the dependence on exchange constitutes the flip side of the freedom linked to circulation. Marx extends and explores the implications of this dependence/freedom couplet in greater detail with the notion of commodity fetishism. Marx argues that the very exchange relations which mutually connect producer-exchangers appear to them not as social relations, but as an outside force they must obey. Even though producer-exchangers *constitute* the market through their interactions, the people involved become beholden to money and exchange-value: they produce commodities for "the market" in order to secure the money they use to purchase commodities from the same. Money and commodities embody social relations and connect individual producer-exchangers, yet they appear as outside forces guiding human action. For these reasons, Balibar argues that "fetishism is fundamentally a *theory of the market* (the mode of subjection or constitution of the 'world' of subjects and objects inherent in the organization of society as market and its domination by market forces)" (1994, 78).

All of the individual acts of buying and selling in circulation constitute mere moments in an endless chain of transactions that mediate the social formation and link the producing-exchanging individuals within it. Circulation implies that all individuals become "to some measure merchants," requiring a host of socially learned beliefs and motivations. The mediation of social interaction via market activity shapes the way in which people relate to each other, seeing each other as potential buyers and sellers of commodities. Consider the following quote from the *Grundrisse* in this regard:

> The general exchange of activities and products, which has become a vital
> condition for each individual—their mutual interconnection—here appears
> as something alien to them, autonomous, as a thing. In exchange value,
> the social connection between persons is transformed into a social relation
> between things; personal capacity into objective wealth. (1993, 157)

Taussig (1980) and Balibar (1995) argue that Marx used fetishism to
critique a particular trope employed in classical political economy: the representation of commercial society and "the market" as natural and self-regulating. The naturalistic quality of these arguments serve "to ratify the
conventions that sustain our sense of reality unless we appreciate the extent
to which the basic 'building blocks' of our experience and our sensed reality are not natural but social constructions" (Taussig 1980, 10). Taussig
further maintains that classical political economy essentially presupposed a
commoditized world, and therefore presupposed (as natural) the beliefs
and motivations behind exchange as well. The naturalness of considering
all things as commodities to be bought and sold, even things like land and
labor, seems normal within commercial society, but there is nothing natural
or inherently normal about it.

Marx argues that a number of presuppositions or prerequisites concerning the subjectivity of exchanging agents need to be present in order for
commodity exchange to assume the role of circulation. To take one example, consider the constant valuation of useful objects in terms of a universal
equivalent, a socially recognized standard of measurement. People employ
certain cognitive abilities when evaluating the use-value (material function-
ality), exchange-value, or cost of commodities. The quantitative relationships, via repetition of the exchange process, become expressed or
'crystallized' into either a universal commodity like metallic coinage or into
a more abstract equivalent such as paper money. Money, like private property, only makes sense given groups of individuals.

Amariglio and Callari provide an excellent summary of the historical
abilities needed by individuals in order to participate in circulation in their
discussion of economic rationality and fetishism:

> The attribute of economic rationality implies that individuals treat the
> objects they possess and trade as quantities that can be calculated. Ratio-
> nal economic agents are so constituted that, first, they conceptualize use
> values as *objects,* separate and distinct from themselves, which potentially
> have the ability to satisfy perceived needs; second, they *quantify,* assign
> numbers to, these objects; third, they construct a set of procedures by
> which the *calculation* of these objects is conducted; and fourth, they

undertake action based on the results of these calculations (actions that are perceived as "rational" because they take advantage of opportunities recognizable only through these calculations). (1993, 208–9)

Marx argues that the attributes of economic rationality are both a precondition for, and an effect of, commodity exchange. Exchanging agents consider commodities in terms of their use-value, or their qualitative aspects, and their exchange-value, or their quantitative aspects. The constant repetition of exchange, as in general circulation, implies the daily performance of such considerations for an entire host of useful objects; the result is, in part, the seeming normality of such calculations, and, in turn, the social validity and objective nature of the calculations. Once this method of thinking has become normalized, producer-exchangers have the cognitive ability to evaluate objects not even produced as commodities, i.e., to consider the exchange-value of things like land, labor, and capital. These normal behavioral traits only make sense given commercial society.[14]

Within circulation, the commodity relation imbues private labor with a social form specifically because all of the qualitatively different forms of labor utilized in the production of commodities become socially valued via exchange.[15] The independent producer-consumer acquires a two-fold social character as a result, for the producer's labor goes toward satisfying a definite social need and the producer's own needs are met through the purchase of someone else's commodities. The constant buying and selling of commodities under circulation results in a social valuation of individual labor expressed in commodities, something which Marx maintained to be the general expression of value. Once useful objects are produced for sale and considered in terms of their price, the money form conceals the social character of private labor, i.e., that each commodity has a value that represents a portion of social production. The commodities simply have a price tag denoting what they are worth. The evaluation of these objects as commodities reinforces the calculation of exchange-value as something normal and socially valid, *even when considering things not produced as commodities.*

We have seen how celebrants of commercial society represent the producers and sellers of commodities as only interacting with each other insofar as they are bearers of property, or possessors/owners of commodities. The theoretical process of interpreting social relations through the lens of circulation, where individual exchanging agents become the starting or entry points of the analysis, is in Marx's eyes fetishistic because it awards powers to the "the market" which is in reality simply a social relation. Fetishism "consists in regarding *economic* categories, such as being a *commodity* or *productive labour,* as qualities inherent in the material incarnations of these formal determinations or categories" (Marx 1991, 1046). Lefebvre represents Marx's notion of fetishism in a similar manner:

> Money, currency, commodities, capital, are nothing more than relations between human beings (between 'individual,' qualitative human tasks). And yet, these relations take on the appearance and the form of *things* external to human beings. The appearance becomes reality; because men believe that these 'fetishes' exist outside of themselves and they really do function like objective things. (1991, 178)

For Lefebvre, such "thingification" exists as a contradictory process, where the social relations surrounding circulation (exchange-value, money) assume the guise or appearance of things, but these things in turn dominate the self-same producer-exchangers that produced them. Individuals decide what to produce and consume based upon the exchange-value of commodities,[16] or in other words, their decisions are predicated upon and dominated by "the market."

Marx presents fetishism as a way in which individuals in commercial society perceive their world, especially the exchange relations which unite these individual and independent producer-exchangers and "the market" as an outside force. Fetishism represents an important supplement to the theory of circulation in that it highlights the domination of exchange over human activity, and the subjection of producer-exchangers by "market forces" (which are after all only social relations) rather than their potential emancipation and freedom. Fetishism also serves as Marx's satirical critique of the celebrants of exchange, whose assumption of the naturalness of circulation Marx calls a religion of the vulgar. Once useful objects assume a commodity form, the evaluation of these objects as commodities reinforces the calculation of exchange-value as something normal and socially valid. Yet, normality, except for the vulgar, does not equate with natural and to treat it as such simply serves to perpetuate the existing *status quo*.

POLANYI'S CRITIQUE OF MARKET SOCIETY.

Polanyi shared Marx's concern with economists who considered commercial society natural; he saw it as an impossible, and dangerous, utopic vision. Like most of the theorists considered in *Market Sense,* Polanyi wrote about commodity exchange in a time of great social upheaval. Trained as an economist prior to WWII, Polanyi worked primarily on economic history. Fleeing Hungry to escape the Nazis, he came to the United States where he wrote most of his most famous work, *The Great Transformation* (2001). At the heart of his opus lies a burning question: how can we, in an age of enlightenment and reason, account for the rise of the oppressive, totalitarian and fascist regimes sweeping Europe? His answer indicted commodity exchange and, in doing so, he produced a radically different vision and analysis of "market society" than liberals and left a critical market sense in his wake. The next chapter presents Polanyi's (and Marx's) analysis of how an "unnatural" market economy came about, but for now we will focus upon his vision of what it entails.

Polanyi defined a market economy akin to how Smith presented commercial society: people work to maximize their own personal gain in "an economic system controlled, regulated, and directed by market prices" (2001, 71). He also represented people in market society as producer-exchangers who produce (supply) the commodities they profit the most from and use the proceeds to exchange for (demand) other commodities they consume. People respond to the prices of commodities by purchasing and selling more or less, making the provision of goods and services dependent upon an interlocking system of markets "automatically" adjusting supply and demand. Liberals envision such a market system as an ideal, but Polanyi sees it as a fantasy.

All societies have an economy, or human activity that produces goods and services and coordinates their distribution; however, only in an idealized (and ultimately impossible) pure market society does the logic of the marketplace guide this activity completely. An "embedded" economy implies politics, religion and historically evolved social relations determine the distribution of goods and services (largely) to ensure the society's survival. In contrast, Polanyi presents a pure system of markets as a "disembedded" economy, where instead of the provisioning of goods and the marketplace itself being subordinated to the needs of society, (as it has in all previous historical epochs), the marketplace subordinates society, transforming it into an appendage of the market. In a pure market society, "the market" comes to dictate where people live, what they do for a living, what they eat, and even their very survival. It also determines the fate of the natural environment—the quality of the air, water and natural surroundings depends solely upon people's willingness to pay for such "amenities."

Polanyi tells a story similar to Marx's analysis of circulation. He highlights how exchange relations, when serving as the primary means uniting individual and independent producer-exchangers under the rubric of the outside force of "the market," efface prior forms of social interaction. In fact, Polanyi, Marx and Smith all employ a similar thin definition of commodity exchange within commercial society, but each reaches very different conclusions about what it (potentially) entails. For example, Polanyi sees a disembedded, market economy as an impossible utopia that requires human beings and the natural environment to be treated as ordinary commodities—something people will not and cannot accept for any length of time.

Polanyi calls land, labor and capital "fictitious" commodities because unlike "genuine" commodities, they are not produced for sale. Labor constitutes human activity and as such it cannot be divorced or detached from the rest of life. Land comprises nature itself and capital is simply a unit of value. While people labor in every society circumscribed by the natural surroundings, to include labor, labor and capital into the market mechanism subordinates the very substance of society itself, e.g., the people and their environment, to the laws of the market. Yet, Polanyi claims that people cannot and will not accept being treated as pure commodities for any length of time, making a pure market economy an impossibility. Polanyi's claim of the impossibility of a truly disembedded, market economy rests on two broad presuppositions. On the one hand, he views treating nature and humans simply as commodities as morally wrong; on the other hand, treating land and labor as a commodity is a dangerous impossibility. The deepest flaw in liberalism for Polanyi concerns how its market-centric policies subordinate human purposes to the logic of an impersonal market mechanism guided by the profit motive rather than deliberation and negotiation.

Polanyi argues that no economy can ever be completely disembedded from society, although the degree of embeddedness varies. Polanyi attributes the extent to which the economy operates under a market logic to the outcome of an ongoing struggle between two opposing movements: the "laissez-faire movement" to expand the scope of the market and a protective "counter movement" that emerges to resist it. Polanyi calls the movement toward and away from a pure market society a double movement. Liberals constantly strive for "free markets," effectively pushing society to the edge of a cliff. People eventually and spontaneously resist once the consequences of unrestrained markets for society become apparent: "they refuse to act like lemmings marching over a cliff to their own destruction" (Block 2001, XXV). Polanyi developed the double movement to make sense of historical transformations:

> Social history in the nineteenth century was the result of a double movement: the extension of the market organization in respect to genuine commodities was accompanied by its restriction in respect to fictitious ones. While on the one hand markets spread all over the face of the globe and the amount of goods involved grew to unbelievable dimensions, on the other hand a network of measures and policies was integrated into powerful institutions designed to check the action of the markets relative to labor, land and capital. (2001, 79)

Whenever society moves toward a greater reliance on market self-regulation, ordinary people bear higher, ultimately unsustainable costs, forcing spontaneous resistance. Workers, farmers and small business people will not tolerate for any length of time a pattern of economic organization that subjects them to periodic and dramatic fluctuations in their daily economic circumstances. "Robbed of the protective covering of cultural institutions, human beings would perish from the effects of social exposure; they would die as the victims of acute social dislocation through vice, perversion, crime and starvation" (Polanyi 2001, 76). Treating land as a commodity like any other facilitates its annihilation, for it becomes valued only as an input into production and a repository for waste. People will not stand by passively watching the environment become degraded and they themselves reduced to disposable inputs in production.

Fred Block aptly likens the double movement to a giant rubber band. Efforts to induce a purer market economy stretch the band and society will either ease the tension by reverting to more embedded (less tense) state or the band will snap. A spontaneous counter movement always emerges to prevent an economy from becoming truly disembedded, but the question is what form the resistance will take and how the state will react. Polanyi saw danger in the movement toward a pure market society due to how society responds to these questions. People resisted the push toward a pure market economy historically by demanding things like a social safety net, minimum wage laws, safety codes, and environmental regulation. The state responded to these demands in one of two ways: through sweeping policy changes that ushered in the modern welfare state, e.g., the New Deal in the USA, or through active suppression of such changes, leading to the rise of fascism and state authoritarianism. If either response fails to contain the demands, the rubber band snaps and the counter movement will precipitate revolution with untold consequences.

Polanyi carefully studied the role liberal economic theory played in the design, implementation, and ideological entrenchment of a system of markets. The systemic efforts of neoliberals today within the World Bank, IMF and WTO today to dismantle restraints on trade and capital flows and reduce governmental "interference" in the organization of economic life resemble the liberal efforts in the nineteenth century to no small degree. Polanyi likens economic liberalism to a political project, but one not as a means toward an end, but an end in itself. Liberals at least since the time of Smith see the implementation of a pure market economy as a great social project which, if realized, will result in the greatest happiness for the greatest number. Nothing less than a self-regulating market on a global scale will ensure the proper function of a self-regulating marketplace. Liberals build

on the work of Smith and envision commercial society as a natural development; however, the restrictions placed upon the marketplace (and bemoaned by liberals as protectionist) Polanyi presents as a social response to
the impossible demands the free market places upon citizens.

By 1944, when Polanyi wrote *The Great Transformation,* the trauma
of the great depression had discredited liberalism and he essentially con-
signed it to the dustbin of history. Yet, given the dominance of neoliberals
in policy circles today, liberalism today seems stronger than ever before.
The partial eclipse of post-depression liberalism enabled its defenders,
notably Friedman and Hayek, to argue that the economic woes associated
with the welfare state resulted from state interference in the operation of
the marketplace. Contemporary liberals share the same market sense as
their historic counterparts, making Polanyi's critique seem as fresh as when
he wrote it over 60 years ago.

Liberals still envision Smith's commercial society as a natural development being held back by state interference in the economy, and claim
that if it weren't for "the unholy alliance of trade unions and labor parties,
monopolistic manufacturers and agrarian interests, which in their short-
sighted greed, joined forces to frustrate economic liberty, the world would
be enjoying today the fruits of an almost automatic system of creating
material welfare" (Polanyi 2001, 150). Liberals today make strikingly similar arguments in favor of a pure market economy, repeating:

> in endless variations that but for the policies advocated by its critics,
> liberalism would have delivered the goods; that not the competitive sys-
> tem and the self-regulating market, but interference with that system
> and interventions with that market are responsible for our ills. . . . The
> economic liberal is thus enabled to formulate a case which links the
> present with the past in one coherent whole. For who could deny that
> government intervention in business may undermine confidence? Who
> could deny that unemployment would sometimes be less if it were not
> for out-of-work benefit provided by law? That private business is
> injured by the competition of public works? That deficit finance may
> endanger private investment? That paternalism tends to damp business
> initiative? This being so in the present, surely it was no different in the
> past. (Polanyi 2001, 150)

Despite a similar focus upon the oscillation toward and away a pure
market system, Polanyi interprets the movement in a radically different way
than liberals. Liberals see the system of natural liberty being constantly
thwarted by reactionary, self-serving policy and unceasingly push for a system

of self-regulating markets, even calling upon the state to establish it, by force if necessary.[17] Polanyi argued that the growth of state regulation and "interference" in the market arose as a spontaneous response by the population to the crises and disjunctures caused by liberal policy to create a more pure market economy; liberals on the other hand argue that the growth of state regulation and "interference" in the market lies at the root of the crises and disjunctures in market societies today. Critics of liberalism—then and now—argue that a pure market economy makes impossible demands on ordinary people around the world and predict people will mobilize to protect themselves. The 1930s witnessed the rise of the welfare state and fascism to respond and contain these demands. Today, one can use Polanyi to read fundamentalist movements of various stripes and "anti-globalization" struggles as responses to the impossibility of market society.

CONCLUSION.

Smith's vision and analysis of commodity exchange provides a foundation for contemporary liberalism, and policy makers continue to evoke the exchange entailments he enunciated to justify a wide range of economic policy.[18] Both Marx and Polanyi explored and criticized his market sense in detail. The immanent critique presented here challenges the one-sided positive, liberal associations of commodity exchange by highlighting the contradictions found within the liberal analysis. The individual freedom, independence and liberty liberals celebrate as entailed by exchange also imply, for the same reasons, subjugation, dependence, and tyranny.

Stepping outside of the rigid confines of Smith's analysis, we also considered Marx's commodity fetishism and Polanyi's critique of market society, highlighting their social and theoretical implications. Beyond explicating the essentialisms underpinning liberal market sense, Marx investigated what he saw as the particular consequences of it, including the stifling of the possibilities of social change and the perpetuation of the *status quo*. With the concept of fetishism, Marx brought to the fore how the social nature of commodity exchange becomes obscured under the liberal analysis, with the exchange-values and money necessary for it to function taking on a 'god-like' status. Just as European and, in particular, British anthropology considered the worship of material objects as the lowest form of religion in the early nineteenth century, Marx derided political economists for fixating upon the market and representing it as a natural, automatic regulator of the economy.

Polanyi saw liberal attempts at creating a pure market economy as impossible and dangerous. His notion that giving commodity status to land, labor and capital is a fiction countered the naturalness liberals ascribe to commercial society. Polanyi characterized the last 200 years of society as a double movement, with liberals consistently pushing society toward a pure market economy and a spontaneous counter movement demanding restraints on the marketplace. Danger lurks in the liberal agenda because the social tension that a pure market economy engenders may be met with either reforms like a modern welfare state, totalitarian suppression of popular demands, or complete social meltdown.

Finally, we also noted some ontological implications of Marx's immanent critique of circulation. Rather than take umbrage at any notion of social dependence, Marx criticized only the particular form of dependence entailed by circulation. The ubiquitousness of dependence or unfreedom found within any society implies that true freedom or independence requires the recognition of social ties. Liberals ignore circulation's contradictions, seeing only freedom, liberty and independence in their utopic vision of commercial society, rather than the indirect dependence, unfreedom and even tyranny a market system also entails. Accepting the unavoidableness of dependence within any complex society opens up, however, an entire new way of thinking; instead of attempting to eradicate social ties via the marketplace or other arrangements, energy becomes directed at transforming oppressive relations into socially acceptable forms.

Chapter Five
Simple Exchange, Merchant Capital and Augmented Circulation.

There are in principle innumerable possible types of market economy, distinguished from each other in extraordinarily diverse and consequential ways.

—George DeMartino, *Global Economy, Global Justice.*

Liberal market sense flows directly from a narrowly bounded understanding of human nature: the supposed innate human desire and ability to truck, barter and trade for individual gain. Liberals follow in Smith's footsteps by treating market activity in a singular fashion, seeing all instances of commodity exchange as particulars of a universal type. Liberals represent exchange prior to commercial society as quantitatively circumscribed but qualitatively the same as today. Regarding the future, liberals envision something akin to Smith's natural path of progression with all societies moving toward the system of natural liberty, despite state economic policy occasionally slowing it down.

The central question motivating liberal economic history involves why a developed system of exchange took so long to emerge, given that it flows directly from our shared DNA. Smith's answer rested upon the incomplete specialization and division of labor, along with misguided state policy hampering the emergence of the system of natural liberty. Modern liberals like Douglass North (1990) blame things like ill-defined property rights and imperfect information, essentially updating Smith's story by utilizing the latest tools of mainstream economic theory. Critics of liberal analyses reject their "flattening" of the market landscape. Instead of seeing one homogenous field of exchange, critics envision many types and ascribe different thick meanings to each.

George DeMartino elucidates some of the ways critical scholars distinguish types of commodity exchange by looking at: "the institutions and rules that govern price formation, distribution, property rights (both the

kinds of goods in which private and/or public property rights may be established, and just what the rights may entail), and, particularly, the scope and
scale of the market" (2000, 85–6). Although it is possible to differentiate a
vast array of market activity, four broad types regularly stand out in the literature. The first, circulation, refers to the liberal understanding of commodity exchange culminating in commercial society. On the other hand,
simple exchange and merchant capital parallel Aristotle's natural and unnatural exchange. Simple exchange refers to specific acts of exchange undertaken to fulfill needs, whereas merchant capital concerns profit motivated
exchange—buying cheap and selling dear. The final category considered here,
augmented circulation, derives mostly from Marx's *Capital* and couples capitalist production with circulation; i.e., capitalist enterprises, rather than liberal individual producers, comprise the primary producers of commodities
and most individuals must sell their labor-power to earn a living.

Differentiating various types of exchange gives us insights into why
people have so many contradictory feelings about the marketplace. Buying
a used car from a friend, shopping at a farmer's market and looking for a
job all constitute acts of commodity exchange, but people often associate
different feelings and meanings with each. Buying directly from individual
producers often elicits different feelings than when merchants mediate a
transaction or when one purchases commodities directly from a corporation. Selling things on eBay feels different than trying to sell your ability to
work. People may enjoy producing and selling handcrafted goods independently but dread selling their laboring abilities to corporations. Seeing
these transactions as different types of commodity exchange broadens our
conception of the marketplace and helps explain the variety of often contradictory feelings commodity exchange evokes in general.

An expansive view of the marketplace also helps us make sense of the
conflicting views of the global economy today. People may be in favor
international trade when they think it's "fair" but dislike it when it's envisioned to enrich merchants and impoverish the poor. People may enjoy the
cheap prices giant merchant corporations like Wal-Mart provide but fear
the perceived impacts of "sweatshops." The following chapter explores the
thick and thin meanings of simple exchange, merchant capital and augmented circulation and helps explain why people often embrace conflicting
ideas about the marketplace.

SIMPLE EXCHANGE.

In their readings of historical economic activity, Marx and Polanyi both
acknowledge that contemporary theory shapes our interpretation of history,

but reject the liberal flattening of the market landscape. "Categories of bourgeois thought possess a truth for all other forms of society, but this is to be taken only with a grain of salt. They can contain them in a developed, or stunted, or caricatured form, etc., but always with an essential difference" (Marx 1993, 106). Commodity exchange in historic societies possesses similarities, e.g., a familial resemblance, to liberal circulation, but we need to recognize the resemblance results from our gaze rather than any inherent or essential features. Just as we can see apes as precursors of humanity, we can see prior forms of exchange as nascent versions of circulation. Yet, apes are not humans waiting in the wings and the same holds for the relationship between simple exchange and circulation.

Marx developed a useful notation to describe simple exchange in historical settings and to differentiate it from circulation in contemporary society. Simple exchange consists of C-C and/or C-M-C, where C represents commodities and M a socially recognized unit of value. To illustrate simple exchange, Marx depicted a weaver exchanging linen for £2 which he, "being a man of the old school," exchanges in turn for a bible (1990, 199). The weaver began with linen (C_1) and exchanged it for a bible (C_2). Analytically, the weavers foray into the marketplace corresponds to C_1-C_2, with commodities *of equal value* constituting both the beginning and the end of the process. Money often serves as an intermediary but does not change the qualitative nature of the transaction when commodities of equal value still constitute the beginning and end of the process: e.g., the weaver sells the cloth for £2 and uses the money to purchase a bible worth £2 $(C_1$–M-$C_2)$.

Circulation, as a process with no beginning or end, lacks the discreteness of simple exchange on a quantitative level. Expressed analytically, circulation looks like the following:

$$\ldots C_{n+1}\text{-}M\text{-}C_{n+2}\text{-}M \ldots C_{n+n} \ldots$$

Circulation comprises the *totality* of exchanges that link commodity buyers and sellers who make simple exchanges in society. Our industrious weaver exchanging linen for a bible constitutes a simple exchange, and in the context of circulation it comprises a singular act within an endless web of buying and selling commodities. The weaver purchasing a bible gives the seller the means to purchase commodities as part of endless cycle of transactions. A constant addition and subtraction of commodities characterizes circulation, linking people in a vast network of buyers and sellers.

Marx qualified simple exchange with adjectives like sporadic or spontaneous to highlight the specificity of circulation, for the mere occurrence of simple exchange does not imply that circulation's systemic series of exchanges will link all individuals in society. Circulation presupposes that commodity exchange serves an important role in the distribution of social product, but the mere existence of commodity exchange in society does not. Polanyi explored how redistribution, gift exchange, bonds of reciprocity and so forth performed the dominant distributive role prior to the advent of market society (e.g., circulation), and simple exchange (what takes place in "local," "regional" or "long distance" markets) merely supplements them, playing a minor role in people's economic life.

Since commodity exchange outside of circulation does not mediate the social metabolism as the primary means of distribution, production does not generally assume a commodity form. Consequentially, exchange-value does not constitute the primary goal or object of social production. When societies do not employ commodity exchange as a primary means of distribution, "the aim of work is not the *creation of value*—although they [producers] may do surplus labor in order to obtain *alien*, i.e., surplus products in exchange—rather, its aim is sustenance of the individual proprietor and of his family, as well as of the total community" (Marx 1993, 471–2). In a similar vein, Polanyi argues that all societies prior to market society subsumed production under a wide range of cultural norms that were designed to ensure community survival and subsistence. The use-values that assumed a commodity form typically derived from the superfluous product of society, the extra goods produced above and beyond producers' and community's needs.[1]

The peasant mode of production literature inspired by Chayanov's *The Theory of Peasant Economy* (1966) and by other more Marxian accounts of peasant production (de Janvry 1981; Schejtman 1988) exemplify the above characterization of commodity exchange within pre-commercial societies. These scholars attribute self-subsistence as the paramount motivation amongst the producing population, with only the *extra* use-values produced, e.g., those useful objects *surplus* to subsistence needs, finding their way to market. Some commodity exchange takes place to be sure, but given the self-sufficiency of these households it serves primarily as either an incidental supplement toward household provisioning when surplus product arises, or as a means to acquire whatever use-values the household cannot produce internally.[2] Liberals on the other hand see all production as essentially commodity based even outside of circulation. For instance, Sol Tax (1953), in an influential anthropological study, represented Guatemalan peasants as "penny capitalists" who produced for exchange after undertaking careful cost/benefit calculations. Samuel Popkin (1979) and Theodore Schultz (1964) similarly envision peasants as "rational maximizers" producing for exchange and itching for increased market opportunities.

Many scholars outside of the liberal tradition see quantitative and qualitative differences in commodity exchange prior to the rise of market society, and I chose the term *simple exchange* with these differences in mind. Quantitatively, simple exchange refers to the non-pervasive material scope/scale of commodity exchange found in many historic and present societies. Qualitatively, *simple* expresses the marginal role of commodity exchange in economic life within historic societies. Within circulation, simple exchange connotes trade motivated by household provisioning rather than profit. Simple exchange parallels Aristotle's representation of natural exchange qualitatively and quantitatively in historic societies because it functions primarily as an incidental means of household provisioning.

Complex rules and norms governed simple exchange in different historical settings to ensure communal provisioning. Cultural rules and norms typically circumscribed what things could become commodities, when they could be sold, and often the prices they could be traded. Igor Kopytoff discusses in detail for instance how the Tiv ethic group separated exchange into three separate spheres: subsistence items, prestige items and rights-in-people: "Items within each sphere were exchangeable, and each was ruled by its own kind of morality" (1986, 71). Local markets provided a space once a week for growers of different agricultural goods to exchange, and less frequent regional markets involved a broader range of subsistence items. The Tiv could freely exchange items within each sphere, but trading prestige goods for means of subsistence rarely occurred, and only under extreme duress of the people involved.

The big difference between liberal scholars and those working within the institutionalist tradition rests with how they interpret cultural stipulations on exchange like the Tiv's. Liberals see such rules and norms as impediments on the "natural" exchange process grounded in human nature. Institutionalists reject liberal reductionism and understand commodity exchange as an instituted process firmly embedded within, and defined by, social relations. Institutionalists like Polanyi see economic activity (i.e., production, distribution and consumption) as always subsumed politically, socially and culturally. To make sense of any facet of the economy, including exchange, institutionalists suggest that one must first examine the broader social context embedding it. The three spheres of the market for the Tiv constituted parts (and only parts) of their economic system, serving specific goals and objectives. From an institutionist perspective, the rules and norms enmeshing Tiv exchange do not *constrain* but *define* it within a specific context.

Many if not most of exchange activity today takes the form of simple exchange, albeit within the context of circulation. People often must engage in exchange to procure their means of subsistence, even if they often buy from merchants trying to make an extra buck. Sellers on eBay, at farmer's markets or at tag sales usually seek a "fair" value for the commodities they vend and use the proceeds to purchase things they need. People sell their ability to work and seek a "fair" wage for their labor for similar reasons. Yet, merchants also participate in exchange by buying cheap and selling dear, inducing a constant worry of being swindled among producers of commodities and consumers. Let us consider exchange for profit, i.e., merchant capital, in more detail.

MERCHANT CAPITAL.

Aristotle's unnatural exchange bears a striking similarity to Marx's writings on merchant capital. Marx uses the terms merchant capital, commercial capital, and commodity-dealing capital interchangeably, for they all refer to the same process of M-C-M,' where an increase in money (M' > M) motivates the buying and selling of commodities.[3] The increase in money (e.g., profit) arises from disproportionate transactions, where exchangers receive more or less for their commodities than is customary. Exchange undertaken for profit often results in someone getting cheated, something Aristotle linked with social conflict and "the source of quarrels and accusations" (*Nicomachean Ethics*, 1131a).[4] Commodity exchange in the hands of merchant capital becomes simply a vehicle, a means of increasing wealth, "and not just wealth, but wealth in its general social form as exchange value" (Marx 1991, 443). Whereas exchange-value facilitates simple exchange and serves as a *means* to an end, it becomes the *end* in and of itself in the hands of merchant capital. Buying a bible from the maker for 1£ and selling it to our weaver for 2£ constitutes merchant capital, for the 1£ difference in purchase and sale price motivates the transaction.

Aristotle saw the ne'er-do-wells pursuing individual gain in exchange as parasites upon the population at large, amassing wealth solely at the expense of others in society. Marx similarly notes how profits gleaned from exchange amass in merchant's hands (or rather their pockets) and infuse the exchange process with a vague notion of general swindling.[5] Merchants and tradespeople comprise personifications of the merchant capital relation, and it shaped pre-commercial society and simple exchange in positive and negative ways.

Marx and Aristotle analytically separated simple exchange from merchant capital rather than conflating them as liberal scholars do. Marx dubbed merchant capital the historic form of capital, because even simple exchange provides all the conditions necessary for its existence: "no further conditions are needed for its existence . . . than are necessary for the simple circulation of commodities and money. Or, one might say that precisely the latter is *its* condition of existence" (Marx 1991, 442). Merchants do not produce commodities, they simply buy and sell them. Hence, merchant capital depends on the existence of commodities in society and the willingness of the population to buy and sell. Merchant capital is "the first form of capital, i.e., of value, which comes exclusively from circulation (from exchange), maintains, reproduces and increases itself within it, and thus the exclusive aim of this movement and activity is exchange value" (Marx 1993, 856). The wealth gleaned from merchant capital relations finds its way into someone's pocket and trading peoples, individuals, groups and even entire societies have amassed wealth as a result of merchant capital relations, "existing like the gods of Epicures in the *intermundia*" (1991, 447)

Since simple exchange provides all of the conditions of existence for merchant capital, the possibility of merchant capital mediating transactions through its "parasitical" insertion between the producers and consumers of commodities exists wherever commodity exchange takes place. As a consequence, merchant capital "appears in the most various forms of society and at the most various stages of the development of the forces of social production" (Marx 1993, 858). The realm of exchange provides the conditions of existence for merchant capital but also serves as its prison. Merchant capital simply mediates the movement of extremes, or negotiates the terrain between production and consumption.[6]

The analytical notation Marx employs to describe merchant capital consists of M-C-C-M' or M-C-M.' Merchant capital connotes the process of deploying exchange-value (M) to purchase commodities (C) only to resell them above the purchase price (M'>M). In the process, M is increased by the profits that arise from buying in order to sell dearer. Both the buyer or seller may be potentially swindled in exchange, but Marx attributed merchant capital's profit primarily with the "frauds practiced on the producers of commodities" (1990, 267); this foreshadows his treatment of merchant capital under the conditions of augmented circulation (see below). Merchant capital in pre-circulation societies often manifests itself within the "carrying" or "truck" trade, such as that conducted by Arabic traders of the middle ages, the mercantile empires of the Dutch, Venetians, Genoans, and Phoenicians, to name but a few. Trading peoples concentrated sales and purchases spatially and often temporally by acting as a locus of exchange between societies.

The wealth of the great trading enclaves arose due to their intermediary role between less developed social formations: "Most of the independent trading peoples or cities attained the magnificent development of their independence through the *carrying trade,* which rested on the barbarity of the producing peoples, between whom they played the role of money (the mediators)" (Marx 1993, 858).[7] The triangle trade between Africa, the Caribbean and Europe provides an excellent example of merchant capital relations, for traders took advantage of the distances involved to buy commodities cheap in one location and sell them dear elsewhere. The less developed the system of exchange in societies, the more likely merchant capital orientated itself, spatially and temporally, around the arrival of (largely) foreign merchants.

Merchant capital interacts only with the guardians of commodities and their potential buyers, purchasing commodities from slave owners, feudal lords, and petty-bourgeois capitalist producers whenever profitable. For analytical purposes, we can label commodities by the means of their production, e.g., slave commodities, but "the character of commodities themselves is in no way altered if they are a product of primitive community, slave production, small peasant and petty-bourgeois production, or capitalist production" (Marx 1991, 442). Merchants buy commodities without regard to the specifics surrounding production or consumption; they are interested solely in the money differential between the purchase and sale price.

WHAT SIMPLE EXCHANGE AND MERCHANT CAPITAL ENTAIL.

Prior to circulation, commodity exchange played a supplementary role in the distribution of the social product. Many thick differences in meaning between simple exchange and circulation arise due to the dissimilarities in scale and scope of exchange inside and outside of circulation. The positive entailments that liberals ascribe to commodity exchange—i.e., freedom, equality, and independence—only become possible when exchange relations achieve a certain critical mass or scale within society and function as the primary means of distribution. An individual economic agent within circulation "relates to himself as proprietor, as master of the conditions of his reality . . . and relates to others in the same way" (Marx 1993, 471).[8] However, being a master of one's conditions of reality only becomes possible when the social caste or hierarchy no longer ensures a certain means of subsistence. With commodity exchange being only accidental and sporadic, other means of social distribution such as central distribution, kinship networks, patriarchy and so forth connect and dominate the social metabolism. The freedom and independence associated with the marketplace evaporates outside of a certain scale and scope of exchange, making the *prevalence* of exchange the key rather than its mere existence.

Liberals and radicals often ascribe to commodity exchange the power to dissolve social hierarchies (for better or worse). However, the power rests with the possibilities created by an alternative means of distribution not linked to existing social hierarchies rather than commodity exchange *per se*. Commodity exchange may emerge as a substitute for previous distributional means, and as a consequence, provide a condition of possibility for economic and social life outside of prior distributional boundaries. Yet, this claim implies that *any* alternative to the existing social hierarchies that govern the distribution of use-values within society may also serve in this role.

Without the scope/scale of commodity exchange under circulation, simple exchange may actually *reinforce* the social divisions and distinctions of status, blood, kingroup and so forth rather than induce their dissolution. Simple exchange relations, as part of a broader cultural setting, may restrict (define) who may participate, and replicate social divisions through the process of inclusion/exclusion. The ability to participate in exchange as a proprietor in ancient Rome partially defined citizenship, or rather, exclusion from certain forms of exchange defined non-citizenship: "In Roman law, the *servus* is therefore correctly defined as one who may not enter into exchange for the purpose of acquiring anything from himself" (Marx 1993, 245). Societies where only certain members of society may freely engage in exchange, such as slave owners, feudal lords and others endowed with property rights, commonly exist in history and typically presuppose that much of the population cannot buy and sell commodities at all.

Aristotle inadvertently illustrated another way exchange may reinforce rather than dissolve social stratification. A modicum of equality may exist among exchanging agents based upon the ability to own property, but one's social rank/status may shape the ratio that commodities are exchanged for. Social rank/status becomes cemented or reinforced in such instances, contradicting the notion that commodity exchange always entails a dissolution of social hierarchies. The exchange entailments articulated in commodity exchange depend upon both the social relations enmeshing it in society, as well as the scope and scale of the marketplace.

The emergence of exchange relations shapes the broader social *milieu* just as existing social relations shapes trading activity. For instance, even simple exchange requires some form of property rights and commodity production. Certain social relations provide important conditions of possibility for commodity exchange to take place and these in turn impact the complex web of economic activity found in any society. The rejection of people who possess an innate tendency to truck, barter and trade implies the need to consider the specific conditions facilitating the emergence of trade and its impact upon the social fabric. Marx and Polanyi dug deep into this fertile theoretical terrain in their analysis of commodity exchange in historical settings.

Marx's *Grundrisse* contains many examples of how the representatives of two social formations, after initially coming into contact with one another, spontaneously barter use-values (or engage in plunder or war, depending upon the circumstances). Other examples involve merchants who infiltrate various social formations and promote and facilitate trade between them through their interposition. Marx considered commodity exchange instigated by merchants rather than spontaneously emerging as barter more classic or typical. Merchants scour the globe for profit-making opportunities and arrive in various locales, bearing exotic use-values *qua* commodities to either trade or sell and/or looking for use-values to purchase or barter for. Merchants facilitate the institution of exchange heuristically by bringing with them its conditions of possibility, i.e., through the actual practice of buying and selling commodities. The same merchants directly mediate and profit from the process, giving them an incentive to initiate exchange relations in the first place. Marx envisions merchant capital historically in a rather unflattering light, for "its development in the trading peoples of both ancient and modern times is directly bound up with violent plunder, piracy, and the taking of slaves and subjugation of colonies; as in Carthage and Rome, and later with the Venetians, Portuguese, Dutch, etc." (1991, 449).

When merchant capital instigates exchange, the social relations enabling the process and acting as its conditions of possibility have yet to emerge as constitutive aspects of society, for use-values produced do not assume a commodity form. Producers do not make things for sale outside of a market context, but with the initial onset of exchange, extra use-values or the social overflow can assume the form of commodities.[9] Whether or not the impulse for positing use-values as exchange-values came from outside with foreign merchants or from within the social formation as in spontaneous barter, it "takes place originally at the borders of the natural communities and is restricted to a narrow sphere, and forms something which passes production by, is auxiliary to it; [and] dies out just as much by chance as it arises" (Marx 1993, 204).[10]

The emergence of simple exchange and merchant capital, even when sporadic and isolated, shapes society in particular ways. At a minimum, long distance trade entails "an accidental enlargement of the sphere of satisfactions, enjoyments (relations to new objects)" for the people concerned, even if very little exchange actually takes place (Marx 1993, 204). Simple exchange and merchant capital may also hasten the development of new social needs such as coffee, sugar and spices and increase familiarity with cultural products from other places. Merchant capital of course plays a role in the construction of new needs, for it acts as a facilitator of the exchange process and profits from it. Trade caravans laden with exotic use-values, or ocean-bound ships containing foreign cargo constitute two examples of merchant capital-inspired trade bringing new use-values to social formations.

The goods posited by merchants as commodities are, nevertheless, only of secondary importance to the social formation's economic organization outside of general circulation. Secondary here refers to the importance awarded to commodity exchange as a method of social distribution—e.g., how the productive population in general secures its material conditions of existence. Productive population refers to the people in society actively engaged in producing use-values above and beyond their individual need.[11] If the bulk of productive society employs a distribution network not predicated upon or involving commodity exchange, than it does not directly impact their ability to secure their own means of subsistence. The commodities of any ensuing trade typically involve consumption items for social elites of different societies rather than, say, the means of subsistence for the population at large.

Advanced trading enclaves did import foodstuffs and other basic means of subsistence from the surrounding agricultural lands or from more distant environs, making them dependent upon trade for survival. Yet, trading enclaves existed as islands in a vast sea of generally subsistence production where commodity exchange still played a tangential role in economic life. Merchants in trading enclaves dealt primarily with the elites of different social formations rather than the everyday producers within them. The "principal proprietors of the surplus product the merchant trades with, i.e., the slave-owner, the feudal lord and the state (e.g. the oriental despot), represent the consumption wealth which the merchant sets out to trap" (Marx 1992, 448).

After the initial instance of exchange, from either spontaneous barter or the instigation of merchant capital, commodity exchange may never progress beyond its first phenomenal form or it may become an integral part of the social formation. Traders may depart with their newly acquired use-values never to return and the "barbarians" may cease to participate in any further exchange (barter) relations. Before exchange relations become established, "commodities constantly have to be thrown into it anew from the outside, like fuel on a fire. Otherwise it flickers out in indifference" (Marx 1993, 254–5). The logic behind Marx's statement stems directly from his rejection of any innate tendency of humanity to truck, barter and trade. On the other hand, exchange relations may solidify and become enmeshed within the social relations constituting society, but the scale and scope of exchange may nonetheless be strictly confined. Only certain, select members of society, for example, may be allowed to participate, or some use-values such as land may be placed off-limits with exchange limited to food stuffs and other direct means of subsistence.

The establishment of exchange relations opens the possibility of extending them beyond their original scope. One of the most common entailments ascribed to exchange within in the Marxian tradition concerns the perceived dynamic necessity for its expansion. I read Marx as exploring the social conditions under which an expansion of commodity exchange may take place, but locating the possibility of such an event squarely within the social relations enmeshing exchange. Consider the following quote: "trade will naturally react back to varying degrees upon the communities between which it is carried on [although the influence] depends very much on the nature of the producing communities between which it operates" (Marx 1993, 858).

Even with only a small portion of social production being earmarked for exchange, some of the contradictory linkages associated with commodity exchange *qua* circulation begin to emerge. Within the branches of production subsumed to exchange, e.g., where production takes place specifically in a commodity form, the producers may begin to possess at least some freedom and independence to produce specifically for exchange rather than direct consumption. The branches of production subsumed to exchange, e.g., feudal artisans, must then sell or "realize" the commodities they produce in order to obtain or secure the commodities needed to secure their own existence.

With exchange constituting a marginal role within society, the amount of production assuming a commodity form also remains marginal. Some independent producers and craftsmen may emerge, primarily in cities, and become imbricated within market relations—producing for exchange and consuming via products purchased. Yet, the majority of the population may remain engaged in self-subsistence or feudal agriculture. In such a scenario, simple exchange entails an advancement and/or solidification of city/country social relations, for although the cities procure agricultural commodities from rural areas and manufactured and finished commodities from the cities find their way back into the country, the scale and scope of exchange remain relatively constant and marginal to the production of use-values as a whole. Scholars such as Paul Sweezy (1978) represent Feudal Europe as just such an example, for commodity exchange regularly occurred, but remained peripheral to agrarian life where the majority of the population resided. Sweezy characterized simple exchange within the feudal order as a "peddling system" that was tangential to the reproductive fabric of the order itself.

On the other hand, the establishment of regular commodity exchange facilitates the incorporation of more commoditized use-values, entailing the potential expansion in scope and scale and perhaps even the emergence of circulation proper. "The development of trade and commercial capital always gives production a growing orientation toward exchange-value, expands it scope, diversifies it and renders it cosmopolitan, developing money into world money" (Marx 1991, 449). Marx devotes some of his theoretical energies into exploring occurrences where the commoditization of use-values "no longer just takes hold of surplus production, but gradually gobbles up production itself and makes entire branches of production dependent on it" (1992, 448). Yet, the object of his analysis varied tremendously from Smith's, for Marx did not seek to provide a stagest theory of history with commercial society as the *telos,* but rather explored how and why such an event may take place, given that commodity exchange *does not* arise from any innate human essence and *does not* always entail an expansionist dynamic.[12]

Marx did not simply assume that simple exchange always leads, sooner or later, to circulation as part of a predestined historical pattern. Rather, he explored the changes in social relations and beliefs that allowed the emergence of circulation to trespass within specific social formations in a number of specific contexts. One prominent example concerns the impact of agricultural production in England in reaction to an influx of Netherlands commodities in the sixteenth and seventeenth centuries. Landed elites in England began exchanging more and more wool in order to obtain foreign commodities and, in response, agriculture became transformed from the production of use-values into exchange-value. Beginning with the simple exchange of *surplus* wool for the commodities offered by Dutch traders, "it turned into a production which took place only in circulation, a production which posited exchange values as its exclusive content" (Marx 1993, 257). In *Capital,* Marx's discussion of the enclosure movement in England elaborated the social aspects of the transition in lurid detail.[13] Polanyi also discussed at length the emergence of market society, and envisioned the process as *directed* rather than *constrained* by the strong arm of the state.

Marx's *Theories of Surplus Value* (1971) complemented his discussion in the *Grundrisse* by outlining other reasons (besides the influx of new commodities) why the sphere of commodity exchange may both expand in scale/scope and even morph into circulation. For one, commodity production changes the relationship between the producers and their product. Once it becomes customary or habitual for some social production to be posited as exchange-value, the trading activity, however it originated, may become transformed from an accessory role to production, e.g., an outlet for the overflow, into the primary outlet for at least some production capability. Use-values produced as commodities bear no direct relation to the producers needs, for the products are produced simply for their exchange-value. This situation makes commodity producing agents dependent, at least to some degree, upon exchange. The more and more specialized commodity production becomes, it is only by pure chance that the producer consumes any of the product at all. This stands in marked contrast with simple exchange historically, "where only those products which exceed the amount required by the producer himself become commodities or, at any rate, this is mainly the case" (Marx 1971, 288).

When commodity producers enter into exchange relations as sellers of goods, they also appear as buyers, purchasing goods for their own consumption and/or production. As buyers of commodities, they comprise a demand for products and may potentially spur commodity production in other areas of society in order to meet their demands. Taken together, these events may spawn a dynamic where more and more goods become produced for exchange simply as a means of obtaining exchange-value to purchase other commodities. However, exactly *how* increased commodity exchange and production will impact the existing relations of production (and class structures in particular) fundamentally depends upon the array of social relations which these changes occur. Consider a remarkable passage where Marx explores this possibility:

> Trade always has, to a greater or lesser degree, a solvent effect on the pre-existing organizations of production, which in all their various forms are principally oriented to use-value . . . how far it leads to dissolution of the old mode of production depends first and foremost on the solidity and inner articulation of this mode of production itself. And what comes out of this process of dissolution, i.e., what new mode of production arises in place of the old, does not depend on trade, but rather on the character of the old mode of production itself. In the ancient world, the influence of trade and the development of commercial capital always produced the result of a slave economy; or, given a different point of departure, it also meant the transformation of a patriarchal slave system oriented toward the production of the direct means of subsistence into one oriented toward the production of surplus value. In the modern world, on the other hand, its outcome is the capitalist mode of production. It follows

that this result is itself conditions by quite other circumstances than the development of commercial capital. (1991, 449–450)

This passage carefully qualifies the status awarded to merchant capital and commodity exchange as agents of social change, and argues that what, if any, social relations/changes arise due to the dissolution process associated with increased commodity exchange and production depend upon social relations *outside of the realm of distribution*. The emergence of trade and commodity exchange will impact existing economic relations, but the trajectory of any transformation and what it entails depends upon the "nature of the producing communities."

One possibility for an expansion of exchange concerns an increasing division of labor, with commoditization allowing for a subdivision of final products into many component products which may, in turn, spawn more commodity exchange. Instead of, say, a cart maker making the wheels, axles, hitches and so forth all by himself, he may opt to purchase some or all of the inputs as commodities. Such an event allows the cart maker to specialize in cart assembly rather than working as a blacksmith, cooper, and carpenter. Essentially, instead of a master cart maker constructing all facets of the final product, several people specialize in one aspect of cart making. In this way, the production of a product becomes divided into many branches; i.e., various phases of one product become different commodities. This means that *"successive phases* or *states* of *one product* are converted into *separate commodities"* (Marx 1971, 289). With the emergence of new, separate commodities on the scene, new applications may be found for them, increasing the demand for, and facilitating the production of, even more commodities; for example, the wheels for the carts may be also used on wheelbarrows. Commodity production may promote a specialization of labor in a synergetic manner analogous to the story Smith provided in the *Wealth of Nations*, serving to expand and deepen the scope of goods being exchanged. Although Marx challenged the *necessary* linkage between the specialization of labor and commodity exchange, Sweezy (1942) points out that he never argued against it either. The essentialist logic linking commodity exchange, labor specialization and an increase in social wealth deserves scrutiny. Specialization may occur without exchange, but even if it does occur with exchange, it may entail poverty and economic malaise rather than expanding wealth. One of Marx's primary contributions involves how he portrayed commercial society as contradictory, producing great wealth and great poverty *simultaneously.*

Radical literature on the international division of labor explores similar contradictions. For instance, Paul Baran's *Political Economy of Growth*

(1957) argued that "backward" areas became specialized as primary commodity/exporters at the same time that other regions specialized in sophisticated industrial and capital goods manufacture. The primary commodity producers/exporters in the "periphery" over time became poorer, at least in a relative sense, compared to industrial "core" nations. More recently, Ankie Hoogvelt's *Globalization and the Postcolonial World* (1997) provides a critical account and review of the new international division of labor that, much like the old division among the core, periphery and semi-periphery, results in some regions and enclaves becoming increasingly deskilled and poorer while others become wealthier. Radicals aver that the class structure of production, political and cultural issues play crucial roles in the significance of an international division of labor. Global integration and specialization spearheaded by colonial power, for example, differed qualitatively from current liberal globalization, even though wealth became more concentrated and centralized with each.

Returning to the implications of simple exchange and merchant capital for production, even though "*a large part of the output* never enters into circulation, is never placed on the market, is not produced as commodities, and does not become commodities" (Marx 1971, 112, emphasis added), a small part of output does. Having goods *specifically* produced for exchange-value rather than strictly for use-value implies changes in production that, at a minimum, involve a reorientation of the motivations behind production itself. With established exchange relations, at least some social production becomes directly produced for exchange purposes. This, in turn, feeds back into the exchange process.

> The exchange of the overflow is a traffic which posits exchange and exchange-value. But it extends only to the overflow and plays an accessory role to production itself. But if the trading peoples who solicit exchange appear repeatedly (the Lombards, Normans, etc., play this role toward nearly all European peoples), and if an ongoing commerce develops, although the producing people still engages only in so-called *passive* trade . . . than the surplus of production must no longer be something accidental, occasionally present, but must be constantly repeated; and in this way domestic production itself takes on a tendency toward circulation. (1993, 256)

Both domestic production (assuming, at least in part, a commodity form) and the firm establishment of exchange relations may also entail a variety of subjective changes in society. The population's regular engagement in commodity exchange not only helps naturalize the exchange process, it may also promote a revolution in thinking about what may be considered a commodity. As more and more use-values begin to assume a commodity form, masses of previously "inalienable" possessions may suddenly become alienable or objectified, including landed property, labor power and new forms of property such as shares "which only exist in negotiable papers" (Marx 1971, 289). Although it is normal within modern societies characterized by circulation to represent land, labor and capital as things that possess exchange value, it nonetheless requires extraordinary changes in the subjective outlooks of people.[14] From an institutionalist perspective, such a change in thinking could only take place gradually, facilitated by frequent exchange and hence frequent comparison of commodities as exchange-values. "As soon as the existence of commodities as prices has become a precondition—a precondition which is itself a product of the social process, a result of the process of social production—than the determination of new prices [exchange-values] appears simple" (Marx 1993, 204).

If and when commodity exchange relations become established in society some changes will occur in the social fabric, even if trade only occurs primarily among the surplus appropriators within society and foreign merchants. What commodity exchange will entail precisely depends, however, upon the social relations enmeshing simple exchange and merchant capital. This section considered a wide range of contradictory possibilities, including increased enjoyments of consumers and expanding wealth, increasing dependence and poverty, and the support or dissolution of social hierarchies. Whether commodity exchange will become established or flicker out with indifference also depends upon the social relations imbricating it.

Marx did, however, devote special attention to the expansion (and resulting entailments of) simple exchange, for the objective of investigating ape-like simple exchange is to consider how it may become human-like circulation. The examination of the social relations surrounding and defining simple exchange, even at its most basic level, produced a knowledge the conditions of possibility for the emergence of circulation. Besides enriching our understanding of circulation, it also incorporated a discussion of how production may increasingly assume a commodity form, as well as the subjective changes that this may entail among members of society. Marx very carefully avoided folding or reducing changes in production processes to the expansion (or contraction for that matter) of commodity exchange. In other social epochs, Marx uses Ancient Rome and Greece as examples of how the expansion of commodity exchange solidified slave class structures rather than inducing capitalist production.[15] One should not, of course, conclude that expanding exchange and merchant capital relations have no impact on the social formation within which they exist, and we explored some of the myriad ways how they may shape other social relations in society. Yet, the significance of simple exchange and merchant capital always depends upon the constellation of social relations enmeshing it within society.

AUGMENTED CIRCULATION.

The production, distribution and consumption of useful things happens in all economies, but the specifics of each aspect of economic activity and their interrelations vary tremendously. Commodity exchange falls under the distribution aspect of economic activity and the establishment of circulation means it becomes the primary form of distribution. Liberals focus on commodity exchange in their analyses of society, and tend to individuate production by seeing it as a vast sea of producer-exchangers guided by self-interest. Other scholars approach the productive aspect of economic activity very differently, and how they do so influences their understanding of commodity exchange.

Marx made sense of commodity exchange *through* production relations rather than vice-versa: "He analyzed the production relations of a determined society, namely commodity-capitalist society, and the role of exchange in that society" (Rubin 1972, 85). When Marxists discuss production, they talk about class relations, i.e., the social relations animating the production, appropriation and distribution of surplus labor. Surplus labor results when some portion of society labors longer than necessary to reproduce themselves according to certain socially acceptable living standards. On the aggregate level of society, "social surplus is the residual that arises from the fact that those who perform the labor necessary to provision society produce more than they themselves consume" (DeMartino 2003, 8). Scholars within the Marxian tradition categorize the class relations surrounding the production, appropriation and distribution of the surplus labor into several broad types, including slave, feudal, capitalist or cooperative (communist).

Exploitative class relations like slave and capitalist imply that the portion of the population appropriating and distributing the surplus "fruit" of production differs from the direct producers. The entities constituting the appropriators within a capitalist class relationship typically include individual capitalists, a corporate board of directors, states, or some combination of these. Productive workers in capitalist class relations add more value to the output than they receive in wages, as the surplus is funneled into the hands of the appropriators. The direct producers use their wages to purchase their means of subsistence in commodity form while the appropriators dispose of the surplus how they see fit.[16] Although a Marxian perspective on capitalist production entails exploitation, productive workers enter into capitalist class relations "freely" by selling their ability to work for a certain remuneration. The ability to sell your labor-power differentiates capitalist from slave production and imbues labor contracts with a voluntary and free guise.

Adam Smith's focus on exchange relations led him to call the economy emerging around him commercial society; Marx's focus on class relations led him to call it the "society of wage-labor and capital." I call the combination of commercial society and the society of wage-labor and capital *augmented circulation*. Circulation interacts with capitalist production because capitalist producers in the society of wage-labor and capital purchase inputs in the form of commodities and sell their outputs in commodity form.[17] Capitalist production can be interpreted as dominating circulation because "exchange is the means of finishing the product and making it fit for direct consumption. To that extent, exchange is an act comprised within production itself" (Marx 1993, 99). On the other hand, circulation can be interpreted as dominating production, for when the "market, i.e., the sphere of exchange, expands, then production grows in quantity and the divisions between different branches become deeper" (ibid). Circulation and capitalist production clearly shape one another and contribute to the thick meaning of commodity exchange in contemporary society.

Marx's *Capital* focuses upon capitalist production but begins with a long (and largely liberal) discussion of commodity exchange. Rubin (1972) explains the positioning of commodity exchange alongside or even before class processes in *Capital* through the historical conjuncture that situated Marx as a theorist: the emerging economic order surrounding him involved great increases in the scale and scope of commodity exchange alongside the rise of capitalist production. Beginning a discussion of the economy of his day with commodity exchange functioned as a common ground or bridge between Marxian and liberal theory: commodity exchange receives pride of place to engage with the economic thinkers of his day on their own theoretical terrain. In fact, what makes the first six chapters of *Capital* so striking is Marx's eloquent elaboration of the liberal vision of commodity exchange.

The liberal representation of individual, independent commodity producers exchanging their goods freely in the marketplace with one another vividly and abruptly ends with the conclusion of chapter six, when the analysis turns toward the "hidden abode" of production. People in augmented circulation still face each other as equals in the realm of exchange with the freedom and liberty to buy and sell commodities, but some portion of society alienates their own labor-power. Another portion of society enters the marketplace to purchase labor-power along with the other means of production necessary to produce commodities. Although both the sellers and buyers of labor-power enter the realm of exchange as equals, they do not leave as such:

> He who was previously the money-owner now strides out in front as a capitalist; the possessor of labour-power follows as his worker. The one smirks self-importantly and is intent on business; the other is timid and holds back, like someone who has brought his own hide to market and now has nothing else to expect but—a tanning. (1990, 280)

The inclusion of labor-power as a commodity fundamentally changes the thick meaning of commodity exchange and how people relate to it, but what it entails depends once again upon the social relations embedding its purchase and sale.

AUGMENTED CIRCULATION AND WAGE LABOR.

Marxian scholars often see the existence of labor-power as a commodity as the *differentia specifica,* the primary feature defining capitalist production. Institutionalists like Polanyi also see something particular about labor as a commodity. Polanyi saw wage labor as a radical and recent invention of society, a new institution, prompted by the demands of manufactures, i.e., "the inevitable consequence of the introduction of the factory system in a commercial society. The elements of industry had to be on sale" (1957, 75). For a labor market to exist, people must consider their ability to labor as something to be bought and sold, and under certain conditions Marxists argue that it provides a condition of existence for capitalist production and exploitation. Polanyi worried more about how wage labor makes people's lives more disruptive and precarious than about exploitation *per se.* Whether or not the labor market facilitates exploitation, as in Marxian accounts, or simply makes life more unpredictable and unstable, as Polanyi explicated, many scholars and people see something different in the labor market than other commodity markets, and what they see shapes their perception of commodity exchange in general.

At a minimum, the labor market entails the commoditization of labor power, i.e., "the aggregate of those mental and physical capabilities existing in the physical form, the living personality, of a human being, capabilities which he sets in motion whenever he produces a use-value of any kind" (Marx 1990, 270). One of the salient features of circulation consists of people envisioning use-values and products of labor as commodities. The existence of established exchange relations facilitates the treatment of use-values as alienable things that possess exchange-value. Persistent involvement in circulation and seeing useful objects as commodities provides a condition of possibility for the commoditization of labor-power, land, and other "things" not produced specifically for sale. Over time, selling labor-power as a commodity helps to normalize its alienation, rendering the sale and purchase of it "no more striking than the sale and purchase of any other commodity" (Marx 1992, 114). Nonetheless, for labor-power to assume a commodity form, a thing bought and sold like cloth and bibles, several consequential events need to occur.

Besides the various conditions of possibility for commodity exchange itself, in order to sell labor-power the people owning it must have the ability to dispose of their ability to work as they see fit. Just as merchants possess property rights over their assorted wares, the owners of labor-power must also be its unmitigated guardian. The normalization of labor-power as a commodity on any sort of mass scale also depends upon the ability of wage workers to purchase their means of subsistence in the form of commodities. Even if we assume that members of the population possess exclusive rights over their labor-power, they still must transform it into the consumption items necessary for subsistence in order to make its continual sale viable. Circulation provides the wherewithal for people to secure the material conditions (e.g., commodities) necessary for the reproduction of labor-power itself, facilitating the emergence of labor market. Established exchange relations also help normalize the selling and buying labor-power. The emergence of circulation helps explain the possibility of a labor-market, but what does working for wages entail?

For starters, a certain notion of equality may emerge from the exchange relations among dealers of commodities, and such a notion applies to the sellers of labor-power as well. Equality here concerns the formal character of the relationship: "Each of the subjects of the exchange process [both the seller and buyer of labor-power] has the same social relation toward the other that the other has toward him" (Marx 1993, 241). The common social relation concerns how each recognizes the other as a guardian of private property with the freedom and liberty to dispose of it how they see fit. The formal relationship entails equality because each exchanging agent possesses the same rights over their property and must voluntarily agree to any transaction.[18] Although such formal equality may have profound social implications, the actual content of the exchange, as well as the specific social context within which it takes place, may still be one of stark inequality. In other words, the thick meaning of the labor market, i.e., all the social relations animating its materiality, cannot be deduced from its mere existence. Exploring the interrelations between production and exchange highlights the implications of this distinction.

Mutually independent buyers and sellers constantly face each other in the marketplace in commercial society, freely exchanging commodities such as shoes, bibles or labor-power. The social relations within the sphere of circulation, e.g., freedom, equality, and liberty, formally exist in both Smith's commercial society and Marx's society of capital and wage-labor, but the free purchase and sale of labor power differs in content from other types of exchange.

> It must be acknowledged that our worker emerges from the process of production looking different from when he entered it. In the market, as owner of the commodity 'labour-power,' he stood face to face with other owners of commodities, one owner against another owner. The contract by which he sold his labour-power to the capitalist proved in black and white, so to speak, that he was free to dispose of himself. But when the transaction was concluded, it was discovered that he was no 'free agent,' that the period of time for which he is free to sell his labour-power is the period of time for which he is forced to sell it, that in fact the vampire will not let go while there remains a single muscle, sinew or drop of blood to be exploited. (Marx 1990, 415–6)

Unlike commodities such as bibles and cloth where the buyer and sellers go their own separate ways after the transaction, labor-power cannot be separated from the seller. What the seller of labor-power offers to potential buyers consists of the laborers' capacity to work for a limited duration of time. "The proprietor of labour-power must always sell it for a limited time only, for if he were to sell it in a lump, once and for all, he would be selling himself, converting himself from a free man into a slave, from an owner of a commodity into a commodity" (Marx 1990, 271). In capitalist enterprises, focusing on the freedom surrounding the sale of labor-power elides the distinct lack of freedom and liberty that occurs during the process of its consumption where employees must obey their employers or face dismissal.

The lack of freedom that individuals face when working in capitalist enterprises does not imply the annulment of freedom in society, but it does relegate freedom to specific spheres of economic life. Guardians of commodities interact as independent subjects with the freedom and liberty to do what they want with their goods, all equal in the political/juridical sense. For precisely these reasons, circulation can promote equality in society and erode oppressive existing social hierarchies; if anything, the inclusion of labor-power as a commodity strengthens this possibility, as it allows for greater independence. Yet, the lack of freedom in capitalist production (or slave for that matter) complicates the liberal narrative, for the celebrated freedoms of commercial society do not extend into the sphere of capitalist production.

The very same freedoms and liberties that circulation entails provide the means and the motivations to challenge the unfreedoms of capitalist production, however. Criticizing capitalist production for not being free flows directly from a liberal idea of freedom as non-coercion. Liberals never tire of expounding on how commodity exchange induces popular demands for political freedom and democracy; however, even though the same logic holds, they rarely consider its implications on the workplace. Labor movements historically did not miss the connection, for they rose to challenge oppressive workplace conditions by demanding the liberal rights of freedom, justice and equality for employees in the realm of both exchange *and* production.

The exchange of labor-power for either money or a specified bundle of use-values in and of itself does necessarily entail capitalist or other exploitative forms of production, however. The purchase of labor power is a simple act of exchange, creating the potential for capitalist, but also individual and cooperative production. Self-employed individuals may sell their capacity to labor or perform services just as producer-exchangers make shoes for sale, the only difference being that one sells a finished product and the other sells the ability to perform some service, still constituting a *quid pro quo* exchange. The market for labor-power in the Middle Ages supported primarily individual production, where "tailors, for example, were to be found everywhere" and people were regularly hired out at fairs on a contract basis (Bridbury 1986, 106). Individuals selling their labor-power in the Middle Ages sold a product—tailoring—for a specified price. Individuals producing shirts and cloth on order or making and stockpiling them for retail later comprise acts of individual rather than capitalist production, for hiring a tailor to make you a suit involves only the purchase of a custom-made product, not the labor-power of the individual to produce commodities for resale at a higher price. Even within augmented circulation, not every sale of labor-power entails capitalist production and exploitation:

> In bourgeois society itself, all exchange of personal services for revenue—including labour for personal consumption, cooking, sewing, etc., garden work etc., up to and including all of the unproductive classes, civil servants, physicians, lawyers, scholars, etc.—belong under this rubric, within this category. (Marx 1993, 468)

A market for wage-labor can also provide a condition of possibility for a cooperative or communist production. Cooperative production entails "an association of free men, working with the means of production held in common, and expending their many different forms of labour-power in full self-awareness as one single labour force" (Marx 1990, 171).[19] Freedom here again builds upon a liberal idea of choice or non-coercion, extending it to individuals collectively controlling production. Labor-power still gets expended in cooperative enterprises, just as many commodities may flow from the process, but the direct producers keep the surplus for themselves. The collective appropriation and distribution of the surplus fruits of collective labor extends the realm of freedom to the production process and stands in marked contrast to having another entity, such as a feudal lord, slave master or capitalist, appropriating and distributing it.

Depending on the specific social relations enmeshing cooperative production, sellers of labor-power may be required to become members of the collective body that appropriates and distributes the fruits of production. Cooperative production may require a transformation of employee consciousness, for no longer would they be simply sellers of labor-power, alienated from the final product, but active participants in the production, appropriation and distributional processes. Nevertheless, they still own their commodity labor-power and possess the freedom to sell it as they see fit. Cooperative firms can and do function side by side capitalist enterprises and individual producers, all of whom make use of the market for labor-power.

Polanyi worried about labor being a commodity for reasons not directly related to exploitation and unfreedom in production. The prices of commodities in "market society" can move rapidly up and down, but the impacts of price fluxuations depend upon the goods being traded. Doubling the price of Lamborghinis induces little hardship among the population at large. Halving the price of labor-power entails a profound disruption in the lives of many. Transforming labor into a commodity involved a radical reorganization of society because people's livelihoods became subject to the vagaries of the price system rather than the relative stability afforded by cultural and/or social networks. Polanyi's *The Great Transformation* explores the ramifications of the emergence of labor markets in England. His vivid portrayal of the working conditions in the "satanic mills" of Manchester and the crowded tenements that low wages forced people to live in help explain why life expectancy in England fell dramatically during this time. Frederick Engels' *The Condition of the Working Class in England* (1980) explores the same sordid issues in even greater, documentary detail.

Polanyi represented human society during the industrial revolution as being on the brink of annihilation, saved only by the protective "counter-moves" that spontaneously arose from the population such as labor unions, minimum wages, and state unemployment relief. The growth of these institutions all point to ways in which societies acted to blunt the impact of the commoditization of labor on human life. Labor movements that arise wherever a market for labor emerges generally prioritize a circumscription of the "laws of supply and demand" upon the price of labor "so as to try to insulate workers' livelihoods and health and safety" (DeMartino 2000, 184). Establishing a "wage floor" helps ensure that the price of labor-power never falls below what people need to live a decent life, an idea that underpins the numerous minimum and living wage campaigns proliferating today. State unemployment relief and pension programs also arose due to popular demands to mitigate the pain individuals face due to job loss, disability and other issues precluding the sale of labor-power. All of these institutions temper the full force of the marketplace on people's ability to survive. For Polanyi, the deepest flaw in market liberalism concerned how it subordinated human purposes to the logic of an impersonal market mechanism, something exemplified through the commoditization of human labor.

Writing in the twilight of the great depression and during the emergence of the welfare state, Polanyi had faith that the instruments of democratic governance could control and direct the economy to meet our individual and collective needs. The erosion of labor market "protection" in today's liberal economic environment has once again subjected the working population to greater uncertainty and instability, helping to explain the negative perceptions many labor unions and working people possess about the contemporary liberal global marketplace. The labor-market promotes freedom for individuals to leave entrenched social hierarchies, but also contributes to the precariousness of everyday life, especially when labor-power is abundant or cheap.[20]

The analysis of the labor market presented here first considered how wage labor may facilitate capitalist production relations and exploitation but not necessarily entail them, for the labor market can provide a condition of existence for individual producer-exchangers and cooperative enterprises, as well as capitalist enterprises. Secondly, the freedoms found in selling labor power often create an awareness of the unfreedoms of capitalist, slave and other oppressive class relations that potentially entail a social demand for freedom in the hidden abode of production. Liberal accounts turn a blind eye toward the unfreedoms often found in production and/or the precarious consequences of a labor market on people's livelihoods. On the other hand, critics of liberalism error in exactly opposite ways, equating the labor market with capitalist exploitation and focusing on its negative entailments rather than its potential freedoms and liberties. The new economics of markets and society presented here highlights the contradictions of the labor market, yielding insights into why people celebrate and worry about it.

THE DYNAMICS OF INDUSTRIAL AND MERCHANT CAPITAL.

The second volume of *Capital* contains Marx's most explicit discussion of the relationship between capitalist production and circulation in a dynamic context. Marx divides the movement of commodities under circulation into money, production and commodity "circuits" comprising "the unity of the process of production and the process of circulation" (1992, 180). Marx referred to capitalist production as "industrial capital," and the analytical form for it mirrors merchant capital: M-C-M.' Industrial and merchant capital both refer to buying and selling of commodities for more than the original purchase price, but whereas merchant capital buys cheap and sells dear, industrial capital transforms the original commodities via a production process into new ones worth more than the purchase price.

> Buying in order to sell, or, more accurately, buying in order to sell dearer, M-C-M,' seems admittedly to be a form peculiar to one kind of capital alone, merchants' capital. But industrial capital too is money which has been changed into commodities, and reconverted into more money by the sale of these commodities. Events which take place outside the sphere of circulation, in the interval between buying and selling, do not affect the form of the this movement. (1991, 256)

The newly minted commodities produced by industrial capital embody more exchange value than the ones beginning the process. This process is captured in the following notation, M-C . . . P . . . C'-M', where P represents a production process. Expanding the notation yields the following:

$$
M\text{-}C \begin{cases} \text{lp} \\ \\ \text{mp} \end{cases} \dots P \dots C'\,(C+c)\text{-}M'\,(M+m)
$$

Industrial capitalists begin the process with money (M), purchasing as commodities (C) labor-power (lp) and other means of production (mp), ideally via *quid pro quo* simple exchange.[21] The production process (P) consumes the inputs and yields new commodities (C'), embodying more value than the original ones. C' equals the value of the commodity inputs (C) plus (c), the "extra" value production yields: C' equals C plus c. Industrial capital recoups the initial money (M) plus the extra value of c (m) by selling or "realizing" the commodities produced: M' equals M plus m.

The "money circuit" expressed above begins and ends with money (M). In a similar manner, the "productive circuit" and the "commodity circuit" begin and end with production (P) and commodities (C). The three circuits of capital illustrate the relationship between production and circulation from different angles. The productive circuit highlights how the extra or surplus value originates in production rather than exchange. The money circuit forefronts the increase in exchange value in the hands of industrial capital. The circuit of commodity capital draws attention to circulation as a mediator of the production process. The final commodities entering the realm of circulation sell for M,' but commodities of a lesser value (M) began the process. The commodity circuit resembles the analytical notation describing circulation, but differs because the value of the commodities changes on each iteration. The difference in commodity value arises because some commodities exit the realm of exchange as final or finished use-values for the population, leaving the rest to begin the process anew. All of the circuits assume circulation's scale and scope of commodity exchange and pervasive commodity production, "for articles cannot go into circulation as commodities except in so far as they are produced for sale, i.e., as commodities" (Marx 1992, 117). Each completed circuit connotes another repetition and hence, reproduction of the cycle.

The expansion of the circuits into their component parts highlights their fragility, for interruption can arise anywhere within them. Producing commodities does not ensure their sale given the celebrated liberal freedom of consumer choice. Failing to sell the new commodities leaves the producers with commodities that are of no use to them. If industrial capitalists decide to slow down or halt production, they purchase less labor-power and means of production, thereby impacting the sellers of these commodity inputs. Individual producers who slow or halt production impact the sellers of inputs with the same effect: sellers of commodities can no longer find buyers. The dynamics of the breakdown in the "circular flow" constitute the fodder for many Marxian and Keynesian analyses of economic crises.

Breakdowns may originate in any phase of production, but the possibility of not realizing the value of new commodities brings us to the particular relationship between industrial and merchant capital within augmented circulation. Merchant capital, even prior to circulation, provided an outlet for excess product, often functioning as a "buyer of last resort" for individual producers. Individual producers and/or manufactures often turned to merchants to relieve them of commodities they failed to sell, offering them at a "discount" to at least recoup some of money from production costs. Merchant capital buys and sells commodities to capture the differences in price, and by purchasing goods at "fire sale" prices it hopes to resell them in other markets at a profit. Even when not under immediate duress, individual producers and industrial capital often discount commodities to merchant capital to rid themselves of the time and effort of selling the goods themselves. Industrial capital can of course perform the role of the merchant capital itself, hiring and utilizing purchasing agents and sales departments to procure the means of production and to dispose of finished commodities, and in doing so, unite industrial and merchant capital within one entity. Dell computers, for instance, sells its commodities directly to consumers, performing the merchant role internally.[22]

The symbiotic but fraught relationship between industrial and merchant capital within augmented circulation manifests itself today in the controversy over retail giants like Wal-Mart. The expansion of value animates and defines merchant and industrial capital. The discounting of commodities to merchant capital implies industrial capital "earned" less profit (e.g., it keeps less of the surplus) than selling the final goods at the going price: the bigger the discount, the smaller the profit. Merchant capital makes money by buying cheap and selling dear and larger discounts increase their profits. The relationship between these two branches of capital may be mutually beneficial and harmonious, with each branch providing a condition of existence for the other, but struggles over the size of discount often break out, impacting consumers and the people involved in capitalist production.

When industrial capital gains the upper hand in the relationship, merchants may be forced to accept smaller discounts, lowering profit margins and potentially forcing bankruptcy. Industrial capital may on the other hand conclude that merchants save enough time and expense to warrant selling merchant capital discounted final commodities. The perceived need by various industrial capitalists to do so at any specific conjuncture might allow merchant capital to gain the upper hand in the relationship, placing them in a position to dictate terms to the producers. Merchant and industrial capital engage in a constant struggle with each trying to make the other dance to their tune.

Take for example the case where some industrial capitalists use merchants and consequentially turn over their productive capital quicker then others. Those industrial capitalists who don't make use of merchant capital might quickly find themselves at a competitive disadvantage when it comes to intersectoral competition. Merchants today often have a monopoly in retail outlets and/or specialize in getting rid of commodities to such a degree that industrial capital depends upon them. The emergence of a global marketplace and lower shipping costs arguably increased the power of merchant capital *vis-á-vis* industrial capital. Wal-Mart personifies merchant capital and provides an excellent example of its potential power over industrial capital, for because of its sheer size and market presence, it often finds itself in a position to dictate terms to the producers (capitalist and otherwise) of the use-values it retails.

Wal-Mart's market power allows it to set the price it purchases commodities for, effectively setting the size of the discount for industrial capital. Producers respond to the imposed discount Wal-Mart offers by lowering the costs of the commodities they use in production—i.e., means of production and labor-power. Wal-Mart purchases commodities from around the world and has helped set in motion a ruthless struggle among producers globally to lower their costs, setting in motion the so-called "race to the bottom" in wages and working conditions. Producers may find it cheaper to produce in "low wage" nations, or subcontract out aspects of production to unregulated firms. If one firm decides to shift production to, say, China and its costs fall, other firms may follow suit or be forced out of business.

The struggle between merchant and industrial capital exposes an important contradiction of today's global economy for purchasers of commodities and sellers of labor power. The "everyday low prices" Wal-Mart vends its commodities for potentially benefits consumers (assuming they shop there), but can also negatively the people trying to sell their labor-power if industrial capital faces a profit squeeze. In short, many people enjoy shopping at Wal-Mart because of the cheap prices but fear and dread how it impacts wages. Liberals like Jagdish Bhagwati (2004) celebrate how the low prices benefit consumers and downplay how industrial capital's "outsourcing" of production to firms in China and other low-wage areas impacts sellers of labor-power, but the debate remains unresolved in academic circles. For workers, however, the case seems pretty clear, and it helps inform a market sense linking giant retailers with sweatshops, low wages and job insecurity.

MERCHANT CAPITAL AND THE WORLD (CAPITALIST) SYSTEM.

Immanuel Wallerstein and Andre Gunder Frank populate a branch of the Marxian tradition that focuses on the global economy. Their respective world-system and dependency theories forefront merchant capital and its perceived effects. Both envision the emergence of a capitalist world system with the explosion of trade and plunder following the discovery of the new world in the sixteenth century. Their influential work concentrates on issues surrounding international trade and informs a critical market sense today. Wallerstein (1974) and Frank (1979) represent international trade as a vast swindle stacked in favor of the rich "core" nations at the expense of the poorer "peripheral" nations: "free trade" in their market sense means a perpetuation and entrenchment of the international *status quo*. Although important differences separate Wallerstein from Frank, their treatment of commodity exchange parallels one another, and I concentrate upon Frank's market sense here.

Wallerstein and Frank part ways with more orthodox Marxian analyses in several ways. First, they concentrate on the structure of the world economy, taking nations as their primary unit of analysis. Secondly, they envision capitalism as a system of power relations exercised through market relations rather than the social relations surrounding production. Thirdly, they define exploitation as essentially unequal exchange, making merchant rather than industrial capital the *sine qua non* of capitalism. The inception of the world capitalist system in their analyses instigated a pattern of exploitation on a global level, where surplus value gets extracted from "peripheral" to "core" nations via international trade.

Frank differentiates a mercantilist stage of world capital accumulation (circa 1500–1770) from both industrial and financial, with the differences among them resting primarily with the political institutions involved and the form/type of commodities produced in the peripheral/core areas (1979, 13–24). Imperial powers first combed the world for precious metal, taking it by force or by trading beads and other cheap trinkets for it. Industrialization in the core led colonial powers to structure the economies of peripheral nations to produce and export primarily agricultural goods, raw materials like ore and lumber, and labor intensive commodities to supply their manufactures with inputs. Peripheral nations in return received excess manufactured goods from the core at exorbitant prices. The earliest days of European empire shaped the world economy in particular ways still evident today, for even nominally independent peripheral nations still produce largely the same primary commodities and rely upon the core for imports of manufactured goods.

Frank sees all production as producing a surplus, regardless of whether it's slave, feudal or capitalist; slave sugar production in the eighteenth century Caribbean yields a surplus just as (presumably) capitalist production in modern export processing zones in the periphery and in core industrial production. The question Frank addresses concerns what happens to the surplus. Core nations then and now retain the surplus and employ it for capital accumulation (e.g., it gets invested in better technology and new factories, expanding production), and/or the surplus becomes partially distributed to workers in the core in the form of higher wages, making essentially a classic "labor aristocracy" argument. On the other hand, the surplus flows out of peripheral nations and is extracted to the core via an entire series of unequal exchanges.

Frank in particular envisions international trade between regions of the world, both then and now, as controlled by large merchants who purchase peripheral goods at a deep discount and sell the core's manufactured goods back to them at inflated prices with the profits arising flowing back into core areas. Arghiri Emmanuel's classic work, *Unequal Exchange: A Study of the Imperialism of Trade* (1972), presents a similar argument, characterizing commodity exchange on an international scale as a systemic unequal exchange between low-wage and high-wage regions of the world. Emmanuel maintains that high-wage areas engage in equal international exchange among themselves, but collectively and systemically swindle low-wage areas in their exchange relations, drawing "all wealth toward certain poles of growth" (1972, 263).

Wallerstein, Frank and Emmanuel present sophisticated analyses that are critical of international trade and predicated on their perceptions of merchant capital's intermediation. Their market sense possesses striking similarities to Aristotle's notion of unnatural exchange, with some exchangers profiting at the expense of others. Wallerstein, Frank and Emmanuel essentially modernize Aristotle's insights to make sense of the global economic order, with core regions of the world gaining at the expense of the periphery through the vehicle of unequal commodity exchange. One method of reading their work involves the explication of the chains of equivalence they construct around international trade. In their hands, international commodity exchange entails exploitation (connoted by surplus extraction to the core) and a perpetuation of the *status quo,* entailing a dependency of the periphery on the core.

The conclusions drawn from their analyses vary. Frank advocates peripheral nations' withdrawal from international exchange altogether. Emmanuel's more technical analysis concludes that trade will involve the transfer of surplus from low wage to high wage areas as long as sellers of labor-power remain immobile while capital freely moves around the globe. His solution to the imperialism of trade involves labor mobility, but if this "dangerous dislocation of the established division of labor . . . [does not ensue] . . . it will indeed be necessary to resolve to set up internationally at least such mechanism of redistribution as already exist on a national scale" (1972, 270).

Liberals disregard dependency and world system theory with a vengeance, consistently referring to the development of nations like South Korea and Taiwan as proof poor nations can "make it" into the core. Dependency theorists consider these exemplars as exceptions to the general rule and highlight the growing disparity between rich and poor regions of the world. Dependency and world system theorists present a rather pessimistic vision of contemporary globalization, seeing it as the latest iteration of imperialism stretching back to the Spanish colonial conquest of Latin America. We will explore liberals' optimistic vision of globalization in detail in the following chapter.

CONCLUSION.

Critical scholars distinguish many types of commodity exchange, and we just considered some of the more pervasive ones that yield insights into why people possess contradictory understandings of the marketplace. Marx derided the liberal flattening of the market landscape, calling it a paradise lost of the bourgeoisie, where people did not "confront one another as capitalists, wage-labourers, land-owners, tenant farmers, usurers, and so on, but simply as persons who produced commodities and exchanged them" (1970, 59). His society of "wage labor and capital" augmented liberal circulation by exploring the hidden abode of production, associating it with "a limited freedom coexisting with a structured compulsion to produce surplus for others" (Resnick and Wolff 2002, 90). Polanyi also saw something unique about the labor market and criticized liberal scholars for glossing over the precariousness of market society for sellers of labor-power.

Critical scholars break down circulation into its parts—the production and exchange of commodities—and explore the social relations surround each facet. Circulation entails the production of commodities, but not any specific class form of production. Both historically and today, slave plantations, individuals, cooperatives and capitalist corporations produce commodities for the marketplace. Wage labor can support an array of class relations, including capitalist, cooperative and individual forms of production, and we considered the potential impetus for the freedoms and liberties of the marketplace to extend into the realm of production, e.g., where and when the direct producers collectively control production processes and the fruits thereof. The freedom to sell one's labor-power helped destabilize and delegitmate slave class processes and today may induce demands for freedom to be extended into the hidden abode of capitalist production.

The sale of commodities can also take place under a range of social conditions. We explored the differences between simple exchange and merchant capital historically, and the particular dynamic between merchant and industrial capital in contemporary society. Liberals reject all of these distinctions for they see all exchange as profit-motivated. Nonetheless, nagging fears of being swindled in exchange and associations of greed still haunt the marketplace, albeit in some dealings more than others. Think about how you feel about buying commodities from traveling salespeople and car dealers versus produce at your local farmer's market. Buying commodities directly from direct producers feels different somehow than when merchants mediate the transaction. Marx's association of merchant capital's profits arising from frauds practiced on the producers of commodities helps explain why people possess different thick meanings about buying "fair trade" coffee, cocoa, and chocolate versus purchasing mass marketed brands on the shelves at the grocery store. Liberal perspectives nonetheless dominate the debate on contemporary globalization, and to these we now turn.

Chapter Six
Liberals and Contemporary Globalization.

The neoliberalism that now informs even conventional thinking about globalization has achieved the status of being taking for granted or, more than that, has achieved the supreme power of being widely taken as scientific and resulting in an optimal world. So resistance to neoliberalism is seen as a resistance to globalization in general, a new kind of Luddite opposition to the technically and economically inevitable.

—Richard Peet, *Unholy Trinity.*

As Montesqieu explained, "the natural effect of commerce is to lead to peace." This principle is at work in Iraq today.

—Don Evans, *Speech to the Department of Commerce Iraq Investment and Reconstruction Conference*

Thick and thin meanings of commodity exchange play an enormous role within the vast literature on contemporary globalization, for the debate over the meaning of contemporary globalization largely mirrors the controversy surrounding what commodity exchange entails. Liberals, i.e., neoliberals in today's jargon, envision the global marketplace as the ultimate *telos* of a natural path of social progression that entails expanding wealth and increasing freedom, liberty, and social harmony on a global level. Liberals present their policy proposals as a simple removal of artificial barriers on the marketplace, while representing any and all alternative economic policies as the product of unenlightened and/or misguided thinking.

The thick meanings of commodity exchange explored thus far highlighted the diverse and often contradictory political, economic and cultural associations that cling to the marketplace. These meanings also influence our interpretations of the global marketplace, for commodity exchange often serves as a stand in or proxy for contemporary globalization, centering the debate upon the efficacy of the market. Liberals present only two possibilities regarding globalization: embrace and build upon liberal trade policy and reap the economic and social benefits thereof, or act rashly and inanely to constrain the exchange relations it embodies, thereby inducing conflict, poverty, and the rest of the negative chain associated with restricted exchange since the time of Adam Smith. The liberal market sense dominates discussion on the marketplace today, and people use it to justify specific policy prescriptions and grand policy proposals, making heavy use of particular thick meanings of commodity exchange to sell their policies to the general public.

Reading the globalization debate though the thick meanings of commodity exchange also sheds some light on a peculiar disjuncture in the controversy. After even a casual examination of the highly diverse, vast and multifaceted literature comprising the "antiglobalization" camp, it appears at first quite strange how proponents of liberal globalization collectively address their critics by accusing them of misunderstanding what trade *really* entails. Liberals produce screed after screed on the social and economic benefits of the global marketplace based on their perception that the critics just don't "get it."

THE HEGEMONIC LIBERAL VISION OF CONTEMPORARY GLOBALIZATION.

Liberal exchange entailments emerge as something akin to a ghost in a machine in the discourse on globalization. The specific arguments linking exchange to the range of things liberals associate it with seldom receive detailed explication, but the lacuna does not prevent their consistent evocation in defense of contemporary globalization. Smith produced a particular knowledge of the marketplace that liberals draw heavily upon, and even though the numerous entailments evoked by celebrants of globalization obviously cannot be all traced to Smith or any single thinker, they did not simply fall from the sky or spring from the ground. The outcome of a particular and long-standing theoretical struggle to dominate the thick meaning of commodity exchange explains the resonance of positive exchange entailments in the academic and popular arena today.

Smith employed a simple but seemingly effective strategy to defend his system of natural liberty and liberals use the same scheme for liberal globalization: first, define society as a sea of independent producer-exchangers linked via circulation and secondly, ascribe of a host of positive entailments to the exchange process. For the champions of contemporary globalization, market integration on a global scale simply brings all the positives associated with the exchange process to the world of producer-exchangers at large. The positive linkages of freedom and expanding wealth go unchallenged even in much of the critical literature on globalization, further attesting to the solidification or entrenchment of the positive associations of exchange today.

From Aristotle to Smith to Marx, the various theories discussed all contribute to the webs of meaning enmeshing exchange today. I see the study of the thick meaning of commodity exchange performed thus far as akin to a topographical map charting out the terrain upon which the struggle over the meaning of exchange takes place. Certain regular battlefields were pointed out—e.g., the "valley of greed" and the "trenches of social harmony"—and we explored how theorists marshaled their troops (i.e., their arguments). Even though few if any of the rival armies conceded defeat, the liberal troops today occupy most of the terrain while opponents hole up in well protected forts, remote mountainsides and valleys. Why is it that liberal associations of commodity exchange boldly swagger while others lurk in the shadows cannot be resolved simply through an examination of different market senses, even though such a theoretical procedure highlights the contradictory and multiple meanings imbricating exchange at any given conjuncture.

Gramsci's notions of a war of position, hegemony, and common sense informed his conception of socialist political strategy, but today provides us with a useful way of making sense of the battle over what the marketplace means. For Gramsci, ideological hegemony connoted the ability of one class, by which he meant either capitalist or proletariat, to articulate or incorporate the interests of other social groups to further their own goals and objectives. Ideological hegemony implies the ability of a group to have its world view dominate political myths and the common sense outlook of everyday life (among other things).[1] Maintaining the ideological hegemony necessitates that its champions present their world view as being in everyone's best interest. Smith's *Wealth of Nations* provides an excellent example of such theoretical maneuvering, for he presented his system of natural liberty as being in the interests of the meanest laborer to the wealthiest capitalist. Neoliberals today defend their policy prescriptions in exactly the same manner.

The specifically anti-reductionist understanding of both ideology and hegemony that Gramsci introduced does not necessitate that market common sense need be free from contradiction or unified.[2] In fact, the multiplicity of interpretations surrounding commodity exchange demonstrates the diversity of what it purportedly entails and the contradictions within even dominant representations. The ideological hegemony of liberal market sense does, however, construct the very terrain upon which the debate over the marketplace and globalization takes place, and explains why various forms of dissent become relegated to unscientific and/or fringe positions. In other words, the concept of a hegemonic liberal market sense helps explain why people commonly represent contemporary globalization as simply commodity exchange on a global scale, and also the ease in which liberals employ specific exchange entailments to support their arguments and deflect criticism. Furthermore, it helps us make sense of why even some trenchant critics of globalization today, such as Noreena Hertz (2001), George Soros (2002) and Joseph Stiglitz (2003) rely upon a liberal market sense to make their case, something developed in the following chapter.[3] To be taken seriously as a critic it seems one must first assert allegiance to the liberal world view, something severely curtailing the range of criticism possible.

The theoretical struggle over what commodity exchange entails easily lends itself to being read through the lens of a Gramscian war of position as well. On the one hand, we have the hegemonic associations of commodity exchange busily being entrenched, marginalizing other thick meanings of the marketplace (and today, globalization) and relegating them to the "lunatic fringe." Marx and Polanyi's critique of commercial society sought to dethrone the reigning liberal understanding of markets and society by introducing a different market sense, thereby comprising "counter-hegemonic" theoretical maneuvers in light of Gramsci's war of position. Similar strategies motivate some within the "anti-globalization" camp today, for many within this army challenge the naturalness of liberal globalization and promote alternative market senses. These scholars highlight the multiple potential forms of economic activity and often promote deep global integration, albeit of a different nature than what we have today. The notion of competing market senses draws attention to the contested significance of commodity exchange, while the concept of hegemony helps explain the dominance of the liberal vision of markets and society, i.e., why liberal market sense appears as common sense.

The reliance upon the liberal vision of the marketplace rather than economic theory arises at least in part because contemporary liberal (neoclassical) trade theory possesses several "issues" making it less than compelling.[4] The most influential mainstream model of international trade, the so-called "factor price equalization" (FTE) theorem, examines the impact of various "factors of production" (land, labor-power, capital) on the price when nations engage in trade.[5] The FTE theorem implies that NAFTA, for example, would alter the demand for factors of production in the nations involved by influencing their price thereby benefiting the suppliers of abundant factors and harming the scarce factor suppliers. Because the suppliers of the factor labor-power in the USA are considered scarce relative to the abundant Mexican suppliers, the FTE implies that they will lose under NAFTA while USA suppliers of capital will benefit. In other words, the FPE theorem predicts NAFTA will cause wages for USA workers to fall and Mexican wages to rise until they reach equality.

Science of this sort does not sell well to the potentially disenfranchised members of society, e.g., all the sellers of labor-power in the USA, so moral posturing and expertism becomes in part a cover for an unsavory theoretical argument. Economists are well aware of the "distributional impacts" of the FTE theorem, i.e., the impacts on wages and profits, but nonetheless claim everyone will benefit in the long run due to gains in efficiency. What economists mean by efficiency therefore warrants discussion, for efficiency claims lend a scientific guise to trade agreements and complement liberal moral suasion in the controversy over contemporary globalization.

EFFICIENCY AND NEOCLASSICAL TRADE THEORY.

Claims that international trade entails efficiency comprise another tool in the liberal tool kit to induce support for liberal economic policy. Economists define efficiency in three distinct ways: Pareto efficiency, X-efficiency and Kaldor-Hicks efficiency. Pareto efficiency arose from utilitarian philosophy and connotes an economic outcome where no one could be made "better off" without making someone else "worse off." If I take ten dollars from your pocket and put it in mine, it makes me better off but you worse off, so economists would label the outcome of the action "Pareto inefficient." On the other hand, if I were to trade you my ABBA album for your Iron Maiden disc, economists would say a "Pareto improvement" occurred in our subjective well-being if we both felt we were better off after the exchange.[6]

X-efficiency concerns production processes rather than individual subjective states and serves as a yardstick to compare firms making similar products. Economists call firms "inefficient" if, relative to other firms, they produce less and/or at a higher cost. X-efficiency plays a minor role in the debates over globalization, however. Economists do use X-efficiency when they claim "inefficient" firms will be weeded out by international competition in the Darwinian struggle of the global marketplace, thereby giving the world of consumers lower prices and/or more products.[7] Nonetheless, the globalization debates focus primarily on the overall *social* impact of trade and other economic policies rather than lower prices *per se*.

Pareto efficiency also plays a minor role in the globalization controversy because it only becomes "operational" when economists can judge whether or not an outcome makes everyone better off. Economists recognize trade agreements and economic policy always produces winners and losers. For instance, the FPE theorem predicts that international trade between the United States and Mexico will harm the sellers of labor-power in the USA (wages will fall) while benefiting Mexican sellers (wages rise) until everyone in both nations receives equal remuneration for their labor-power. In a similar fashion, the owners of capital in the United States would reap higher profits while their counterparts in Mexico will see falling returns until profits equaled out. Because *any* economic policy entails a wide range of effects, invariably benefiting some and harming others, liberal economists developed Kaldor-Hicks efficiency specifically to adjudicate such outcomes.

Economists use Kaldor-Hicks efficiency to attempt to assess what they call the total social costs and benefits from any economic action. To determine whether or not a potential economic action is "efficient," such as the expansion of a firm or the building of a new road, economists weigh the perceived "net balance of the positives (total benefits) and negatives (total costs)" (Wolff 2004, 170). If the benefits outweigh the costs, economists deem the action efficient. Suppose, for example, economists predict that NAFTA will cost the United States 10 billion dollars of lost income (due to falling wages) but benefit 15 billion dollars of extra profit (e.g., returns on investment). According to these (hypothetical) numbers, economists would argue NAFTA is efficient because the 15 billion in gains outweighs the 10 billion in loses, resulting in a net gain of 5 billion for the United States as a whole. Bluntly stated, economists justify implementing trade policy when they see the total gains outweighing the total costs, even though they realize some people will become worse off.

Economists defend Kaldor-Hicks efficiency as fair because the winners of NAFTA can theocratically "compensate" the losers and still have some gains left over. Nevertheless, economists say nothing about *actually* compensating the losers and no compensation scheme needs to be in place for a policy to be deemed efficient. Liberal economists circumvent the thorny "distributional issues" (e.g., who gains and loses) involved with any specific economic policy by pointing out the cumulative impact of a series of efficient policy choices over time. Most economists recognize the potentially severe distributional issues involved with a Kaldor-Hicks efficient outcomes, but argue that although a *particular* policy will make some people worse off, in the long run everyone, on average, will likely gain through a series of Kaldor-Hicks improvements. Furthermore, economists and liberal pundits infallibly cite the *net* potential gains when lauding potential trade agreements to the general public, for breaking down the impacts into who wins and who loses does not sell very well. Knowing that "society as a whole" gains from international trade hardly offsets the pain of the potential losers, especially when the winners comprise a relatively small portion of the population (e.g., owners of capital), and the losers a large one (owners of labor-power).

Kaldor-Hicks improvements comprise the "scientific" economic rationale behind international trade, but economists seldom acknowledge the deeply problematic assumptions haunting efficiency calculations. Richard Wolff (2004) highlights how any such analysis depends first and foremost upon the bold notion that someone can actually identify all the myriad impacts of a potential economic action. Secondly, generating a number for the net effects requires those undertaking a cost-benefit analysis to put a dollar figure on all the consequences. Let us consider a relatively small economic act to illustrate the problems with these two assumptions before thinking about the difficulties in assessing the impacts of modern trade agreements like NAFTA, which took over 900 pages to specify everything involved.

Suppose a city council received an "urban renewal" proposal calling for the razing of several blocks of housing to clear space for an office park and they call in a team of economists to provide a cost-benefit analysis of the proposal. The first hurdle the economists face concerns identifying *all* the impacts. After figuring this out, the economists must sit down and figure out how to put a price tag on each and every one. The economists might first consider the "direct" costs and benefits involved for the city. The direct costs involve at a minimum purchasing the land, providing new infrastructure, and the loss of property tax revenue from the displaced population. The direct benefits for the city involve the tax revenue paid by the new office park and the incomes from its construction. These direct costs and benefits do not come close however to exhausting the potential impact of the proposal.

The people evicted will face a number of "indirect" costs, including: the impact upon their children's school performance and potential skill levels; the time and effort to find a new home; the change in commute time upon their quality of life; and the emotional impact of leaving behind friends and neighbors. Moving beyond the people displaced, the economists would also have to consider the indirect impacts of the proposal upon: changing traffic patterns; local housing costs and rents; local merchants and their livelihoods; local teachers and professional services (dentists, doctors, lawyers); and even local sports clubs and little leagues. The very partial list of consequences stated here highlights the thorny nature of identifying all the impacts of the proposal. Even if we assume economists *can* produce the potentially infinite list of all the potential direct and indirect impacts, they then need to decide whether or not they should be placed on the cost or benefit side and attach a price tag to each—a Herculean task given the difficulty of placing dollar figures on many things. How, for example, do we put a dollar value on changing traffic patterns, the emotional strain of relocating for children, or the potential environmental impact of an action?

Economists attempt to circumvent the numerous problems involved in cost-benefit analysis by using established models. Yet, every model only considers *some* of the potentially infinite consequences of any economic action. Further, relying upon prior theory does not mitigate the daunting task of pricing the impacts—it just means they employ someone else's subjective valuation scheme. Mark Weisbrot and Dean Baker discuss at length the differences among models employed by mainstream economists to predict the consequences from international trade and highlight "their ability to project wildly different outcomes when modeling an identical policy" (2002, 3). The primary reason they cite for the stunningly divergent outcomes concerns. not surprisingly "the many different effects of trade economists have sought to model" (2002, 5).[8]

Economists typically measure the impact of trade as a percentage of the GDP (gross domestic product) of the nations involved. When economists estimated the gains from "free trade" between the US and Canada, the range of impacts derived from standard mainstream models went from negative .025% to plus .8% of GDP for the US and negative .25% to plus 9% for Canada.[9] Given the wide and contradictory range of estimates even within mainstream models, Weisbrot and Baker note that "it is difficult to argue that projections of gains from trade that are largely speculative in nature should provide the basis for public policy" (2002, 5). Economists tirelessly cite "efficiency gains" as a justification for international trade policy, but the divergent and contradictory numbers generated by actual cost-benefit analyses illustrate the impact of the bold assumptions underpinning such practice. As Richard Wolff notes, "no efficiency claim can be or ever has been based on a complete or comprehensive identification of all consequences. Nor has any system of measurement (including guesstimates of the future) ever won everyone's agreement. Beauty lies in the eye of the beholder, and efficiency lies in the eye of the economist" (2004, 174).

The largely speculative method of calculating the efficiency of any economic action should give pause to those who claim that cost-benefit analyses are scientific in nature, but liberals still employ efficiency effectively to lend a scientific facade to trade policy. The potentially large and disruptive distributional impacts of international trade and the dismal track record of actual "compensation" schemes help explain why many people worry about international trade agreements. Liberals often evoke efficiency as the scientific rationale behind trade policy, but the inherently subjective nature of cost-benefit analysis and the mere speculation that everyone benefits in the long-run from Kaldor-Hicks improvements demonstrates the weakness of the mainstream economic rationale for liberal trade policy. No wonder liberals resort to tirelessly repeating their hegemonic market sense to defend contemporary globalization!

THE LIBERAL MARKET SENSE IN ACTION: NAFTA AND THE WTO.

The public debates over first NAFTA and then the ratification of the WTO exemplify the specific way liberal globalization advocates employ market sense to frame the debate over international economic policy. Proponents of both NAFTA and WTO consistently portrayed the trade agreements as products of enlightened public policy designed to benefit everyone in global society. The economic benefits liberals claimed for NAFTA primarily concerned greater efficiency via Kaldor-Hicks improvements, something they see as "guided by generally recognized and scientifically established principles of economics, extending and enhancing the freedom and efficiency of the market on a continental scale" (Rupert 2000, 54). The efficiency calculations trotted out in support of NAFTA clearly helped lend it a scientific guise despite the deeply subjective nature of the calculations themselves.

Besides efficiency, liberals mustered a rather familiar list of exchange entailments like freedom, democracy and liberty to rally support for NAFTA. The proponents of NAFTA and the WTO also sought with great success to frame the debate along particular lines that still characterize the discussion of trade agreements today: on the "pro" side we have science and truth, on the other side, sophistry and ignorance. Liberals presented themselves as basing their arguments upon nonpartisan, rigorous and highly respected objective research produced by economists, scientifically demonstrating the merits of international trade (i.e., Kaldor-Hicks improvements) while representing their critics as basing their arguments upon partisan, sloppy and unrespected work performed by people and groups ulterior motives. The similarities here with how Smith distinguished his system of natural liberty from mercantile economic policy are striking. Another, complementary juxtaposition liberals employed to defend NAFTA and contemporary trade agreements like CAFTA (Central American Free Trade Agreement) also has roots in Smith. Liberals maintain that we as global society supposedly face a choice. On the one hand we have "free trade" and the package of exchange entailments they associate with the marketplace, e.g., freedom, liberty, democracy and efficiency. Rejection of "free trade" implies, on the other hand, its very opposite—social conflict, poverty, tyranny and inefficiency.

The work of USA*NAFTA, a lobbying group formed with some of the millions corporations donated to the cause, presents a vivid exemplar of the peculiar coupling of expertism and exchange entailments used to generate support for NAFTA. The lobbying packet that USA*NAFTA provided to legislators contained the now infamous letter signed by over 300 hundred economists who endorsed NAFTA, including several American Nobel prize winners, along with material asserting the nonpartisan, rigorous, and highly respected nature of the efficiency analyses that demonstrated the potential gains from the agreement (Rupert 2000, 59). The overwhelming support for the trade agreements of the last few decades among "serious" economists should not come as a surprise in light of the overwhelming dominance of neoclassical (liberal) theory in the profession, but nonetheless the *New York Times* repeatedly cited the near consensus as exceptionally noteworthy and unusual, suggesting the compelling intellectual power of the argument (Rupert 2000, 54).

Corporate backing for NAFTA extended far beyond USA*NAFTA. Money flowed into liberal think-tanks like the Heritage Foundation and CATO Institute to produce numerous television documentaries, publications, journals and economic research all designed to sway the often skeptical public on trade agreements and the privatization of publicly owned assets, along with, of course, the propagation of liberal market sense in general. The hegemonic liberal market sense became a bridge between private (corporate) interests and public policy. The defenders of liberal globalization achieved great success (e.g., the passage of numerous trade agreements over the last few decades) at least in part through the tireless promotion of certain associations and the ideas surrounding the exchange process.

Kuttner, the cofounder of *The American Prospect* and author of *Everything For Sale* (1997), reflected upon how Milton Friedman and his disciples worked aggressively for decades to establish a connection between the functioning of commodity exchange and extra-market values such as freedom and democracy. Milton Friedman explicitly sought to subvert critics of capitalist (e.g., market) society by proclaiming a necessary linkage between political freedom and markets and attesting in his *Capitalism and Freedom* that the "historical evidence speaks with a single voice on the relation between political freedom and a free market" (1962, 9). Kuttner considers Friedman's project a failure because it cannot account for all of the "free market" fascist states, ruthless dictatorships and autocracies in recent history. Yet, Kuttner misses how the associations Friedman and company articulated dominate the discussion of the marketplace today, despite their contradictions and lacunas. To the extent that such associations graduated from being posited as relationships on the fringes of accepted wisdom to common (market) sense marks the real success of their attempts over the last 30 years.

The positive, extra-market values associated with exchange today constitute one of the primary weapons in the pro-globalization arsenal. Kettle highlights some of the ways in which the Bush administration employed positive exchange entailments in support of various policy initiatives: "Trade brings prosperity, said Evans [the former US secretary of commerce]. Prosperity brings civilization. Civilization brings democracy. Democracy and trade are the pillars of a peaceful world. Every word that Evans said would have been fully understood by the Victorians" (2001, 7). Only with the firm entrenchment of the extra-economic association of democracy with exchange could such a statement become enunciated as common sense rather than a bizarre, non-sense utterance.

Bhagwati, one of the leading and most outspoken liberal champions of "free trade" from within the discipline of economics, consistently evokes a similar array of positive associations of exchange to defend the WTO and liberal globalization in general. The following statement is symptomatic of his deployment of exchange entailments to make his case to those skeptical of liberal trade agreements:

> What these critics often forget is that certain economic freedoms are basic to prosperity and social well-being under any condition, and are thus of the highest moral value. Property rights and markets, for instance provide incentives to produce and allocate resources efficiency, and can in turn strengthen democracy by allowing a means of sustenance outside of pervasive government structures. (2000, 19)

The thin argument behind Bhagwati's association of exchange and democracy is all that is deemed necessary—a gentle reminder of a well-established truism. The constant and relentless repetition of such positive exchange entailments (markets promote democracy, markets mean individual liberty and freedom, markets mean prosperity, markets entail efficiency) helps establish their familiarity and allows them to be simply stated rather than rigorously specified or defended. Bush's speech writers and Bhagwati's prose treat the linkages they evoke as not mere possibilities or conjectures, but obvious. Bhagwati does not waste any ink outlining how property rights and markets "are basic to prosperity and social well-being under any condition," nor does Bush explain how a trade agreement will entail the expansion of political rights.[10] Both statements make an appeal to common (market) sense and assume the audience will nod sagely along.

To cite an even more blatant example of reinforcing positive exchange entailments, consider the following statement from the *New York Times:* "Free trade means growth. Free trade means growth. Free trade means growth. Just say it fifty times and all doubts will melt away" (Baker 1994, 9). The parallels between such a statement and Althusser's representation of ideology in his essay "Ideology and Ideological State Apparatuses" (1971) are striking. Althusser approvingly paraphrased Pascal's formula of "Kneel down, move your lips in prayer, and you will believe" as something akin to the notion of ideology that he (partially and incompletely) developed. Although the constant repetition of certain statements by no means guarantees their ascendancy to common sense, it surely cannot hurt. With some digging one encounters the official rationale behind trade and growth, e.g., the familiar associations of exchange leading to a specialization and division of labor and efficiency gains. Yet the article Baker cites makes no pretense at justifying the linkage, it just asserts it as the common, accepted knowledge of economists, and therefore of science in general.

Rarely does one find such blatant cheerleading in the media as attested in the statement above, but the media's coverage of NAFTA and the WTO accepted, almost without question, the very suggestive statements about the efficacy of these trade agreements put forth by conservative think-tanks, the business community, and mainstream economists.[11] The same may be said of the popular representation of the FTAA and CAFTA. Not surprisingly, the statements surrounding liberal trade agreements and global market integration more broadly defined consisted primarily of the same positive chain of significance that we have already explored, constituting a rhetorical trope with roots back to Adam Smith.

HOW LIBERALS FRAME DISSENT.

Thick meanings of commodity exchange within the general public such as job losses, corporate greed, lower wages and a lack of public accountability dogged international trade agreements and necessitated intense lobbying for NAFTA.[12] Liberals attacked all opposition with vitriol, giving critics two types of treatments in the popular media and mainstream academic literature. First, critical arguments become patronizingly cast as simply uninformed positions, hysterical, or as Mark Rupert puts it, "the common sense of the simple, those uninitiated into the more sophisticated and scientifically valid truths of liberal economics" (2000, 59). This fits nicely within the science/sophistry bifurcation that liberals deploy to marginalize criticism from non-liberal perspectives.[13] Another common strategy involves presenting dissent as simply a self-serving form of protectionism; organized labor's vocal opposition becomes translated thereby into the voice of uncompetitive workers trying to save their jobs at the expense of the greater good of society. This rhetorical framing device flows directly from the dichotomy between free and restricted commodity exchange with roots back to Adam Smith.[14]

Besides writing off their critics as either simple-minded or self-serving protectionists, several prominent economists and pundits made repeated appeals to the morality of free trade in an attempt to persuade skeptics. In doing so they explicitly relied upon positive exchange entailments, the extra-market values sedimented around the exchange process such as freedom, liberty and democracy. Bhagwati, one of the most prominent liberal globalization pundits, provides an excellent example of such posturing, for his messianic zeal to persuade the public sentiment arises from his attempt to make trade agreements a moral endeavor. The liberal globalization project possesses "the highest moral value" (Bhagwati 2000, 19) because, as he points out, common knowledge informs us that trade and exchange create the conditions for the expansion of wealth benefiting everyone in society. He represents those who challenge the spate of trade agreements over the last few decades as ignorant of the scientific truths of economy theory and as unwittingly perpetuators of poverty and social malaise.[15] Like Smith's portrayal of his system of natural liberty, Bhagwati claims the moral high ground in the advocation of freer trade by asserting that it is in the interests of everyone in society. Another similarity with Smith concerns how the advocates of liberal globalization emphasize how trade agreements will benefit the meaner population. Smith's impassioned pleas for the intellectual and wealthier strata of society to perform their moral duty and allow everyone, including the poorest, to exchange commodities freely, even if this came at their own immediate expense, constitutes a well established motif in contemporary literature.

The campaign to make the liberal globalization project an ethical issue features prominently in the speeches and writings of Don Evans, former United States Secretary of Commerce. The following quote is representative:

> As President Bush has said trade is not just about economics; it's a moral imperative. Free and open trade is a foundation for economic development, democracy, social freedom and political stability . . . it's still not clear to many Americans that increasing trade is in their best interests. Highly charged rhetoric that conjures up the specter of job

losses still inflames the debate, but we have the facts on our side. (Evans, 2001)

The disarmingly simple structure of Evans' intonations demonstrates the potential effectiveness of hegemonic entailments in making a moral argument and silencing dissent: he simply asserts that because trade entails these positive aspects of society, more trade must be in our best interests. Whether or not one understands Evans' position as a firm conviction or a blatant hustle to support a corporate agenda, it has little bearing upon how he uses liberal exchange entailments to make his case. By asserting that trade entails democracy, social freedom and political stability, Evans explicitly places those who challenge the particular trade agreements he espouses as anti-democratic, anti-freedom and pro-political instability. The sedimentation of certain exchange entailments and their dominance obviously facilitates his argument, but he recognizes that other notions of what commodity exchange entails still exist. Evans addresses these alterative views by insisting that anyone who believes trade agreements will result in job losses or other undesirable outcomes is simply ill-informed, daft or hysterical since, after all, the facts are on his side.[16]

Bhagwati's *In Defense of Globalization* (2004) provides perhaps the best example of theoretical pigeonholing, resolute use of exchange entailments, and neosmithian zeal in print today, although Thomas Friedman's *The Lexus and the Olive Tree* (2000) comes pretty close. Bhagwati tackles "anti-globalization" head-on in his opening chapter in an attempt to disarm critics of the liberal globalization project before proceeding for the next 200 pages to dispel the "myths" surrounding it. Of particular interest here concerns his representation of skeptics of the liberal globalization project in general and the protest movement in particular. Bhagwati distinguishes two main lines of dissent. The first consists of a loose group of "hard-core" protestors united only in their "anti-capitalist, anti-globalization, and acute anti-corporate mind-set" (2004, 4). The second group encompasses people who basically lack the theoretical sophistication of (neoclassical) economic theory. Bhagwati summarily dismisses the anti-capitalist wing as quite beyond reason and completely incapable of any rational discussion, claiming "there is little that one can do to enter into a dialogue with them" (2004, 17). The second group invites reasoned engagement because, although not explicitly hostile to capitalism (e.g., markets), in their general ignorance they mistakenly attribute a range of negatives to international trade agreements.

Bhagwati's ridicule of, and unforgiving language used to characterize the anti-capitalist protestors typifies the representation of the protest movement found in the popular media and by mainstream economists.[17]

The "idealists" involved (for they must be idealists to believe something other than liberal economic policy) "arrive at their social awakening on *campuses in fields other than economics.* English, comparative literature, and sociology are fertile breeding grounds" (Bhagwati 2004, 15, emphasis mine). Right from the beginning Bhagwati cites ignorance of economic science as one of the rationales behind the criticism of liberal trade policy and the pursuit of profit in exchange generally.[18] He reads the "pocos" and "pomos" involved as being under the influence of new literary theory and old Marxism, making them "susceptible to the bitingly critical view of economics as an apologia for capitalism" (2004, 17). Yet, their lack of knowledge about the real science of economics implies that they lack the intellectual training to rationally deal with the problems they see in the world. As Bhagwati repeatedly asserts, the best and surest path to peace and prosperity involves exactly the policies the highly literate but misguided idealists take umbrage with: "free trade."

Bhagwati professes to constantly seek dialogue with protestors to bring them into the fold and help them see the light. In this regard, he explicitly avows to tirelessly campaign and reach out to those with simple common sense but who, nevertheless, possess the capability for rational thought. He sees the genuine compassion such individuals possess, which makes his need to inform them of what markets *really* entail all the more urgent; while he respects their ethical and normative commitments, he also notes that they, unfortunately and completely, lack "any ability to engage concretely on the issues they take a stand on" (2004, 24). If only they had a better idea of economic theory, such individuals might see the error of their ways. Bhagwati's claim that trade agreements are in our collective best interest, and that being opposed to them both demonstrates ignorance and condemns the meaner classes to perpetual poverty and misery, echoes Smithian rhetoric to a remarkable degree.

The paternalistic strategy of portraying critics of liberal globalization as, at best, in need of some schooling or, at worst, as lacking mental capacity, helps facilitate their dismissal as people or groups to be taken seriously. Furthermore, Bhagwati attempts to steal their thunder by averring his allegiance to the same ideals that they cherish. Even though the anti-capitalist contingent may be a lost cause in Bhagwati's opinion, reasonable but, unfortunately, nescient people constitute a sector of the protest movement reachable by his impassioned pleas. It rapidly becomes clear that the "dialogue" Bhagwati seeks means little more than his bestowal of the collected wisdom of neoclassical economic theory upon them in order for them to see the folly of their ways; to paraphrase Althusser's more colorful phase, the protestors simply need to kneel down and move their lips in prayer.

Thomas Friedman follows exactly the same track in writing off critics of liberal globalization. His OpEd column in the *New York Times* repeatedly ridicules "anti-globalization" positions, and although he seldom goes as far as accusing their proponents as being intellectually challenged, he likewise expresses his dismay at their ignorance of economy science.[19] Whereas Bhagwati's stereotypical protestor consists of an undergraduate English major, Friedman's seems to be a latte swigging dilettante, who ventures out of the local coffee shop just long enough to join the trendy protest movements that shadow the WTO, the G-7 (Group of Seven) and the Bretton Woods sisters (The World Bank and IMF). The bifurcation of societal types into free exchange/trade or planning/autarky underpins his analysis as it does Bhagwati's; for example, Friedman professes disbelief at how people who so avidly slug down imported coffee could possibly be against international trade.[20]

Based upon such a simple dichotomy, Friedman proceeds to accuse the protestors of hurting rather than helping the world's poor due to their protectionist stance. Bhagwati makes exactly the same rhetorical move when he states that critics of globalization essentially want restrictions on the natural functioning of markets and, much to their supposed chagrin, consequentially promulgate poverty and unfreedom. The anti-sweatshop student and labor movement graced with fairly widespread media attention receive similar treatments. Both Bhagwati and Friedman see the promotion of international labor and environmental standards as either well intentioned but simple minded, or a protectionist excuse to block imports from abroad.

By treating dissent in such a manner, liberals implicitly reject alternative ways to constitute international exchange relations, a stance engendered by their reductionist view of human nature and the marketplace. Korten notes something similar, stating that the proponents of global liberalism:

> would have us believe that the only choice available is between a 'free' market unencumbered by government restraint and centrally planned, state-controlled, Soviet-style economy. . . . Similarly, it is implied that we must either throw open national borders to 'free' trade so that goods and capital can cross unimpeded, or erect impenetrable walls that cut us off from the rest of the world. (1996, 188)

The defenders of liberal globalization envision the global marketplace the same way they do commodity exchange in general: singular and ineluctable. Liberals construct a binary opposition between free and restricted exchange and rigidly fix what each entails. Any notion that commodity exchange may assume multiple forms and promote and/or undermine the proffered associations becomes thereby theoretically eradicated. In a similar manner, all alternatives to their policy prescriptions become advocates of protectionism, restrictions on exchange and even central planning. Dissent becomes subtly channeled into either anti-trade or anti-market positions, and either way, becomes summarily relegated to uninformed, misguided or otherwise fringe positions.

Since the days of Smith the celebrants of commodity exchange and market society have presented their vision of market society in a remarkably similar fashion, representing any and all alternatives to what they propose as somehow infringing upon exchange and therefore the natural order of things. As such, criticism becomes summarily cached within the same negative chain of equivalence articulated to restricted exchange, i.e., unfreedom, poverty and social conflict. Such logic helps us understand how the proponents of liberal globalization both interpret and counter dissent, for once international economic integration becomes understood as essentially a global system of exchange, then any critique of globalization, just like commercial society, becomes *ipso facto* an attack upon commodity exchange.

CONCLUSION.

The addition of Kaldor-Hicks efficiency lends a scientific guise to liberal arguments today, but they employ the same rhetorical tropes to defend their vision of the marketplace as Adam Smith. Smith juxtaposed his system of natural liberty to state-sponsored restrictions upon commodity exchange; liberals do the same with free trade and protectionism, representing critics of "free trade" as either self-seeking advocates of restricted exchange or as possessing the common sense of the simpleminded. In either case, the advocates of "restricted exchange" are incapable of seeing what the marketplace really entails. Contemporary liberals also embrace how Smith cast his policy proposals as in the interests of everyone in society, from the meanest laborer to the largest capitalist.

Smith never set out to provide an apologia for the *status quo*, however, and in *The Wealth of Nations* he provides numerous, forceful critiques of the emerging social order. Smith took aim at those economic policies that he perceived as primarily benefiting the wealthy at the expense of the poor—just the opposite of what he argued proper policy should do. Smith decried economy policy favoring large merchants and manufactures at the expense of the meaner strata of society, but many see contemporary globalization doing exactly this. It is with some irony therefore that liberals today make use of the market sense Smith developed as a critique of the emerging order to defend a *status quo* that many perceive as predicated upon economic policies favoring large merchants and manufactures. The following chapter begins by exploring how many critics of contemporary globalization use Smithian market sense against its liberal celebrants and ends with an exploration of the other market senses that animate "antiglobalization" today.

Chapter Seven
The Market Sense of Contemporary Globalization's Critics.

My goal in writing this book is not only to shed light on how global capitalism works but also to suggest ways in which it could be improved.

—George Soros, *On Globalization*

The challenge today is how to reform globalization, to make it work not just for the rich and more advanced industrial countries, but also for the poor and least developed.

—Joseph Stiglitz, *Globalization and its Discontents*

Generally speaking, those who wish for free trade desire it in order to alleviate the condition of the working class. But strange to say, the people . . . are very ungrateful. The people see in these self-sacrificing gentlemen . . . their worst enemies and the most shameless hypocrites.

—Marx, *On the Question of Free Trade.*

Critics of contemporary liberal globalization are proliferating today, expressing themselves in scholarly works, best-selling literature and a range of activism. The issues they raise go far beyond the divergent understandings of the marketplace discussed thus far, and the sheer volume of "anti-globalization" literature makes providing a detailed survey of all the dissenting views next to impossible. In what follows, I first explore and evaluate the "neosmithian" perspective that animates the mainstream dissent on contemporary globalization and then do the same for the market senses informing some of the other strands of criticism today. The specific rationales behind the condemnation of the latest "free trade" agreement, CAFTA (Central American Free Trade Agreement), illustrate how diverse market senses inform the voices of dissent today.

Neosmithian critics embrace a market sense that is similar to liberals, but differ in their evaluation of the present historical conjuncture. Neosmithians see contemporary international trade policy as favoring certain groups of exchangers over others; in particular, multinational corporations and finance capital[1] over small businesses and farmers. They also interpret trade agreements such as the WTO, NAFTA and CAFTA as hypocritical, since they promote the ability of wealthier nations to export commodities freely while simultaneously protecting their own markets. For neosmithians, corporate influence over public policy emerges as the primary problem with contemporary globalization, with "special interests" skewing the global marketplace in their favor.

Other critics with non-liberal market senses often share with neosmithians a disdain for corporate influence upon public policy, but present a much harsher assessment of contemporary globalization. This diverse set of critics reject the typical liberal arguments in support of trade policy and tend to focus on specific issues and markets, such as the impact of trade policy on jobs, income inequality and corporate power. While not hostile to international trade *per se,* these critics see the "free trade" agreements concluded in the last few decades, CAFTA being the most recent example, as involving much more than simply trade, and worry about their implications for the issues they champion.

Besides presenting these critical perspectives, I provide an analysis of their political implications. Neosmithians, although providing valuable analyses of corporate influence on public policy, reduce the problems of global society today to violations of the economic contract. They also implicitly support the *status quo* by accepting the liberal Ideal vision of society. Other critics condemn contemporary trade agreements because they interpret them as being part of a larger liberal project they reject. Resistance to CAFTA can be seen as part of a movement to redefine the institutional structure embedding the marketplace based upon alternative visions of what the marketplace entails. I identify some of the strengths and weaknesses of this "counter movement" before concluding with some summary notes on our journey toward providing a new economics of markets and society.

NEOSMITHIAN CRITICS OF LIBERAL (CORPORATE) GLOBALIZATION.

Perhaps surprisingly, some of the most prominent critics of contemporary globalization in print today, including George Soros (2002), Joseph Stiglitz (2003), and Noreena Hertz (2001) share with liberals a similar understanding of what commodity exchange entails.[2] Neosmithians embrace the supposed fundamental linkages between commodity exchange and freedom, liberty and expanding wealth found in liberal market sense, but they nonetheless do not indorse contemporary globalization. The neosmithian label reflects how these critics see violations of the Smithian economic contract as the primary problem with the global economy today.

Smith managed to reconcile his positive assessment of what exchange entails with the poverty and conflict in society he saw around him by introducing the concept of restricted exchange and what *that* entails; Smith's reconciliation animates the neosmithian critique. Smith developed the negative chain of significance for restricted exchange specifically to chastise advocates of economic policy who favored certain individuals and groups. Merchant monopolies and large industrialists received his full wrath for using their political influence to ensure the passage of economic policy, such as rules that allowed them preferential access to certain markets (e.g., trade monopolies, barriers for competing imported goods, etc.) and gave them profits at the expense of large sectors of society. Soros, Stiglitz, and Hertz employ the same rhetorical motif when they indict finance capital and multinational corporations today for unduly influencing the policies and actions of international policy makers such as the IMF, WTO, and the US government.

The hegemony of liberal market sense sheds light upon the criticisms and proposed solutions that neosmithians embrace. Like Smith in his *Wealth of Nations,* neosmithians do not turn a blind eye to social tensions induced by the grinding poverty that exists side by side the explosion of merchant and industrial wealth, but in fact make such issues the centerpiece of their arguments. For instance, neosmithians highlight the growing disparity in incomes, both domestically and globally. Joseph Stiglitz claims "A growing divide between the haves and have-nots has left increasing numbers in the Third World in dire poverty, living on less than a dollar a day" (2003, 5). Similar statements may be found in Hertz (2001, 45–59) and Soros (2002, 10).

Liberals accuse their critics of advocating protectionism, e.g., restricted exchange, who thereby tacitly condemn the world to conflict, poverty and despair. Neosmithians essentially reverse the liberal argument by claiming that contemporary liberal policy favors corporations and wealthy nations in the global marketplace at the expense of the world's poor. Neosmithians in effect maintain that the chain of equivalence Smith associated with hindered commodity exchange better characterizes the present conjuncture than what he articulated to free exchange. The celebrants of liberal globalization represent the existing order as moving toward or embodying something akin to Smith's Ideal, e.g., his system of natural liberty. Neosmithians embrace the same Ideal, but view contemporary globalization as moving in the opposite direction.

One of the specific issues raised by neosmithians, especially Stiglitz, concerns how the IMF supposedly changed from promoting fair international trade and financial stability to implementing policy that serves the narrow interests of the international financial community.[3] Another issue is how the existing global economic environment favors those who purchase labor-power over those who sell it. Neosmithians also see contemporary trade agreements as favoring wealthier nations (and the corporations within them) at the expense of poorer ones.[4] The argument that corporations today have managed to co-opt economic policy to enrich themselves at the expense of the broader public runs through a range of critics of contemporary globalization. This, along with their focus upon the have-nots, helps explain the resonance of neosmithians within progressive, activist audiences.

Noreena Hertz, for instance, provides a scathing appraisal of corporate power today in her text *The Silent Takeover* (2001), the main thread being the desperate need today for us, as in global civil society, to reclaim the state from corporate interests. Arianna Huffington's *Pigs at the Trough* (2003) makes a similar argument, although it's focused primarily upon the United States. The neosmithian argument resonates within activist circles and helps explain its popularity today; for example, the *Guardian Weekly*, a British paper with a leftish/liberal bent, noted "The rational that underlies much of the protest movement is that multinational corporations have become too powerful, and the nation state little more than a puppet to pursue their interests" (21–27 June 2001). With prominent mainstream economists like Nobel Laureate Stiglitz making similar arguments, it is harder to dismiss such claims as being on the "lunatic fringe."[5]

Neosmithians challenge the liberal *status quo and* often present a dichotomy between the interests of society at large and that of industrial, merchant and finance capital. This "radical moment" within neosmithian analyses strikes a chord within activist circles and seems to imply that any solutions to the problems of contemporary globalization require some fundamental changes in the interaction between corporations and the state and/or the institutional structure of the global economy. The writings of Paul Krugman (1993; 2003), another prominent neosmithian, often lean in this direction, making him a darling of the left (at least on this issue). Although neosmithians identify corporate influence over public policy as the key problem within contemporary globalization, they see nothing inherently flawed about market society, the liberal Ideal, and/or existing economic institutions.[6] Smith attributed the problems haunting commercial society solely to violations of the economic contract, and neosmithians follow suit. Even though neosmithians focus upon and highlight corporate power and its abuses, they steer widely away from considering a reconfiguration of the corporate sector or a restructuring of international economic institutions.

Two things explain the neosmithian stance. First, they attribute the problem of undue corporate influence on policy to a few "bad apples" spoiling the rest of the barrel: e.g., "crony capitalism." In other words, rather than indict market society in general, neosmithians see corruption as a recent, exceptional phenomena rather than systemic.[7] Secondly, I argue that neosmithians largely embrace the hegemonic liberal market sense in order to interpret the world around us, and this severely limits the range of possibilities they see for change. Neosmithians critique the *status quo* and in doing so they share some affinity with more radical critics of contemporary globalization. Nonetheless, neosmithians largely engage the liberals squarely within their own theoretical terrain and embrace a similar vision of an Ideal society, even as they see a need to end corporate influence on public policy to achieve it.

JOSEPH STIGLITZ AND THE NEOSMITHIAN MARKET SENSE IN ACTION.

Nobel Laureate Joseph Stiglitz's best selling *Globalization and its Discontents* (2003) features prominently in the globalization debates. Stiglitz wrote his trenchant critique of the policies and practices of the IMF after stepping down as the chief economist and senior vice president for the World Bank. Stiglitz claims that a "simplistic" free market ideology permeates the IMF and provides "the curtain behind which the real business" of serving the interests of global finance and creditors takes place (2003, 207). Stiglitz claims that the "bad economics" guiding IMF policy has its roots in corporate influence on public policy.

Stiglitz's arguments fit squarely within the hegemonic liberal market sense, something apparent almost from the first page of *Globalization and its Discontents*. Stiglitz constantly uses the terms market society, capitalism, and globalization interchangeably, and proclaims his faith in "the market" as being behind the good aspects of globalization: efficiency, economic prosperity and democracy.[8] The immense faith Stiglitz has in the market (e.g., capitalism and globalization) depends upon the supposed fundamental linkage between it and freedom, liberty and prosperity. He differs from the celebrants of contemporary globalization, however, by claiming corporations violating the economic contract are presently undermining progress toward Smith's Ideal. Stiglitz's primary example of such policy involves the excessive zeal the IMF demonstrated in liberalizing capital markets, which, in his opinion, clearly benefited only a few financial corporations and wealthy individuals and came at the expense of the population at large (2003, 195–213).

Stiglitz's allegiance to capitalist society and Smith's utopian vision, albeit with a deep suspicion toward capitalists and corporations, manifests itself in how he represents any alternative economic arrangements. For Stiglitz, one either has "the market" and therefore freedom, liberty and prosperity alongside (perhaps unfortunately) corporations, or a Soviet-style planned society and everything *that* entails. Stiglitz hints at the alternatives to the market in the following statements:

> Karl Marx, aware of the adverse effects that capitalism seemed to be having on workers of his time, provided an alternative model [to that of the market] . . . But with the collapse of the Soviet empire, its weaknesses have become all too evident. And with that collapse, and the global economic dominance of the United States, the market model has prevailed. (2003, 217)
>
> As a consequence of the 1917 Revolution and the Soviet hegemony over a large part of Europe after WWII, some 8 percent of the world's population that lived under the Soviet Communist system forfeited both political freedom and economic prosperity. (2003, 133)

Although Stiglitz does proceed to qualify various types of market economies, for instance, the American "model" versus the more welfarist European versions, he clearly argues that the market constitutes the basis of any free and prosperous society.[9] Since Stiglitz equates the market with capitalism, his theoretical stance helps (re)produce the peculiar social dichotomy put forth by liberal celebrants of commodity-capitalist society: one either has capitalism, prosperity and freedom, or planning, Uncle Joe and the gulag. As the specter of Stalin does not constitute an attractive option, Stiglitz seeks some sort of middle ground in order to save capitalism, and now the global capitalist economy, from itself. The fundamental entailments of commodity exchange that Stiglitz assumes, coupled with his identification of commodity exchange, capitalism and globalization means that, as global civil society, we must reestablish Smith's economic contract or else face the sinister specter of the Soviet Union, something Stiglitz sees Keynes also arguing back in the 1930s:

> Today, the system of capitalism is at a crossroads just as it was during the Great Depression. In the 1930's, capitalism was saved by Keynes,

who thought of policies to create jobs and rescue those suffering from the collapse of the global economy. Now, millions of people around the world are waiting to see whether globalization can be reformed so that its benefits can be more widely shared. (2003, 249–50)

Neosmithians essentially see the deepening of commodity exchange on a global level as *a necessary but not sufficient* condition of possibility for all of the positive aspects of society that its celebrants applaud. Stiglitz's accusation that liberal celebrants of contemporary globalization deploy a simplistic free market ideology essentially serves to posit himself as objective and presumably beyond ideology, yet, he shares the same vision of an Ideal society as liberals.[10] In fact, Stiglitz even embraces the same, reductionist rhetorical motifs employed by liberal scholars to make his case. Both he and the backers of contemporary globalization equate commodity exchange with a slew of positive aspects of society and bifurcate social forms into two types, market-based or planned. The (sometimes) subtle theoretical differences between liberals and neosmithians hinges upon whether or not they consider the existing form of globalization as promoting or hindering movement toward Smith's Ideal. Stiglitz identifies large corporations influencing public policy as the fly in the ointment today, implying that the best course of action to alleviate the "discontents" of globalization is for global civil society to devise ways to ensure that corporations obey the economic contract.[11]

Like liberals, neosmithians essentialize the connection between commodity exchange and freedom, liberty and prosperity, with the consequence that they both reduce the problems of the global economy to misapplied policy distorting the marketplace. The source of the misapplied policy varies between liberals and neosmithians—liberals like to blame "protectionist" policy upon labor unions and others ignorant of economics while neosmithians single out corporate influence over public policy. Stiglitz in particular has received a great deal of attention from those critical of liberal globalization, but he basically advocates and makes a strong case for "what is more or less Keynesian social democracy" (McIntyre 2004, 102).

For Stiglitz, the solution to the problems of contemporary globalization emerges directly from his market sense: a "reinstatement" of good, prudent economic policy that mitigates corporate influence and preserves the economic contract. Neosmithians engage liberals on their own terrain and, by doing so, lend support to the hegemonic market sense and the Ideal vision of society underpinning liberal globalization. Many critics, while sympathetic to neosmithians, reject liberal arguments behind contemporary trade policy and the liberal (neosmithian) Ideal. The condemnation of

CAFTA provides insights into the market sense of the non-neosmithian critics and their alternative vision of the optimal role of the marketplace in society.

BACK INTO THE THICK OF THINGS: CAFTA AND ITS CRITICS.

In early August, 2005, U.S. President Bush, signed CAFTA into law, uniting under a common trade agreement the following countries: the U.S., Costa Rica, the Dominican Republic, El Salvador, Guatemala, Honduras, and Nicaragua.[12] CAFTA was modeled after NAFTA and was largely seen as a stepping stone to the larger FTAA (Free Trade Agreement of the Americas). The debate over CAFTA began early in 2002 soon after a tentative agreement had been reached among the countries involved and largely echoed the controversy over NAFTA, FTAA and the WTO. The liberal defense of CAFTA mirrored that of other contemporary trade agreements: its proponents claimed that it would support democracy in Central America and lead to greater prosperity, freedom and efficiency. As the debate evolved, the Bush administration added to the standard liberal rhetoric the notion that passing CAFTA is a "vital national security interest" for the U.S., since the growing prosperity and democracy will slow down immigration and counter the "desperate acts of a few who cling to dead ideas" (Zoellick 2004).

The hegemony of liberal market sense allowed CAFTA backers to state their grand claims as facts, their vision of an Ideal economy as universal, and to paint dissent as ill informed, naive or "protectionist." While liberals championed CAFTA as a win-win for all involved, its opponents represented it as a net loss for the majority of the populations involved and a win for corporate interests. Numerous voices in Central America and the U.S. opposed CAFTA, including trade unions and a wide range of progressive social movements. CAFTA barely passed through the U.S. House of Representatives, with a final vote of 217 for and 215 against; in the Senate, it passed with a final vote of 54 for and 45 against.[13]

Although liberals attempted to frame discussion on CAFTA as being for or against international trade, the dissent largely took issue with the *specifics* of the agreement—*not* trade itself. Several key issues dominated the dissenting views. Many critics singled out and condemned the corporate influence behind the specifics of the trade agreement and represented U.S. multinational corporations as CAFTA's primary winners. The phrase "corporate globalization" features widely in activist circles, who present the corporate quest for profits (often identified in an Aristotelian fashion as greed) and the expansion of market opportunities as the primary motivating force behind CAFTA and other contemporary trade agreements. Non-neosmithian critics went far beyond condemning the corporate influence behind CAFTA, however, for they also challenged the liberal vision of the marketplace upon which it is based.[14]

Labor unions tended to raise the specter of job losses and presented CAFTA as accelerating the "race to the bottom" for wages and living standards globally. Others (Kyer 2002; *Stop* CAFTA 2005; *Public Citizen* 2005) bemoaned the "economic reforms" contained in the agreement, such as the privatization of public assets and procedures to rigidly enforce intellectual property rights.[15] One of the economic reforms in CAFTA touted by liberals would promote the selling of publicly owned assets like utility companies in Central America to U.S. multinational corporations. Many Central American groups see the privatization as an encroachment upon their national sovereignty and condemn it on nationalist grounds, but many also reject it because they see it as introducing the profit motive behind the distribution of vital human needs like water and health care. The intellectual property rights provisions were seen as a major victory for corporations at the expense of the needy, for they will force nations to stop purchasing generic pharmaceuticals; protestors fear that the cost of needed medical treatments, like AIDS medication, will rise dramatically.

Many also highlighted the detrimental impacts of the investment clauses in CAFTA that are similar to NAFTA's chapter 11, which, as Mark Engler writes, allow "corporations to sue governments for regulations (including the enforcement of local environmental laws) that they believe infringe on their rights" (2004, 1). The investment clauses were intended to spur foreign direct investment, for (primarily) U.S. multinationals will now be able to operate freely in Central America with "ironclad" guarantees. Activists see this as an invitation to take advantage of the cheaper labor costs and weaker environmental standards relative to the U.S.

CAFTA was pitched as a trade agreement, but the economic reforms it contains were one of the most heavily protested aspects of the treaty. For activists, the reforms represent a major shift in the political and economic climate in Central America, legally entrenching corporate "rights" at the expense of the population at large. The arguments articulated by dissenters illustrate how the alternative market senses they embrace informed opposition. The logic behind the "race to the bottom," for instance, concerns the impact of having labor and environmental standards subject to market competition. Liberals claim that such competition leads to efficient economic outcomes, and therefore Kaldor-Hicks improvements, but many dissenters reject the idea of having labor and the environment subject to competition and the profit motive.

Competition *per se* is neither good or bad, because what it entails always depends upon the full set of circumstances defining the "political and economic rules of the game that delineate the conditions under which competition is allowed to unfold, and the set of attributes of social life that it is permitted to implicate" (DeMartino 2000, 186). People may applaud competition when it leads to better designs and greater X-efficiency, but bemoan it when safety standards, wages and the environment become subject to it. Critics of CAFTA highlighted how it, like other liberal trade agreements, will serve to alter the present conditions situating competition and the aspects of social life it implicates, by allowing and promoting corporations and other businesses to take advantage of lower wages and lax environmental standards to gain a competitive advantage over their rivals.

Firms consider wages and environmental standards to be costs of production; over the last hundred years, however, almost every society enacted rules and regulations to prevent them from being objects of competition. Taking wages out of competition, for instance, through the implementation of (enforced) minimum wage laws or via a strong labor union presence, means that all firms must pay at least a minimum price for labor-power. Establishing (and enforcing) a minimum wage helps ensure that the price of labor-power never falls below what people need to live a decent life. Labor movements generally prioritize a circumscription of the "laws of supply and demand" upon the price of labor "so as to try to insulate workers' livelihoods and health and safety" (DeMartino 2000, 184). State unemployment relief and pension programs—the result of long struggles by common people to mitigate the pain they face due to job loss, disability and other issues precluding the sale of labor-power—provide a "fall-back" wage level, and also help establish a wage floor. Minimum wages, labor unions and unemployment programs temper competition over the price of labor-power and, in doing so, alleviate the precariousness of daily life for its sellers.

In a similar manner, consumer safety laws were put in place to prevent firms from lowering the costs of commodity inputs via adulteration; after their passage, firms were no longer able to undersell their competition by using inferior or contaminated products. Societies the world over enacted rules so competition will not come at the expense of human health, or even life. Environmental standards that ensure all firms face the same rules and regulations regarding their interaction with nature imply firms cannot gain a competitive advantage by polluting. Liberal trade agreements like CAFTA effectively change the political and economic rules of the game by allowing, and providing incentives for, competition based on wages, environmental standards, and in some cases, consumer safety laws in the name of greater efficiency.[16]

What critics of liberal globalization mean by the race to the bottom is how firms today are effectively rewarded by, and actually given an incentive for, finding ways to drive down wages and externalize pollution costs to the lowest common denominator. Businesses that pay relatively high wages in certain regions or countries will be punished in the global marketplace since they face higher costs than other firms that do not. Businesses that manage to externalize pollution costs (e.g., dump their effluent instead of treating it), and/or locate in areas with lax environmental rules, can produce output at a cheaper cost than those paying to clean up their mess. Firms that produce in areas or countries with relatively high wages and environmental regulations that face tariff-free imports from other places will be at a competitive disadvantage to firms that do not, providing them an incentive to relocate. Furthermore, when regions or countries attempt to enforce wage and environmental standards, businesses have a choice (thanks to the investment clauses in recent trade agreements): relocate to places that do not and thereby face lower costs, or stay put and lose their competitive advantage by paying higher costs of production.

Regarding CAFTA, activists fear that multinational corporations located within the signatory countries will relocate production to these nations where labor is cheaper and environmental rules are lax or not enforced. Not only do corporations have an incentive to do just this, but countries desperately seeking foreign investment also have an incentive to *provide* such an investment climate by suppressing labor movements and lowering environmental regulation. In short, activists fear that decades of labor organization and hard-fought environmental standards will be fundamentally challenged by CAFTA (like NAFTA and the WTO) once wages and environmental rules become subject to international competition.

Environmentalists also take issue with the investor clauses in CAFTA that are similar to those (Chapter 11) in NAFTA. Chapter 11 has been used by corporations to sue governments that enact and enforce environmental rules and regulations that they perceive as damaging to their bottom line. A vivid example from NAFTA concerns how the Canadian Methanex Corporation sued the U.S. over California's ban of MBTE in gasoline. MBTE promotes the clean burning of fuel, but is also a carcinogen that contaminates the water supply. Methanex contended the ban "expropriated parts of its investments in the United States in violation of Article 1110, denied it fair and equitable treatment in accordance with international law in violation of Article 1105, and denied it national treatment in violation of Article 1102" (U.S. Department of State).[17]

In the law suit filed under Chapter 11, Canadian Methanex demanded close to one billion dollars in damages, for they argued that the ban on MBTE will cost the company that much in future lost profits. Methanex had invested heavily in producing methanol, a key ingredient in MBTE, and argued the ban unfairly expropriated its investment. Chapter 11 was intended to protect foreign investors when undertaking projects in other NAFTA signatories, but Methanex versus the U.S. proved that corporations could challenge any and all environmental laws they consider harmful to their bottom line. CAFTA contains similar "investor protection" clauses, leading many environmentalists to conclude that the agreement will undermine existing environmental regulation and/or prevent new regulation from being implemented.

CAFTA AND CRITICAL MARKET SENSE TODAY.

We can understand some of the concerns raised about the environmental and labor impact of CAFTA by using the market senses explored thus far. Polanyi's market sense is particularly helpful in comprehending a range of contemporary dissent. Recall that Polanyi attributed the extent to which the economy provides goods and services based on the profit motive as the outcome of an ongoing struggle between two opposing movements: the "laissez-faire movement" to expand the scope of the market and a protective "counter movement" that emerges to resist it. Whenever society moves toward a greater reliance on market self-regulation, e.g., the profit motive to distribute goods and services, ordinary people bear higher, ultimately unsustainable costs. Spontaneous resistance will erupt whenever people feel their livelihoods have become too precarious or uncertain as a result.

Polanyi predicted that people will resist liberal attempts to make living standards, jobs, and the environment determined purely by the profit motive, because it makes life more precarious and leads to environmental degradation. From a Polanyian market sense perspective, CAFTA does just this by increasing competition among the sellers of labor-power and eroding national environmental standards. The active participation of labor unions and environmental activists within the "antiglobalization" movement and protesting liberal trade agreements like CAFTA comprises a perfect example of a Polanyian counter movement, for the goal of many protesters is to limit the scope of competition on various aspects of social life, especially labor-power and the environment.

A Polanyian market sense also helps explain the resistance to the privatization of public utilities. For Polanyi, the deepest flaw with liberalism concerns how its market-centric policies subordinate vital aspects of human life to a profit motive rather than need. The 2000 "water war" in Bolivia arose as a response to the privatization of the public water supply in the city of Cochabamba to a U.S. corporation. Today, Cochabamba's response to the privatization serves as a rallying cry for activists resisting liberal policies. The water war comprised a popular, spontaneous resistance to the impact of privatization of public resources on the livelihoods of common people, and ultimately resulted in the reinstatement of democratic control over a vital natural resource.

The origins of the water war stem from the purchase of the water distribution rights in Cochabamba by *Aguas del Tunari*, a subsidiary of U.S. *Bechtel*. Oscar Olivera, who emerged as one of the lead organizers against the action, provides some background behind the popular resistance, explaining how, in Bolivia:

> The people look at water as something quite sacred. Water is a right for us, not something to be sold. The right to water is also tied to traditional beliefs for rural people, as it has been since the time of the Incas. The traditional social practices and ideas behind the use of water go far beyond the distribution of water to encompass the idea that water belongs to the community and no one has the right to own the water (2004, 8).

The privatization of water fundamentally challenged the notion that people have a right to water and that it belongs to the people. Locals in Cochabamba said *Aguas del Tunari* was "leasing the rain" for a profit (Finnegan 2002).

Discontent with *Aguas del Tunari* began to arise when the corporation dramatically raised the price of water soon after it assumed ownership to fund infrastructure improvements and ensure a profit of several million dollars. The rate increases made water, a vital human need, unaffordable to a vast swath of the population. The spark which ignited the war, however, occurred when they informed the people of Cochabamba that the corporation now owned the rights to *all* water distribution and would start metering the water drawn from private wells. After numerous weeks of intense protest going all the way to the capital city, *Aguas del Tunari* pulled out of Bolivia, something hailed by the protestors and activists elsewhere as a major victory against corporate globalization.[18]

Privatization represents, in the eyes of activists, essentially an enclosure of the commons, making public goods like water, health care, and education commodities like any other: things to produce and distribute only when profitable. Liberals cite efficiency as the rationale behind privatization, but the protesters interpret such actions as rationing basic needs via the ability to pay. Producing and distributing ties and tutus for profit is one thing, but "leasing the rain" represents something else entirely—immense hardship and even death for those unable to afford it. The privatization of utilities, education, and health care means that profit rather than need guides their production and distribution. As Polanyi predicted, Cochabamba demonstrates how people will not sit idly by while their livelihoods are threatened.

The inclusion of investment clauses and other "economic reforms" in CAFTA, NAFTA and the WTO means these agreements involve much more than simply international commodity exchange: they are *intended* to change the climate situating market activity for numerous aspects of society. Activists within the counter movement deny being against trade or the marketplace *per se,* but do object to the political and economic rules of the game implied by the contemporary liberal policy regime, of which CAFTA serves as a case in point. They seek better, "fairer" trade agreements with clauses allowing societies to enact the means to protect labor and the environment and not subject them to global competition. They also resist the encroachment of the profit motive behind the distribution of basic needs, such as water. The alternative market senses discussed over the course of *Market Sense* help us understand some of the beliefs behind contemporary dissent over liberal trade policy, for they arise from visions of the marketplace that differ from the one posited by liberals.

Many activists reject the liberal Ideal of having every aspect of life dictated by the profit motive. Liberals flatten the market landscape by seeing all commodity exchange and the motivations behind it as universal, but dissenters often differentiate the marketplace by the commodities being traded and the rules and norms governing their exchange. The latter's understanding of the marketplace dovetails with the notion of commodity exchange advocated here, for I see market activity as a complex ensemble of economic, political and cultural practices, always capable of assuming a vast array of forms. Every non-liberal market sense examined here does not in fact condemn market activity in the abstract, but considers the implications of various types of market activity within specific contexts.

The market senses discussed thus far help shed light on why the resistance to CAFTA does not necessarily imply an opposition to commodity exchange, but the specific forms of exchange being propagated under liberal trade agreements. Liberals represent the demand for fair trade as basically codifying "distortions" of the marketplace, but others "recognize that the market is not *constrained* but actually *defined* by the rules, norms, and institutions that give rise to it" (DeMartino 2000, 86). Many of the so-called distortions of the marketplace are mechanisms devised by societies after decades of struggle to ensure people have the means to life a decent life. The criticism of liberal globalization arises not, as liberals claim, because the people just do not "get" what the market really entails, but because they get something very different than liberals.

I should note, finally, that the dissent is, of course, very diverse and only a fraction of the issues they raise has been discussed here. Furthermore, the dissent seldom speaks with one voice, and the ensuing cacophony opens the door for numerous interpretations. Nonetheless, many of the positions they articulate resonate with the various market senses discussed thus far. While liberals see the institutional structure situating contemporary international trade as entailing efficiency, democracy and freedom, others see it entailing an increase in the precariousness of everyday life, environmental degradation, and an intrusion of the profit motive into areas where it does not belong.

TOWARD A NEW ECONOMICS OF MARKETS AND SOCIETY.

In the first chapter, I stated that people possess conflicting meanings of what commodity exchange entails. I also stated that the controversy over contemporary globalization needs to be severed from sterile debate over the essential significance of "the market" as a singular universal type. This will allow space for a more productive discussion on *types* of markets and potential forms of economic integration globally. As I also mentioned in the introduction, a partial list of the social relations animating exchange activity, and hence lending it specific meaning, includes: all of the beliefs motivating exchange activity, whether or not prices are set or bargained, whether or not money mediates the exchanges, the specific constitution of the property rights involved, the scope of exchange (e.g., what may or may not be sold), the scale or pervasiveness of exchange, and so on (and on).

The liberal market sense, on the other hand, presents "the market" and/or a "market economy" as a singular monolith, with an innate logic. Based on this reductionist account, liberals argue that contemporary trade agreements simply allow "the market" to flourish as nature intended. Liberals, and even neosmithians like Stiglitz, essentially equate "the market" with capitalism and today, contemporary globalization. The framing aspect of liberal market sense allows for the critics of contemporary globalization to become labeled as anti-capitalist or anti-globalization when they are actually championing a different form of economic integration than propounded by liberals. Although liberals have managed to frame positions on contemporary globalization as being either for or against it, the real issue at stake is the *type* of globalization, for many types of market economy and market activities are possible, and each will possess different, probably contradictory, consequences for society.

Commodity exchange *qua* international trade serves largely as a red herring in the globalization debate, for the current controversy has little to do with being for or against trade, but rather what forms of trade people wish to see emerge. Critics of contemporary globalization, for example, oppose liberal trade agreements like CAFTA and the economic reforms they contain because they see them as setting back the social agendas they seek. I see a real need to move beyond liberal market common sense to engender a more meaningful discussion about the role of the market in promoting and/or undermining certain economic, political and cultural outcomes. The neosmithians provide an example of the consequences of embracing an essentialist understanding of commodity exchange, for it thwarts a more profound investigation into the very things they see as problems in society. That multiple forms of market activity exist, each replete with often contradictory impacts on society, makes advocating or denouncing market activity in terms of abstract entailments an empty platitude, one we need to move beyond.

To their credit, many (although certainly not all) people involved in the so-called "antiglobalization" struggle argue that the market in the abstract is not the problem, but rather the rules situating it within contemporary liberal globalization—i.e., what they refer to as corporate globalization. The stress on the *form* of international economic integration is important because it both challenges the inevitability of the existing, liberal economic regime and it opens up the space and possibility to consider various alternatives based on other market senses. Given that powerful criticism of liberal market sense has existed for centuries, the real question the globalization controversy poses is how and why have liberals managed to dominate the conversation in policy circles and frame the debate in the particular ways outlined here?

On a purely utilitarian level, Rupert explores how corporations have donated millions to support the passage of contemporary trade agreements and funded numerous liberal think-tanks to spread the liberal market sense. He also examines in some detail the specific constellation of dominant social forces propelling liberal globalization, and interprets them via a traditionally grounded Marxist lens. Predicating his analysis on the supposed innate tendency of capital to expand, he writes that globalization "represents the ongoing, if episodic development of the capitalist organization of production" (2000, 43). In effect, Rupert (along with many others) sees the hegemonic liberal market sense as an ideology that supports capitalist interests, the implication being that the common folk who "buy it" have been duped. His analysis resonates with many, especially those who represent contemporary globalization as corporate globalization.

Another reason behind the sedimentation of liberal market sense however concerns how aspects of it strike a chord in our daily lives. Commodity exchange always entails contradictions, and the liberal market sense emphasizes the positives while eliding the negatives in any particular conjuncture. Simply condemning commodity exchange misses how it can serve as a means of liberation from oppressive social hierarchies, how it can expand the realm of freedom in society, and how it can broaden the useful objects we take pleasure in consuming. Even trade agreements like CAFTA can prompt progressive social change, such as greater unity of labor movements in the U.S. and Central America, and create an awareness of some of the common problems people in all the countries involved face.

Marx carefully avoided equating the marketplace and capitalist exploitation because doing so implies that ridding society of commodity exchange is a necessary precondition for a socialist society.[19] In a similar manner, Marx famously dismissed Proudhon's equation of money with exploitation because essentializing the link between the two implies that ridding society of money will therefore eradicate exploitation as well.[20] Marx also provides us with some examples of how to build upon the contradictory entailments of commodity exchange to push for social change. The market in human labor-power may, in certain circumstances, entail capitalist exploitation and make life more precarious and uncertain, but it many also be liberating and produce a sense of equality among its participants. Rather than build analyses of the present conjuncture that are predicated on a blanket condemnation of "the market," activists could celebrate along with the liberals its potential positives, but stress its potential negatives as well. People use their market sense to attack economic policy like CAFTA, but such a practice effectively precludes any exploration of how such policy may entail a wide, and even contradictory range of political, cultural and economic practices at any given point in time and place.

CAFTA, like the WTO and NAFTA, will undoubtedly have contradictory effects for all the societies involved. By simply painting CAFTA or other trade agreements as entirely negative, energy becomes focused on stopping them, leaving activists demoralized when they pass. However much contemporary trade agreements have instilled the race to the bottom for labor and living standards, they have also provided many poorer people in the U.S. with access to cheap consumer goods, potentially increasing their standards of living. The challenge is to figure out how to create a new economics of markets and society, in other words, how to revise the rules and norms situating commodity exchange in all aspects of social life so as to reap its potential positive implications while mitigating its negatives.

The Transition from Feudalism to Capitalism Debate.

The debate among various prominent Marxists and Marxian historians over the movement from a society characterized by simple exchange and feudal class relations to one characterized by circulation and capitalist exploitation raged for quite some time. It centered on Dobb's treatise *Studies in the Development of Capitalism* (1947) and Sweezy's (1976) pointed response, although several Marxian scholars contributed in all.[1] Paul Sweezy fingered merchant capital as the "prime mover" behind both the collapse of the feudal order and the rise of the capitalist exploitation, lucidly illustrating what merchant capital and simple exchange may entail for society in such a context. He also provides an explanation of how merchant capital and simple exchange potentially create the conditions of possibility for both the emergence of circulation and the rise of capitalist as opposed to feudal exploitation.

The crux of the debate rested on whether feudalism collapsed due to internal contradictions or as a result of the influence of foreign merchants and expanding exchange relations. Although both sides agreed merchant capital and expanding exchange played some role in the transition, disagreement arose over what commodity exchange entailed in the transition. Maurice Dobb contended merchant capital and commodity exchange only served as the handmaidens of the transformation, facilitating but not inducing change, while Paul Sweezy maintained that merchants were directly responsible for the dissolution of the feudal order and the establishment of commodity-capitalist society. Since circulation and wage labor often serve as proxies for capitalist social relations, the rationale for the transition of simple exchange relations to circulation also foreshadowed the significance awarded to simple exchange and merchant capital in the world today.

Feudal society in the debates intimated a society with primarily feudal production relations with commodity exchange only taking place within a very limited sphere of society. Feudal*ism* connotes a social formation characterized or dominated by feudal class and non-class relations. Although they did not engage directly in the debate, Resnick and Wolff explicate some of the feudal class relations commonly put forth as representative of European Feudal society:

> Individual serf households or, more commonly, groups of serf households, organized in villages or communes, functioned within relationships of loyalty and fealty to "their" landlords, that is, the private lords or "state-lord" of the lands to which they "belonged." Religion and tradition enshrined these as fixed relationships entailing specific patterns of necessary and surplus labor performance and specific deliveries of surplus labor (or its fruits) by serfs to "their" lords. (2002, 134)

Such a thin definition of feudalism serves primarily to highlight some commonalities among feudal production relations, not to mask or deny the tremendous thick variations of feudalism(s) which existed. In fact, Dobb argued that the diversity of feudal forms prohibited a general theory of feudal transformation. From such a perspective, the differences among the broader constellation of social relations enmeshing any relations of production and distribution serve to make *any* story regarding the transformation to capitalism site and context specific. Sweezy took issue with Dobb for this, accusing him of defining feudalism as "not *one* social system but a family of social systems" (1976, 34) and introduced a rather static, self-contained notion of a feudal mode of production in its stead to facilitate his sweeping narrative of the transition process.

Throughout the debate, Sweezy's maintained that increased commodity exchange, chiefly promoted by merchant capital, was the prime mover behind the transition. Sweezy's theory rests therefore upon a specific understanding of the significance of commodity exchange and merchants for such a society. Sweezy points out several changes as the driving force behind the transition, including the increasing dependence of production upon exchange, the increasing specialization and division of labor, and myriad subjective changes regarding what may be considered a commodity. However, they all ultimately boiled down to the increased commodity exchange spearheaded by foreign merchants.

The first argument Sweezy introduces to support his contention concerns the changing role of commodity production within feudal society. Sweezy argues that, long before any fundamental transition in the class structure occurred, local and long-distance trade constituted only a minor role within feudal society. Trade and the associated merchants functioned as "props rather than threats to the feudal order: they supplied essential needs without bulking large enough to affect the structure of economic relations," e.g., the relations and forces of Feudal production (Sweezy 1976, 41). Sweezy's argument here echoes many statements by Marx, such as the following from *Theories of Surplus Value:* "the *merchant* in the Middle Ages was simply a *dealer in commodities* produced either by the town guilds or by the peasants" (1971, 469). Bridbury supports such an interpretation of exchange in feudal society, arguing that markets in the middle ages were either "local in range and narrow in provenance" or "cosmopolitan" and associated with foreign wares and merchants (1986, 96). In all of these examples, markets performed at best a supplementary role to social distribution.

Given the relatively stable relationship among merchants, commodity exchange, and the social relations and forces of feudal production that are supposedly characteristic of the feudal mode of production, Sweezy needed to provide an explanation as to why feudal relations began to fall apart. In other words, what changed such that the merchant props of the feudal order became, instead, its nemesis? The answer he provides revolves around the expansion of long-distance trade which took place for reasons outside of the logical of the feudal mode of production. As Hilton notes "Sweezy, following Pirenne, had found the outside force in the merchant capital accumulated in the Middle Eastern-Mediterranean trading area, which was, as it were, injected into the stable feudal system through the agency of a set of traders of unknown social origin" (1976, 26).

Sweezy claims that Dobb, for all of his nuanced arguments, never succeeded "in shaking that part of the commonly accepted theory which holds that the root cause of the decline of feudalism was the growth of trade" (1976, 41). Sweezy's fundamental objection to Dobb, and the one he predicated his argument upon, concerns his ambivalent relation with the role of exchange and merchant capital. Let us look at the specifics of Sweezy's argument in more detail, for although essentialist, many of the issues he raises have parallels in the elucidation of simple exchange discussed thus far. Further, as Sweezy's account contrasts markedly with the more 'Dobbian' stance this project embraces, the specifics and implications of both knowledges become highlighted through their comparison.

In brief, Sweezy's argument maintains first that even the meager amount of exchange induced by long-distance trade induced an increasing division and specialization of labor in feudal society. The resulting efficiency gains precipitated a dramatic fall in price for locally produced manufactured commodities. Once manufactured goods could be purchased from towns for less than it cost the feudal manors to make them on site, feudal lords came under increasing pressure to come up with the money to purchase rather than make these goods "in house." Feudal estates began producing more and more agricultural commodities for sale simply in order to generate the exchange value necessary for purchasing such commodities.

The resulting growth in agrarian commodity production induced more manufactured commodities as well and therefore led to an expansion in the scope and scale of commodity exchange in society. Merchant capital consequentially became empowered and enriched, for it mediated, concentrated, and profited from the exchange taking place. Further, increasing local sales and purchases created the space for more long-distance and foreign trade. The resulting wealth that became concentrated in the hands of merchant capital eventually posed a challenge, both politically and economically, to the feudal order.

Sweezy also theorizes how commodity exchange's expansion in scope and scale shaped the consciousness of individuals in particular ways. The growth of commodity exchange induced a shift in the attitude of exchangers in Sweezy's story in a way strikingly reminiscent of Aristotle's arguments on unnatural exchange. Exchanging agents, primarily comprised at least originally of feudal lords and petty commodity producers, gradually became intoxicated by the possibility of amassing wealth via exchange. Such a "psychological transformation" meant commodity exchange became no longer simply a means to acquire use-values and/or redistribute the social product, but, at least for the afflicted individuals, also a means to amass exchange-value. As the feudal lords devoted more and more of their time and energy into the amassment of wealth, they neglected their other social and political duties, sacrificing their own feudal obligations. The expansion of exchange escalated the number of afflicted individuals throughout all strata of society, and as the desire to amass wealth for the sake of wealth spread throughout society, feudal obligations steadily eroded.

Sweezy's third argument concerns another specific psychological transformation purportedly undergone by the feudal lords as a result of foreign commodities: a desire for luxury. Merchants displaying finery and exotic goods corrupted or bewitched feudal lords into desiring ever more luxurious consumption. The increasing luxury among the feudal elites necessitated ever-increasing revenues to finance. Although the greed and desire for wealth driving Sweezy's story originally stemmed from commodity exchange and merchants, once in place, these desires created the conditions of possibility for expanding exchange. In effect, as more and more feudal commodities found their way to market in order to put exchange-value into the pockets of the (newly) rapacious feudal lords, the growing trade fueled an enlargement of their own desires, resulting in a dynamic cycle.

Maurice Dobb also argues that the desire for more revenue among feudal lords provided an impetus behind the breakdown of the feudal *regime,* but locates the origin of such wants with the rise of the towns rather than with exchange *per se:*

> So far as the growth of the market exercised a disintegrating influence on the structure of Feudalism, and prepared the soil for the growth of forces which were to weaken and supplant it, the story of this influence can largely be identified with the rise of towns as corporate bodies, as these came to possess economic and political independence in varying degrees. (Dobb 1947, 70)

Keeping with his own understanding of the transformation, Dobb provides no essential reason behind the growth of the towns, citing the unclear and controversial rationale behind the urban communities. After exploring several explanations, he concludes by stating: "with the limited knowledge in our possession, we shall probably have to be content for the present with an eclectic explanation of the rise of mediaeval towns: an explanation which allows a different weight to various influences in different cases" (1947, 75).

Sweezy does not share Dobb's druthers, however, and ironically provides an explanation for the town's expansion which could have been scripted by liberal economists. Towns, being "breeders of the exchange economy, opened up the servile population of the countryside the prospect of a freer and better life" (Sweezy 1976, 43). The growth of commodity exchange production in the urban areas instigated a mass migration, for the feudal peasants fleeing from the increased exploitation of the feudal estates flocked to the cities. The peasants became free in the double sense of both lacking any instruments of production, as well as being free from feudal obligations and hence free to sell their labor-power.[2] Although both Dobb and Sweezy maintain that the flight from the land became a decisive factor in the ultimate break down of the feudal order, Sweezy attributes this migration primarily to a desire for the (albeit contradictory) freedom commodity exchange entails in opposition to the increasing feudal exploitation and misery.

Both Dobb and Sweezy agree that, at the same time the exploitation in feudal estates began to rise, commodity exchange deepened in scope and scale and production became increasing geared toward exchange-value. Feudal lords lost the ability to maintain control over social production as serfs fled from the land and production expanded in cites. Sweezy ascribes this process to the rise of merchants and exchange, as the following statement illustrates: "no doubt the rise of the exchange economy had other effects on the old order, but I think that the four which have been mentioned were sufficiently pervasive and powerful to ensure the breaking up of the pre-existing system of production" (1976, 43). Dobb weighs in more on the expansion of cities as gradually undermining the feudal system, but assigns a complex rationale for such expansion; merchants and exchange play at best a supporting role.

From a Marxian theoretical perspective, both Sweezy's and Dobb's narratives highlight some of the ways in which merchant capital and exchange may influence society. Sweezy's essentialist reduction of the transformation to an entailment of exchange ignores, however, Marx's analysis of the phenomena, where he argues that although "there can be no doubt [that the] great revolutions in trade . . . were a major moment in promoting the transition from the feudal to the capitalist mode of production . . . this very fact has led to false conceptions" (Marx 1991, 450). When considering the transformation, Marx provides a long list of some of the processes which all made a 'fundamental contribution' to the dissolution of the former economic order, including many of the ones mentioned above, and mulls their impact:

> The sudden expansion of the world market, the multiplication of commodities in circulation, the competition among the European nations for the seizure of Asiatic products and American treasures, the colonial system, all made a fundamental contribution toward shattering the feudal barriers to production. And yet, the modern mode of production in its first period, that of manufacture, developed only where the conditions for it had been created in the Middle Ages. . . . (1991, 450)

Although all of the events and changes he describes here may have facilitated some changes in the feudal order, manufacture, and in particular, capitalist production, still only developed in isolated, special cases. Although commodity exchange and merchant capital contributed to the breakdown of the old order, they cannot by themselves explain the growth of capitalist social relations. Commodity exchange, even if expansive, in and of itself does not entail any particular class process or relationship. Marx specifically argues this point, stating that "whatever mode of production is the basis [in society], trade promotes the generation of a surplus product designed to go into exchange . . . [and] thus it gives production a character oriented more and more toward exchange-value" (1991, 443). Yet, as any class process may produce commodities, all the deepening of the scale and scope of exchange entails is a social distribution of use-values increasingly assuming a commodity form.

Notes

NOTES TO CHAPTER ONE

1. *The Economist,* June 11th-17th 2005.
2. Akerlof's first paper on this was "The Market for 'Lemons': Quality Uncertainty and the Market Mechanism" published in 1970.
3. Michel Foucault grappled with a similar problem in his attempt to define madness. In the end, Foucault concluded "mental illness was constituted by all that was said in all the statements that named it, divided it up, described it, explained it, traced its developments, indicated its various correlations, judged it, and possibly gave it speech by articulating, in its name, discourses that were to be taken as its own" (1972, 32).
4. Bloor, the editor of Wittgenstein's text, notes how this approach is radically different from more traditional ways of defining categories, which typically assert that we can grasp the intrinsic properties or essences of them, despite the disagreement on the correct procedure to do so.
5. See Held and McGrew (2002) for a detailed survey of contemporary literature on this connection.
6. The chain of equivalence is adapted from Laclau and Mouffe (1985, 183–6).

NOTES TO CHAPTER TWO

1. For a critical review of the mainstream notion of individual desires, see Staveren 1999. Moore (1993) and McNally (1993) link, in an essential manner, commodity exchange and exploitation. Tomlinson (2004) explores commodity exchange as cultural imperialism.
2. Peter Dicken (2003, 198–314) provides a detailed survey of the literature on multinational corporations. George DeMartino (2000, 207–15) compares and contrasts a number of fair trade approaches, including social charters, social tariffs, and the Sullivan Principles.

3. Plato and Aristotle employed very different notions of an Ideal state however. For Plato, the Form or Idea of the *polis* could never be reached, for reality will always be a flawed, imperfect image of the Form or Idea. Aristotle presented society as capable of moving toward the Ideal in a similar manner of how Smith presented society as progressing toward the system of natural liberty. The important difference between Aristotle and Plato does not mitigate how they both utilized an Ideal to compare/contrast the present.

4. For a detailed discussion of Karl Marx's classical scholarship, see de Ste. Croix (1981) *The Class Struggle in the Ancient Greek World,* especially chapter's 1 and 2. Scott Meikle (1991) takes the strong position that Marx's analysis of exchange was explicitly based on Aristotle. Lowry (1979) provides a concise summary of how economists, including Schumpeter and Marx, interpreted Aristotle's work, as well as more contemporary accounts.

5. This discussion is located within a notoriously difficult section of book V in the *Nicomachean Ethics,* which Lowry notes "puzzles and intrigues scholars to this day" (1987a, 183). The 'standard' interpretation embraced by Lewis (1978) maintains that proportionality did not imply equality for Aristotle, for social standing was seen to play a role in exchange along with the customary price. Finley (1970), assuming the voluntary nature of exchange, maintains that there cannot be an unjust or disproportionate transaction and argues that the passage under question concerns a 'breach of contract.' Meikle states that systemic proportionate exchange is an impossibility, for "private property could not conceivably be exchange in anything like this way. If, because of hierarchy, one man could command in the market more for his goods than another, who would choose, without compulsion, to exchange with him?" (1991, 194). For an in-depth discussion of this from a neoclassical perspective, see Josef Soudek (1952). This position is critiqued in Polanyi (1968a).

6. Staveren (1999) provides a lucid and detailed study of the importance of excess and deficiency in Aristotle's notion of justice; see especially chapter 7.

NOTES TO CHAPTER THREE

1. Numerous scholars (Brown 1994; Callari 1981; Hirschman 1986; Lux 1990) note that Smith's aim was not to provide an apologia for capitalist society, and that, in fact, the *Wealth of Nations* provides numerous, forceful critiques of the emerging social order. The invisible hand constitutes Smith's most famous legacy, but he introduced this concept to counter and discredit state sanctioned trade monopolies such as the East India Company and colonial economic policy in general.

2. Rodney Hilton's (1976) text collected several essays comprising the lively debate over the role of commodity exchange in the emergence of capitalist society.

3. Callari argues that the classical theorists (Smith, Ricardo, Malthus) "adopted wealth as an entry point and their theory of distribution (of the means and products of laboring activity) as a justification for the framework of private property" (1981, 102).

4. Regarding the poster child aspect, the Liberty Fund, a right-leaning think tank which encourages the study of 'the ideal of a society of free and responsible individuals,' subsidizes the reprinting and distributing of the *Wealth of Nations*.

5. Avarice as a concept underwent a transformation during this process as well, and became increasingly referred to as individual advantage, economic interests, or as the love of gain (Hirschman 1977, 37). Hume, a close and influential friend of Smith and a powerful protagonist of this perspective, boldly averred that "Avarice, or the desire of gain, is a universal passion which operates at all times, in all places, and upon all persons" (1898, 176).

6. Hirschman also argues that the main impact of Smith's *Wealth of Nations* was to establish a theoretical justification for the untrammeled pursuit of individual self-interest.

7. Weber's classic *The Protestant Ethic and the Spirit of Capitalism* (1958) is a detailed argument of this 'Puritan economic ethic.'

8. Whether or not economic self-interest constituted the entire subjectivity of humanity (Hume 1898; Mandeville 1962) or simply one fundamental aspect of it became the subject of much debate. Tensions between these competing understandings of humanity may even be found in Smith's work. Whereas Smith's *Theory of Moral Sediments* outlines a host of human passions, including sympathy, benevolence and economic self-interest, his *Wealth of Nations* reduces individuals to being motivated entirely by self-interest. These competing understandings of individuality lie at the root of the so-called "Adam Smith problem."

9. Vico implied that the Ancient Greeks lived in an age of reason and after a long detour, society was once again moving toward one. Hence, the tripartite system he developed is not a simple teleology.

10. Tawney notes that "Not the least fundamental of divisions among theories of society is between those which regard the world of human affairs as self-contained, and those which appeal to a supernatural criterion" (1954, 15).

11. Typically, this was stated as the need of the state to insure proper 'balances' of trade and money flows in and out of the state. The statesman had to exercise constant vigilance in order to provide a series of countermeasures that would prevent the balances from deteriorating.

12. Tawney (1954) notes in this regard that foreign merchants in Antwerp wrote in a letter to Phillip II (1527–98, king of Spain) that "No one can deny that the cause of the prosperity of this city is the freedom granted to those who trade there."

13. Smith defines wealth as "the annual produce of the land and labor of the society" (1981, 12).

14. Exactly the same sort of idea may be found in much of early economic development literature; Rostow's depiction of society passing through various stages to finally reach the 'age of high mass consumption' exemplifies this tendency (1960).

15. Brown provides an excellent summary of Smith's argument: "In the absence of restrictions, the natural course of development will be from agriculture, to manufacturers, to foreign trade. This course of development is a naturalistic one, deriving partly from the stadial theory of history, where societies progress in a linear sequence through the stages of hunting, pasturage, agriculture and finally commerce. It also derives from a notion of a natural division of labour between the country and the town, in which agricultural activity is prior to and proportioning of the manufacturing activity of the towns. Just as a surplus of agricultural goods can be exchanged for manufactures from the town, so a surplus of manufactured goods over and above this exchange with the countryside will be required before foreign trade becomes feasible" (1994, 176).

16. As Rubin notes, "the victory of one social system over another (the bourgeois order over the feudal) appears to Smith as a victory of man's 'natural' immutable nature over the 'artificial' social institutions of the past" (1989, 169).

17. The rest of the quote reads as follows: "When the division of labour has been thoroughly established, it is but a very small part of a man's wants which the produce of his own labour can supply. He supplies the far greater part of them by exchanging that surplus part of the produce of his own labor, which is over and above his own consumption, for such parts of the produce of other men's labour as he has occasion for. Every man thus lives by exchanging, or becomes in some measure a merchant, and the society itself grows to be what is properly a commercial society" (Smith 1981, 37).

18. "In the series of binary opposites deployed in these comparisons, it is the derogated term that is systematically applied to the mercantile system [Smith's moniker for physiocratic and mercantilist thought]. Pairs such as prejudice/reason, sophistry/common sense, disorder/order, and unnatural/natural, map out a discursive space in which the system of natural liberty is presented as reasonable and self-evidently superior to all those who are not blinded by prejudice" (Brown 1994, 194).

19. "By extorting from the legislature bounties upon the exportation of their own linen, high duties upon the importation of all foreign linen, and total prohibition of the home consumption of some sorts of French linen, they endeavour to sell their own goods as dear as possible. By encouraging the importation of foreign linen yarn, and thereby bringing it into competition with that which is made by our own people, they endeavour to buy the work of the poor spinners as cheap as possible. They are as intent to keep down the wages of their own weavers, as the earnings of the poor spinners, and it is by no means for the benefit of the workman, that they endeavour either to raise the price of the compleat work, or to lower that of the rude materials. It is the industry which is carried on for the benefit of the rich

and the powerful, that is principally encouraged by our mercantile system. That which is carried on for the benefit of the poor and the indigent, is too often, either neglected, or oppressed" (Smith 1981, 644).

20. In this vein, consider the following exemplar: "Soldiers and seamen, indeed, when discharged from the king's service, are at liberty to exercise any trade, within any town or place of Great Britain or Ireland. Let the same natural liberty of exercising what species of industry they please be restored to all his majesty's subjects, in the same manner as to soldiers and seamen; that is, break down the exclusive privileges of corporations, and repeal the statute of apprenticeship, both which are real encroachments upon natural liberty, and add to these the repeal of the law of settlements, so that a poor workman, when thrown out of employment either in one trade or in one place, may seek for it in another trade or in another place, without the fear either of a prosecution or of a removal, and neither the publick nor the individuals will suffer much more from the occasional disbanding some particular classes of manufacturers, than from that of soldiers" (Smith 1981, 470–1).

21. "Most of what is considered political economy rested upon the assumption that without a large state presence to promote various sectors of the economy, and to regulate economic life, the state and society would fall apart. Typically, this was stated as the need of the state to insure proper 'balances' of trade and money flows in and out of the state. The statesman had to exercise constant vigilance in order to provide a series of countermeasures that would prevent the balances from deteriorating" (Brown 1994, 157).

22. The Physiocrats are important in another facet of Smith's intervention in that, like them, he argued that increases in wealth are not due to unequal exchange, but the laboring activity which produces commodities for sale: commodity exchange for both Smith and the Physiocrats was seen to involve the exchange of equivalents. As we will see in the following section, this served implicitly to counter the negative exchange entailment that profits are due to unequal exchange, or what Aristotle deemed to be the root of all social conflict.

23. An important corollary of this concerns the subsumption of the social into the individual, or in other words, constructing the national interest as simply the summation of individual interests. See Callari (1981) for more on this issue.

24. Yet, as Callari notes, "Smith's own *Wealth of Nations* and *Theory of Moral Sentiments* were very cautious in the presentation of this thesis: they promoted the thesis that workers, as well as capitalists and landlords, being rational human beings, had a stake in the progress of wealth; they also strongly suggested that where a non-commonality of interests between workers and the other classes existed, then this was to be resolved in favor of the workers" (1981, 198).

25. This political entailment of commodity exchange is often used today; for example, Bush, while on the campaign trail said that "The case for trade is not just monetary, but moral . . . Economic freedom creates habits of

liberty." Trade freely with China, he added, and the political rights will follow (Kettle 2001, 7).

26.   Another difference is that for Quensay and his followers, locating the production of wealth in the agrarian sector implied that the state should only tax landlords in this sector as a means of *public* wealth. Hence, Smith deems the Physiocrats political economists as they are still seen to be looking out for the provisioning of the state (public wealth) as their central problematic. Smith on the other hand was interested in the expansion of *private* wealth, for this alone would ensure social harmony. The emphasis awarded to the agrarian sector as both the sole source of *produit net* and landlords as a cash cow for state revenue by Quensay in the *Tableau économique* was seen by Smith as serving to hinder the expansion of wealth for society at large: "Such a political economy, though it no doubt retards more of less, is not always capable of stopping altogether the *natural progress of a nation towards wealth and prosperity,* and still less of making it go backwards" (1981, 674, emphasis mine).

27.   For Smith, profit is a reward given to owners of capital for advancing their capital stock. The pursuit of profits would lead the owners of capital to move it where they would get the highest rate of return. As we have seen, this will 'naturally' lead to the pattern of social evolution Smith 'described.' Yet, Smith also maintained that labor is the source of all wealth. Hence, Smith introduced exploitation in that laborers produce all the wealth but part of this wealth is deduced from them and given as a 'reward' to advancers for 'hazarding their stock.' Perhaps troubled by this, Smith also introduced another notion of wealth where value is resolved into the value of its component parts, the so-called 'adding up' theory of value. While this adding up theory of value excised the notion of exploitation, it left Smith without a coherent theory of value; something Marx and others would take him to task for.

28.   This transition did not abolish theoretically or socially the previously articulated links between greed and self-centered individualism and either private property or exchange. In relation to private property, witness Prodoun's understanding of "property as theft" leading to social conflict or Rousseau's (1973) arguments that private property is at the root of social conflict. The Aristotelian negative exchange entailments are thriving in the contemporary anti-globalization movement, as we will see in chapter seven.

NOTES TO CHAPTER FOUR

1.   The freedom associated with exchange should not be construed as a statement that general circulation *necessarily* precludes or abolishes these social networks however; it is more appropriate to consider that general circulation opens up the space for a radically different social alignment, for better or worse.

2.   One needs caution and modesty with such a statement, for there are no guarantees that the pain and suffering involved will bring about 'socialist' society or anything of the sort. Marxist scholars such as Warren (1980)

essentially transformed the possibility into a necessity (and in the process provided an apologia for colonization).

3. For example, see Marx and Engel's *New York Tribune* articles on India and Persia, collected in *On Colonialism* (1972).

4. The unbridled optimism expressed here related to the date of its publication in 1848 on what looked like the eve of revolution in Europe. Jani (2002), in a provocative essay on Marx's writings on India for the *New York Daily Tribune,* argued that over the decade of the 1850's Marx became much more reserved in the idea of "capitalist progress." Jani demonstrates how Marx in his later articles on India emphasized how the smashing of Indian social relations by British colonialism produced lots of pain with little gain.

5. The reciprocal dependence upon circulation becomes more pronounced the more society becomes specialized: "The division of labour within society brings into contact independent producers of commodities, who acknowledge no authority other than that of competition, of the coercion exerted by the pressure of their reciprocal interests, just as in the animal kingdom the 'war of all against all' more or less preserves the conditions of existence of every species" (Marx 1990, 477).

6. Beck (2000) writes about the paradox of individualism and dependence to critique liberal understandings of the contemporary global marketplace.

7. C.B. Macpherson expresses the contradiction succinctly. "The market makes men free; it requires for its effective operation that all men be free and rational; yet the independent rational decisions of each man produce at every moment a configuration of forces which confronts each man compulsively. All men's choices determine, and each man's choice is determined by, the market" (1962, 106).

8. See also Sweezy (1942); David Harvey (1982); and Resnick and Wolff (2002).

9. These two examples by no means exhaust the potential hierarchical arrangements.

10. The freedom found in circulation may provide a condition of possibility for the realization of productive freedom by increasing the desire for cooperative production.

11. Amariglio and Callari argue that Marx and Marxists have long insisted upon "the critical importance of scrutinizing the historical production of economic subjectivities" (1993, 187). Marx consequentially maintained that the independent individual participating in exchange could only be a social product.

12. "In this society of free competition, the individual appears detached from the natural bonds, etc. which in earlier historical periods make him the accessory of a definite and limited human conglomerate. Smith and Ricardo still stand with both feet on the shoulders of the eighteenth-century prophets, in whose imaginations this eighteenth-century individual—the product on one side of the dissolution of the feudal forms of society, on the other side of the new forces of production developed since the sixteenth century—appears as an ideal, whose existence they project into the past.

Not as a historic result, but as history's point of departure. As the Natural Individual appropriate to their notion of human nature, not arising historically, but posited by nature" (Marx 1993, 83).

13. Many if not most of these Marxian accounts of commodity fetishism rely upon an essentialist base/superstructure representation of society however, or are at a minimum, as Amariglio and Callari argue, "infected by an economic determinism" (1993, 189).

14. See Taussig (1980) for a modern representation of "enforced normality" in the context of South American mining towns.

15. Production in the form of commodities does not, however, imply any particular class process. Marx treated production, distribution (exchange) and consumption as "the members of a totality, distinctions within a unity" (1993, 99). The similarities and differences among social formations regarding these three moments of a single unity led him to construct a rich understanding of the interaction of various modes of distribution and production. Although the class processes involved in the production of useful objects shape distributional processes, no one-to-one mapping of particular distribution and class processes exists.

16. Even though exchange value seems to be a product of the commodity itself, i.e., what the commodity is worth, Marx argues that the valuation represents equal and universal labor—the abstract labor—expended in the production of the object. Hence, even though labor is private and independent in the production of commodities, labor still assumes social form in the exchange-value linked to commodities, which serves as a symbol of the socially necessary abstract labor time involved in the commodity's production. This exists in contrast to, as Balibar puts it, "an 'anatomy' of value based entirely on the quantification of labour" (1995, 78). As Marx notes, "exchange-value of commodities is indeed nothing but a mutual relation between various kinds of labour of individuals regarded as equal and universal labour, i.e., nothing but a material expression of a specific social form of labour" (1970, 35).

17. The public policy "adopted" by Iraq after the latest U.S. invasion is a striking case in point. The new rules governing Iraq's economy have been welcomed by liberal observers as the most "open" in the world; the liberal *Economist* magazine went as far as calling them a "capitalist's dream" (2003)

18. The BBC news service, in an article on "globalisation," noted that "increased trade has made us wealthier and allowed us to lead more diverse lifestyles. . . . For consumers and avowed capitalists, this [trade] is largely a good thing. Vigorous trade has made for more choice in the High street, greater spending, rising living standards and a growth in international travel" (14 September 2000).

NOTES TO CHAPTER FIVE

1. Of course, the commodities traded could be simply appropriated from producers, implying that they actually constituted part of the subsistence

bundle of their producers. Colonial "hut taxes" for instance often forced communities to sell goods to obtain the means to pay, even if the "commodities" sold induced depravation.

2. The limited exchange constitutes the realm of interaction between peasant producers and other "modes of production" and distribution argued to dominate society at large. See Laclau (1971) for a critical review of the "articulation of modes of production" discussion.

3. Other forms of capital include industrial capital, where the increase in value is located in the production process, and finance or financial capital, where money breeds money directly—M-M.'

4. Recall also that Aristotle linked unnatural exchange with individual perversion because the agents who partake in exchange to seek profits become corrupted and end up devoting or centering their existence and abilities upon amassing exchange-value.

5. The addenda to the third volume of *Theories of Surplus Value* concentrates on financial capital, but contains some illustrative notes on merchant capital as well: "Profit in this field [merchant capital] is in part linked with a vague notion of general swindling, or more specifically, with the idea that the merchant swindles the industrial capitalist in the same way that the industrial capitalist swindles the worker, or again that the merchant swindles the consumer, just as the producers swindle one another. In any case, profit here is explained as a result of exchange, that is, as arising from a social relation and not from a thing" (Marx 1971, 454).

6. "The independent and preponderant development of capital in the form of commercial capital is synonymous with the nonsubjection of production to capital, i.e., with the development of capital on the basis of a social form of production that is foreign to it and independent of it" (Marx 1991, 445).

7. Marx argues that "in antiquity, exchange value was not the *nexus rerum;* it appears as such only among the mercantile people, who had, however, no more than the carrying trade and did not, themselves, produce" (1993, 223).

8. Marx presents this thesis in numerous ways in the *Grundrisse*. Consider the following: "As subjects of exchange, their relation is therefore that of *equality*. It is impossible to find any trace of distinction, not to speak of contradiction, between them" (1993, 241). A little later, Marx notes that: "When the economic form, exchange [as general circulation], posits the all-sided equality of subjects, then the content, the individual as well as the objective material which drives toward the exchange, is *freedom*. Equality and freedom are thus not only respected in exchange based on exchange values but, also, the exchange of exchange values is the productive, real basis of all *equality* and *freedom*. As pure ideas they are merely the idealized expressions of the basis; as developed in juridical, political, social relations, they are merely this basis to a higher power. And so it has been in history. Equality and freedom as developed to this extent are exactly the

opposite of the freedom and equality in the world of antiquity, where developed exchange value was not their basis, but where, rather, the development of that basis destroyed them" (1993, 245).

9. The concept of social surplus should be understood here as the use-values above and beyond the means of subsistence. The social surplus, like the concept of subsistence, is (over)determined within each social formation and does not refer to any biological threshold.

10. "Capital as merchant capital is found in the earliest conditions of economic development; it is the first movement in which exchange value as such forms the content—is not only the form but also its own content. This motion can take place within peoples, or between peoples for whose production exchange value has by no means yet become the presupposition. The movement only seized upon the surplus of their directly useful production, and proceeds only in the margin" (Marx 1993, 253).

11. I use productive population in a broader sense than how Marx used the term to discuss capitalist production, e.g., "The concept of a productive worker therefore implies not merely a relation between the activity of work and its useful effect, between the worker and the product of his work, but also a specifically social relation of production, a relation with a historical origin which stamps the worker as capital's direct means of valorization" (Marx 1990, 644).

12. For a modern example of such a teleological narrative, consider the new institutionalism of Douglass North. North identifies a 'shopping gene' as motivating humanity and he maintains that commodity exchange underpinned the "success story entitled *The Rise of the Western World*" (1990, 96). The relatively late emergence of circulation in human history for North results from ill-defined property rights and therefore artificially high transaction costs, which, taken together, stymy the innate human desire to accumulate and exchange property.

13. See the appendix for a discussion of the feudalism-to-capitalism transition debate.

14. Polanyi explores the subjective changes and their consequences in vivid detail in *The Great Transformation* (1957), where he deems land, labor and capital as "fictitious commodities" because they are not produced as such, but only take on the guise of commodities within certain social formations. His essay "The Self-regulating Market and the Fictitious Commodities: Land, Labor, and Money" (1968) explores both the objectification of these "commodities" as well as what he sees as the social consequences thereof.

15. Marx 1991, 449–51; Marx 1993, 471–79 passim.

16. Some of the ways the appropriators distribute the surplus includes taxes, research and development, advertising, dividend payments in the case of corporations, bribes, payments to "unproductive" workers like managers and so forth. For a detailed discussion of surplus distributions, see Resnick and Wolff's *Knowledge and Class* (1987).

17. The production of commodities does not necessarily entail capitalist class relations, for individuals, slave plantations and even communist cooperatives can produce use-values in commodity form. Circulation can mediate the social metabolism of slave societies, individual producers as envisioned by liberal scholars, or capitalist production.

18. "A worker who buys a loaf of bread and a millionaire who does the same appear in this act only as simple buyers, just as, in respect to them, the grocer appears only as seller. All other aspects are here extinguished. The *content* of these purchases, like their *extent,* here appear as completely irrelevant compared with the formal aspect" (Marx 1993, 251).

19. "The total product of our imagined association is a social product. One part of this product serves as fresh means of production and remains social. But another part is consumed by the members of the association as means of subsistence. This part must therefore be divided among them. The way this division is made will vary with the particular kind of social organization of production and the corresponding level of social development attained by the producers" (Marx 1990, 171–2).

20. Many new books and articles discuss contemporary liberal globalization and increasing insecurity. The witty and perceptive *The Age of Insecurity* (1998) by Larry Elliott and Dan Atkinson is one of the best.

21. The inputs do not need to be capitalist commodities. "Within its circulation process, in which industrial capital functions either as money or as commodity, the circuit of industrial capital, whether in the form of money capital or commodity capital, cuts across the commodity circulation of the most varied modes of social production, in so far as this commodity circulation simultaneously reflects commodity production. Whether the commodities are the production of production based on slavery, the product of peasants (Chinese, Indian ryots), of a community (Dutch East Indies), of state production (such as existed in earlier epochs of Russian history, based on serfdom) or of half-savage hunting peoples, etc.—as commodities and money they confront the money and commodities in which industrial capital presents itself, and enter both into the latter's own circuit and into that of the surplus-value borne by the commodity capital, in so far as the latter is spent as revenue; i.e., in both branches of the circulation of commodity capital" (Marx 1992, 189).

22. Gateway on the other hand, one of Dell's primary competitors, recently began selling its computers at a discount to merchants because of the cost savings involved.

NOTES TO CHAPTER SIX

1. Mouffe (1979) provides an excellent account that situates Gramsci within the debates of his day and fleshes out some of the categories he worked with.

2. Aristotle's representation of exchange for example, in both its positive and negative forms, constituted the common market sense in his day and for centuries thereafter.

3. Consider Hertz's statement in her introduction: "Capitalism [read markets] is clearly the best system for generating wealth, and free trade and open capital markets have brought unprecedented economic growth to most if not all of the world" (2001, 12).

4. Critics often point out how every "developed" nation after England employed a range of tariffs and trade barriers explicitly to cultivate manufacturing and other sectors of the economy (Amsden 1989; Gerschenkron 1962; Khor 2001).

5. Several problems haunt the FTE theorem, perhaps the most important being the vague notion of capital as a factor of production as pointed out by Joan Robinson (1973). We will consider the FTE notwithstanding these problems.

6. In fact, since liberals assume all exchange is voluntary, then *all* trades lead to a Pareto improvement, for why would someone voluntarily engage in an exchange if they did not feel they benefited from it?

7. The concept of increasing returns to scale, e.g., when a firm's costs fall when production expands, complicates the X-efficiency story. Today's "inefficient" firms may well in the long run have lower costs than their contemporary rivals if given the time and opportunity to increase the scale of production.

8. Economists who base their analysis upon Kaldor-Hicks efficiency disregard how economic policy analysis is always a cultural, political and social endeavour rather than the study of the application of proven, scientific truth, and how policy serves many, often contradictory, economic and social interests.

9. Data cited in Weisbrot and Baker (2002).

10. Bhagwati also does not explain why he portrayed critics of globalization as being anti-exchange or property rights.

11. Arjo Klammer and Jennifer Meehan discuss the role of academic economists in the NAFTA debate in some detail. Their main argument is about how certain ideas from academia were latched on to, but they also paraphrase George Stigler, stating that "the public is willing to hear [only] those economists who supply what they demand" (1999, 71).

12. Amariglio and Ruccio examine both the popularity and prevalence of ersatz economics (where many of the less flattering representations of exchange and trade exist today) and the serious and vitriolic campaign undertaken by professional economists to (re)educate the population as to the truth of the neoclassical position. They represent everyday economics as transgressive because its proponents "simply do not accept and obey" (1999, 33).

13. See Amariglio and Ruccio (1999) for a detailed exploration of the science gambit employed by mainstream economics. Keen notes something similar in the following: "Economists, we are told, know what is best for society

because economic theory knows how a market economy works, and how it can be made to work better, to everyone's ultimate benefit" (2001, 2).

14. Rupert summarizes this strand very nicely: "From the perspective of liberal economic theory, the universe of possibilities is defined in terms of a continuum stretching between the poles of free trade (individual liberty within a market context) or protectionism (external constraint hampering individuals in the market). Insofar as critics were opposed to NAFTA's definition of free trade, they must therefore be protectionists; and in the light of the (putatively self-evident) lessons of Smoot-Hawley, that could hardly be a respectable position" (2000, 59).

15. Keen provides an excellent elaboration of how critics of trade become represented as "simply special interest groups, at best misunderstanding the mechanisms of a market economy, at worst pleading their own special case to the detriment of the larger good" (2001, 4).

16. Bhagwati takes such a line of reasoning even further, stating that "it would require a wild imagination, and a deranged mind, to think that such freeing of trade leads to debilitating economic crises" (2000, 20).

17. Amariglio and Ruccio (1999) provide numerous examples of the harsh language employed.

18. Amariglio and Ruccio's (1999) work on ersatz economics charts this tendency and the hostility to "common place" understandings of economics in some detail.

19. Similar arguments have repeatedly been made by Krugman on the OpEd pages of the Times. Krugman, like Bhagwati, posture themselves as spokesmen for the science of economics, giving "pop" lectures on internationalism to demonstrate the gains from trade.

20. See for example his OpEd piece in the *New York Times* on FTAA (24 April 2001).

NOTES TO CHAPTER SEVEN

1. Finance capital consists of firms and institutions, such as hedge funds, large international banks, and the financial arms of major corporations involved in moving capital around the globe for investment and speculative purposes.

2. Consider the following quotes by Soros in this light: "Globalization is indeed a desirable development in many ways. Private enterprise is better at wealth creation than the state. Moreover, states have a tendency to abuse their power; globalization offers a degree of individual freedom that no individual state could ensure. Free competition on a global scale has liberated inventive and entrepreneurial talents and accelerated technological innovations" (2002, 5).

"In spite of its shortcomings, I am an ardent supporter of globalization. I support it not only because of the extra wealth it produces but even more because of the freedom it can offer" (2002, 7).

3. Writing about the IMF, Stiglitz argues that "Simplistic free market ideology provided the curtain behind which the real business of the 'new' mandate could be transacted. The change in mandate and objectives, while it may have been quiet, was hardly subtle: from serving global economic interests to serving the interests of global finance" (2003, 207).

4. "The global protests over globalization began at the WTO meetings in Seattle, Washington, because it was the most obvious symbol of the global inequities and the hypocrisy of the advanced industrial countries. While these countries had preached—and forced—the opening of the markets in developing countries to their industrial products, they had continued to keep their markets closed to the products of the developing countries, such as textiles and agriculture" (Stiglitz 2003, 224). See also Krugman (2003).

5. Even the leading liberal scholar Bhagwati cites undo corporate influence behind the "Trade Related Aspects Intellectual Property Rights" (TRIPS) provision within the Uruguay round of the WTO. See especially his chapter "Corporations: Predatory or Beneficial?" in his *In Defense of Globalization* (2004, 162–197).

6. Soros writes for example that "Antiglobalization activists are woefully misguided when they try to destroy the IFTIs [international financial and trade institutions]. . . . To "sink or shrink" the WTO would be counterproductive; it would destroy the goose that lays the golden eggs" (2002, 14).

7. Henwood provides a timely critique of the notion that corporations have only recently corrupted politics, to wit: "when was this Golden Age? The 1960s, when GE was filling the Hudson with PCBs? The 1930s, when Chase was banking with Nazis? Or in the 1890s, when Carnegie's Pinkertons shot strikers? . . . the Golden Age myths belong to literature, not nonfictions, but even there they vanish on close inspection" (1996, 2).

8. Hertz concurs, arguing that "no other system has proven as effective in generating wealth" as free market capitalism (2001, 32).

9. The differences in the market models he discusses essentially boil down to more or less regulation of the corporate sector and more or less social safety nets for the disenfranchised.

10. See McIntyre (2004) for a similar reading of Stiglitz's text.

11. "Many years ago the former president of GM and secretary of defense Charles E. Wilson's famous remark to the effect that what's good for GM is good for the USA became a symbol of a particular view of American capitalism. The IMF often seems to have a similar view—'what the financial community views as good for the global economy is good for the global economy and should be done.' In some instances, this is true; in many, it is not." (Stiglitz 2003, 195).

12. As of the writing of this essay, not all the countries involved in CAFTA have approved the agreement.

13. This vote tally represents a much smaller margin of victory than NAFTA, (which passed in the House with a final vote of 234 for and 200 against

and had the support of 61 senators), and perhaps indicates some slippage in the liberal hegemony.

14. To quote one activist: "In the era of globalisation, the pyramid of power has been verticalized so strongly, that in the reality, there exists no representative democracy anymore. This is not only a matter of formalities, but it's also about the contents of the decisions. The civil society, millions of people, are concerned about the fate of migrants, the inhabitants of poor countries, the excluded people of the rich North and the environment, as the neoliberal policies are deepening. These concerns cannot be answered only by saying that the market will do its job" (*Indymedia* 5 April 2001).

15. See the AFL-CIO's Global Fairness 2005 report "CAFTA: A Two-Way Street To Job Loss In The Americas" for a clear statement. *Public Citizen,* founded by Ralph Nader, claims CAFTA's passage would "serve to push ahead the corporate globalization model that has caused a 'race to the bottom' in labor and environmental standards and would promote privatization and deregulation of key public services" (2005)

16. A good example of the latter concerns the debate over genetically modified (GMO) foods. Most nations in Europe and Latin America passed laws strictly regulating or even banning such foods due to the uncertain impacts upon human health and the environment. The U.S., the world's leading producer of GMO food, is presently suing the European Union through the WTO to allow their importation, claiming the GMO ban represented an unfair barrier to trade.

17. The articles mentioned here are part of NAFTA's Chapter 11, section A.

18. William Finnegan notes that "water privatizations have been backfiring all over Latin America. In Panama, popular anger about an attempted privatization helped cost the President his bid for reelection. Vivendi, the French multinational, had its thirty-year water contract with the Argentine province of Tucumán terminated after two years because of alleged poor performance. Major water privatizations in Lima and Rio de Janeiro have had to be cancelled because of popular opposition. Trinidad recently allowed a management contract with a British water giant to expire. Protests against water privatization have also erupted in Indonesia, Pakistan, India, South Africa, Poland, and Hungary" (2002).

19. See for example McNally (1993) and Moore (1993), who both condemn exchange for its perceived fundamental connections with exploitation.

20. See *The Poverty of Philosophy* (1973)

NOTES TO THE APPENDIX

1. Rodney Hilton (1976) gathered several essays on this debate in a collected volume.

2. Bridbury (1986) discusses the labor market in the middle ages at some length, see especially pages 105–8.

Bibliography

AFL-CIO. 2005. CAFTA: A Two-Way Street to Job Loss in the Americas. www.afl-cio.org/globaleconomy (accessed June 20, 2005).

Akerlof, George. 1970. The Market for 'Lemons': Quality Uncertainty and the Market Mechanism. *Quarterly Journal of Economics* (August): 488–500.

Althusser, Louis, and Etienne Balibar. 1979. *Reading Capital*. New York: Verso.

Althusser, Louis. 1971. Ideology and Ideological State Apparatuses (Notes toward an Investigation). *Lenin and Philosophy*. New York: Monthly Review Press.

Amariglio, Jack, and Antonio Callari. 1993. Marxian Value Theory and the Problem of the Subject: The Role of Commodity Fetishism. In *Fetishism as Cultural Discourse*, ed. Emily Apter and William Pietz, 186–216. Ithaca: Cornell University Press.

Amariglio, Jack, and David F. Ruccio. 1999. Transgressive Knowledge of "Ersatz" Economics. In *What do Economists Know: New economics on knowledge*, ed. Robert Garnett, Jr., 19–36. New York: Routledge.

Amsden, Alice. 1989. *Asia's Next Giant: South Korea and Late Industrialization*. New York: Oxford.

Anderson, Alan Ross, and Nuel D. Belnap, Jr. 1975. *Entailment: The Logic of Relevance and Necessity*. Vol. 1. Princeton: Princeton University Press.

Aquinas, Thomas. 1981. *Selected Political Writings*. Translated by J.G. Dawson. Totowa, NJ: Barnes & Noble Books.

Aristotle. 1982. *The Politics*. Translated by T.A. Sinclair. Suffolk, UK: Penguin Books.

_____. 1985. *Nicomachean Ethics*. Translated by Terence Irwin. Indianapolis: Hackett Publishing Company.

Avineri, Shlomo. 1971. *The Social and Political Thought of Karl Marx*. Cambridge: Cambridge University Press.

Baker, Dean. 1994. Trade Reporting's Information Deficit. *Extra!* (November-December): 8–9.

Balibar, Etienne. 1995. *The Philosophy of Marx*. New York: Verso.

Baran, Paul. 1957. *The Political Economy of Growth*. New York: Modern Reader.

Bastiat, Frédéric. 1964. *Economic Harmonies*. Translated by W. Hayden Boyers. Princeton, NJ: D. Van Nostrand Company, Inc.

Bauman, Zygmunt. 1988. *Freedom*. Minneapolis: University of Minnesota Press.

Beck, Ulrich. 2000. Living Your Own Life in a Runaway World: Individualisation, Globalisation and Politics. In *Global Capitalism*, ed. Will Hutton and Anthony Giddens, 164–174. New York: New York Press.

Bhagwati, Jagdish. 1993. The Case for Free Trade. *Scientific American* (November): 42–49.

———. 2000. Globalization: a Moral Imperative. *UNESCO Courier* (September): 19–20.

———. 2004 *In Defense of Globalization*. New York: Oxford University Press.

Block, Fred. 2001. Introduction to *The Great Transformation*. Boston: Beacon Press.

Bloor, David. 1983. *Wittgenstein: A Social Theory of Knowledge*. New York: Columbia University Press.

Bock, Kenneth. 1994. *Human Nature Mythology*. Chicago: University of Illinois Press.

Bowles, Samuel, and Herbert Gintis. 1987. *Democracy and Capitalism: Property, Community, and the Contradictions of Modern Social Thought*. New York: Basic Books.

Bridbury, A.R. 1986. Markets and Freedom in the Middle Ages. In *The Market in History*, ed. B.L. Anderson and A.J.H. Latham, 79–120. Dover, NH: Croon Helm.

Brown, Viviennne. 1994. *Adam Smith's Discourse: Canonicity, Commerce and Conscience*. New York: Routledge.

Callari, Antonino. 1981. The Classical's Analysis of Capitalism. Ph.D. diss., University of Massachusetts, Amherst.

Chayanov, A.V. 1966. *The Theory of the Peasant Economy*. Homewood, IL: Richard D. Irwin, Inc.

Coase, Ronald. 1988. *The Firm, the Market, and the Law*. Chicago: University of Chicago Press.

Colletti, Lucio. 1974. *From Rousseau to Lenin*. New York: Monthly Review Press.

de Janvry, Alain. 1981. *The Agrarian Question and Reformism in Latin America*. Baltimore: The Johns Hopkins University Press.

DeMartino, George. 2000. *Global Economy, Global Justice: Theoretical and Policy Alternatives to Neoliberalism*. New York: Routledge.

———. 2003. Realizing Class Justice. *Rethinking Marxism* 15(1):1–32.

de Ste. Croix, G. E. M. 981. *The Class Struggle in the Ancient Greek World: From the Archaic Age to the Arab Conquests*. Ithaca, NY: Cornell University Press.

Dicken, Peter. 2003. *Global Shift: Reshaping the Global Economic map in the 21st Century*. New York: Guilford.

Dobb, Maurice. 1947. *Studies in the Development of Capitalism*. New York: International Publishers.

Economist. 2003. Let's all go to the yard sale. September 25th. http://www.economist.com/displaystory.cfm?story_id=2092719

———. 2005. Meg and the power of many. June 9th. http://www.economist.com/displaystory.cfm?story_id=4054876

Elliott, Larry, and Dan Atkinson. 1998. *The Age of Insecurity.* New York: Verso.

Emmanuel, Arghiri. 1972. *Unequal Exchange: A Study of the Imperialism of Trade.* New York: Monthly Review.

Engardio, Pete, Aaron Bernstein, and Manjeet Kripalani. 2003. Is Your Job Next? *Business Week,* February 3: 50–60.

Engels, Frederick. 1980. *The Condition of the Working Class in England.* Moscow: Progress Publishers.

Engler, Mark. 2004. The Trouble with CAFTA. *The Nation* (web only), February 2. http://www.thenation.com/doc.mhtml?i=20040202&s=engler (accessed on July 22, 2005).

Evans, Don. 2001. Remarks by Secretary of Commerce Donald L. Evans Before the Woodrow Wilson Center for International Scholars. June 12, Washington, DC. (As Prepared For Delivery).

———. 2004. Secretary of Commerce Don Evans' Speech to the Department of Commerce Iraq Investment and Reconstruction Conference, Wednesday, February 11. (As Prepared for Delivery).

Evensky, Jerry. 1992. Ethics and the Classical Liberal Tradition in Economics. *History of Political Economy* 24, no. 1 (Spring): 61–77.

Ferguson, Adam. 1767. *History of Civil Society.* Edinburgh. Quoted in Karl Marx. *Capital,* 474, New York: Penguin Classics, 1990.

Finley, M.I. 1970. Aristotle and Economic Analysis. *Past and Present* 47, May: 3–25.

Finnegan, William. 2002. Leasing the Rain. *The New Yorker.* April 8. http://www.newyorker.com/fact/content/?020408fa_FACT1 (accessed May 10, 2005).

Fisch, Max. 1970. Introduction to *The New Science Of Giambattista Vico.* Ithica: Cornell University Press.

Frank, Andre Gunder. 1967. *Capitalism and Underdevelopment in Latin America.* New York: Monthly Review Press.

———. 1979. *Dependent Accumulation and Underdevelopment.* New York: Monthly Review Press.

Frei, Eduardo. 1967. Christian Democracy in Theory and Practice. In *The Ideologies of the Developing Nations,* ed. Paul Sigmund, 384–90. New York: Frederick A. Praeger.

Friedman, Milton. 1962. *Capitalism and Freedom.* Chicago: University of Chicago Press.

Friedman, Thomas. 2000. *The Lexus and the Olive Tree.* New York: Anchor Books.

Foucault, Michel. 1972. *The Archaeology of Knowledge and the Discourse on Language.* New York: Pantheon Books.

Gerschenkron, Alexander. 1962. *Economic Backwardness in Historical Perspective.* Cambridge, MA: Harvard University Press.

Gordon, Cyrus. 1965. *The Ancient Near East.* New York: Norton.

Hardt, Michael and Antonio Negri. 2000. *Empire.* Boston: Harvard University Press.

Harvey, David. 1982. *The Limits to Capital.* Chicago: The University of Chicago Press.

Heilbroner, Robert, and William Milberg. 1995. *The Crisis of Vision in Modern Economic Thought*. New York: Cambridge University Press

Held, David, and Anthony McGrew. 2002. The Great Globalization Debate: An Introduction. In *The Global Transformations Reader*, eds. David Held and Anthony McGrew, 1–46. Malden, MA: Blackwell Publishers, Ltd.

Henwood, Doug. 1996. Antiglobalization. *Left Business Observer* 71:1–2.

————. 2002. Bubble accounting. *Left Business Observer* 102:1–2.

Hertz, Noreena. 2001. *The Silent Takeover: Global Capitalism and the Death of Democracy*. New York: Harper Business.

Hilton, Rodney, ed. 1976. *The Transition from Feudalism to Capitalism*. London: Verso.

Hirschman, Albert. 1977. *The Passions and the Interests: Political Arguments for Capitalism before its Triumph*. Princeton, NJ: Princeton.

————. 1986. Rival Views of Market Society. *Rival Views of Market Society and Other Recent Essays*, 105–41. New York: Viking.

Hobbes, Thomas. 1986. *Leviathan*. New York: Penguin.

Hoogvelt, Ankie. 1997. *Globalization and the Postcolonial World: the new Political Economy of Development*. Baltimore: Johns Hopkins University Press.

Huffington, Arianna. 2003. *Pigs at the Trough: How Corporate Greed and Political Corruption are Undermining America*. New York: Three Rivers Press.

Hume, David. 1898. *Essays Moral, Political, and Literary*. Vol. 1. ed. T.H. Green and T.H. Grose. London: Longmans, Green and Co.

Jani, Pravav. 2002. Karl Marx, Eurocentrism, and the 1857 Revolt in British India. In *Marxism, Modernity and Postcolonial Studies*, ed. C. Bartolovich and N. Lazarus, 81–100. Cambridge: Cambridge University Press.

Kauder, F. 1953. Genesis of the Marginal Utility Theory, from Aristotle to the End of the Eighteenth Century. *Economic Journal* 63: 638–50.

Keen, Steve. 2001. *Debunking Economics: The Naked Emperor of the Social Sciences*. New York: Pluto Press.

Kern, William. 1983. Returning to the Aristotelian paradigm: Daly and Schumacher. *History of Political Economy* 15: 501–12.

Kettle, Martin. 2001. Blind Spots Blight Bush's Rosy Vision of the World. *Guardian Weekly*, April 26-May 2: 7.

Keynes, John Maynard. 1973. *The General Theory of Employment, Interest and Money*. Cambridge: Cambridge University Press.

Khor, Martin. 2001. *Rethinking Globalization: Critical Issues and Policy Choices*. New York: Zed Books.

Klammer, Arjo and Jennifer Meehan. 1999. The crowding out of academic economists. In *What do Economists Know: New economics on knowledge*, ed. Robert Garnett, Jr., 65–85. London and New York: Routledge.

Kopytoff, Igor. 1986. The Cultural Biography of Things. In *The Social Life of Things: Commodities in Cultural Perspective*, ed. Arjun Appadurai, 64–91. New York: Cambridge University Press.

Korten, David. 1996. The Mythic Victory of Market Capitalism. In *The Case Against the Global Economy*, ed. Jerry Mander and Edward Goldsmith, 183–91. San Francisco: Sierra Club Books.

Krugman, Paul. 1999. *The Return of Depression Economics*. New York: Norton.
_____. 2003. America the Scofflaw. In *The Great Unraveling: Losing Our Way in the New Century,* 385–37. New York: Norton.
Kuttner, Robert. 1997. *Everything for Sale: The Virtues and Limits of Markets*. New York: Alfred A. Knopf.
Kyer, Krystal. 2002. Another Bad Trade Pact: From NAFTA to CAFTA. *Counterpunch*. http://www.counterpunch.org/kyer0912.html (accessed March 12, 2004).
Laclau, Ernesto. 1971. Feudalism and Capitalism in Latin America. *New Left Review,* 67: 19–37.
Laclau, Ernesto, and Chantelle Mouffe. 1985. *Hegemony and Socialist Strategy*. London: Verso.
Lefebvre, Henri. 1991. *Critique of Everyday Life*. Translated by John Moore. London: Verso.
Lewis, W. Arthur. 1954. Economic Development with Unlimited Supplies of Labor. In *The Manchester School*. Reprinted in *The Economics of Underdevelopment,* ed. A.N. Agarwala and L.P. Singh, 400–449. New York: Oxford University Press, 1963.
Lewis, T.J. 1978. Acquisition and Anxiety: Aristotle's Case Against the Market. *Canadian Journal of Economics* 11: 69–90.
Locke, John. 1960. *Two Treatises of Government*. New York: Cambridge University Press.
Lowry, S. Todd. 1974. Aristotle's 'Natural Limit' and the Economics of Price Regulation. *Greek, Roman and Byzantine Studies* 15(1): 57–62.
_____. 1979. Recent Literature on Ancient Greek Economic Thought. *Journal of Economic Literature* 17(1), March: 65–86.
_____. 1987a. *The Archaeology of Economic Ideas: The Classical Greek Tradition*. Durham: Duke University Press.
_____. 1987b. The Greek Heritage in Economic Thought. *Pre- Classical Economic Thought,* ed. S. Todd Lowry: 7–31. Boston: Kluwer Academic Publishers.
Lukács, Georg. 1994. *History and class consciousness: studies in Marxist Dialectics*. Translated by Rodney Livingstone. Cambridge, MA: MIT Press.
Lux, Kenneth. 1990. *Adam Smith's Mistake*. Boston, Shambhala.
MacLeod, Colin. 1998. *Liberalism, Justice, and Markets: A Critique of Liberal Equality*. Oxford: Clarendon Press.
Macpherson, C.B. 1962. *The Political Theory of Possessive Individualism: Hobbes to Locke*. London: Oxford University Press.
Mandeville, Bernard. 1962. *The Fable of the Bees*. New York: Capricorn Books.
Marx, Karl. 1969. *Theories of Surplus-value, Part I*. Moscow: Progress Publishers
_____. 1970. *A Contribution to the Critique of Political Economy*. New York: International Publishers.
_____. 1971. *Theories of Surplus-value, Part III*. Moscow: Progress Publishers.
_____. 1973. On the Question of Free Trade. Appendix in *The Poverty of Philosophy,* 180–195. Moscow: Progress Publishers.
_____. 1973. *The Poverty of Philosophy*. Moscow: Progress Publishers.

_____. 1990. *Capital, Volume I.* New York: Penguin Classics.

_____. 1991. *Capital, Volume III.* New York: Penguin Classics.

_____. 1992. *Capital, Volume II.* New York: Penguin Classics.

_____. 1993. *Grundrisse.* New York: Penguin Classics.

Marx, Karl and F. Engels. 1972. *On Colonialism.* New York: International Publishers.

McCloskey, Deirdre. 2000. Postmodern Market Feminism. *Rethinking Marxism* 12(4):27–36.

McIntyre, Richard. 2004. Globalization Goes for Therapy. *Rethinking Marxism* 16(1):101–108.

McNally, David. 1993. *Against the Market: Political Economy, Market Socialism and the Marxist Critique.* London, New York: Verso.

Meek, Ronald. 1956. *Studies in the Labor Theory of Value.* New York: Monthly Review.

Meikle, Scott. 1991. Aristotle on Equality and Market Exchange. *The Journal of Hellenic Studies* CXI: 193–6.

_____. 1995. *Aristotle's Economic Thought.* Oxford: Clarendon Press.

Mirowski, Philip. 2002. *Machine Dreams: Economics Becomes a Cyborg Science.* New York: Cambridge University Press.

Mishkin, Frederic. 1997. The Causes and Propagation of Financial Instability: Lessons for Policymakers. In *Proceedings of the Federal Reserve Bank of Kansas City* Aug: 55–96.

Monroe, Arthur. 1924. *Early Economic Thought.* Cambridge: Harvard University Press.

Moore, Stanley. 1993. *Marx Versus Markets.* University Park: The Pennsylvania State University Press.

Mouffe, Chantal. 1979. Hegemony and Ideology in Gramsci. In *Gramsci & Marxist Theory,* ed. Chantal Mouffe, 168–204. Boston: Routledge & Kegan Paul.

Myint, Hyman. 1954. An Interpretation of Economic Backwardness. *Oxford Economic Papers* 6(2): 132–63.

Myrdal, Gunner. 1953. *The Political Element in the Development of Economic Theory.* Translated from the German by Paul Streeton. London: Routledge & Paul.

North, Douglass. 1990. *Institutions, Institutional Change and Economic Performance.* Cambridge: Cambridge University Press.

Nurske, Ragnar. 1953. *Problems of Capital Formation in Underdeveloped Countries.* New York: Oxford University Press.

O'Brian, Robert. 2004. Globalisation, Imperialism and the Labour Standards Debate. In *Labour and Globalisation: Results and prospects,* ed. Ronaldo Munck, 52–70. Liverpool: Liverpool University Press

Olivera, Oscar. 2004. *Cochabamba: Water War in Boliva.* Boston: South End Press.

Ollman, Bertell. 1971. *Alienation: Marx's conception of man in capitalist society.* Cambridge, MA: Cambridge University Press.

Pack, Spencer. 1985. Aristotle and the Problem of Insatiable Desires: a comment on Kern's interpretation of Aristotle, with a reply by William S. Kern. *History of Political Economy* 17(3): 391–3.

Peet, Richard. 2003. *Unholy Trinity: The IMF, World Bank and WTO*. New York: Zed Books.

Plato. 1983. *The Republic*. Translated by Desmond Less. Bucks, UK: Hazell Watson & Viney Ltd.

————. 1976. *Protagoras*. Translated by C.C.W. Taylor. Oxford: Clarendon Press.

Polanyi, Karl. 2001. *The Great Transformation: The Political and Economic Origins of our Time*. Boston: Beacon Press.

————. 1968a. Aristotle Discovers the Economy. In *Primitive, Archaic and Modern Economies: Essays of Karl Polanyi*, ed. George Dalton, 78–115. Garden Cite, NY: Anchor Books Doubleday & Company, INC.

————. 1968b. The Self-regulating Market and the Fictitious Commodities: Land, Labor and Money. In *Primitive, Archaic and Modern Economies: Essays of Karl Polanyi*, ed. George Dalton, 26–37. New York: Anchor Books Doubleday & Company, INC.

Popkin, Samuel. 1979. *The Rational Peasant: the Political Economy of Rural Society in Vietnam*. Berkeley: University of California Press.

Public Citizen. 2005. CAFTA: Part of the FTAA Puzzle. http://www.citizen.org/trade/cafta/ (accessed May 10, 2005).

Resnick, Stephen, and Richard Wolff. 1987. *Knowledge and Class: A Marxian Critique of Political Economy*. Chicago: The University of Chicago Press.

————. 2002. *Class Theory and History: Capitalism and Communism in the U.S.S.R.* New York: Routledge.

Robinson, Joan. 1973. *Economic Heresies: Some Old-Fashioned Questions in Economic Theory*. New York: Basic Books.

Roll, Eric. 1946. *A History of Economic Thought*. New York: Prentice-Hall.

Rostow, W.W. 1960. *The Stages of Economic Growth: A Non-Communist Manifesto*. Cambridge: University Press.

Rousseau, Jean-Jacques. 1973. *On the Social Contract* and *The Discourses*. Translated by G.D.H. Cole. New York: Alfred A. Knopf, Inc.

Rubin, I.I. 1972. *Essays on Marx's Theory of Value*. Detroit: Black and Red Press.

————. 1989. *A History of Economic Thought*. London: Pluto Press.

Rupert, Mark. 2000. *Ideologies of Globalization: Contending visions of a New World Order*. New York: Routledge.

Samuelson, Paul and William Nordhaus.1989. *Microeconomics: A Version of Economics*. New York: McGraw-Hill Book Company.

Saunders, T.J. 1981. Reviser's introduction to *The Politics*, by Aristotle. Bungay, Soffolk: Richard Clay (The Chaucer Press) Ltd.

Schejtman, Alexander. 1988. The Peasant Economy: Internal Logic, Articulation, and Persistence. In *The Political Economy of Development and Underdevelopment*, ed. Charles Wilber, 364–391. 4th ed., New York: Random House Business Division.

Schultz, Theodore W. 1964. *Transforming Traditional Agriculture*. Chicago: University of Chicago Press.

Schumpeter, Joseph. 1954. *History of Economic Analysis,* ed. Elizabeth Boody Schumpeter. New York: Oxford University Press.

Sims, Kimberly. 2002. Political Community and Individual Gain: Aristotle, Adam Smith and the Problem of Exchange. Ph.D. diss., University of Massachusetts, Amherst.

Smith, Adam. 1981. *An Inquiry into the Nature and Causes of the Wealth of Nations.* Indianapolis: Liberty Classics.

————. 2000. *The Theory of Moral Sentiments.* Amherst, New York: Prometheus Books.

Sinisi, John. 1992. Economic Struggles and Economic Development: Transformations in the Development of a Theme. Ph.D. diss., University of Massachusetts, Amherst.

Soros, George. 2002. *On Globalization.* New York: Public Affairs.

Soudek, Josef. 1952. Aristotle's Theory of Exchange: An Inquiry into the Origin of Economic Analysis. *Proceedings of the American Philosophical Society* 96(1): 45–75.

Stace, W.T. 1955. *The Philosophy of Hegel.* New York: Dover.

Staveren, Irene van. 1999. *Caring for Economics: An Aristotelian Perspective.* CW Delft: Eburon.

Stiglitz, Joseph. 2003. *Globalization and its Discontents.* New York: W.W. Norton. *Stop CAFTA.* 2005. An Activist's Guide to Stopping CAFTA. http://www.stopcafta.org/article.php?list=type&type=2 (accessed July 20, 2005).

Sweezy, Paul. 1942. *The Theory of Capitalist Development.* New York: Modern Reader.

————. 1976. A Critique. In *The Transition from Feudalism to Capitalism,* ed. Rodney Hilton, 33–56. Old Woking, Surrey: Verso.

Taussig, Michael. 1980. *The Devil and Commodity Fetishism in South America.* Chapel Hill: University of North Carolina Press.

Tawney, R.H. 1954. *Religion and the Rise of Capitalism.* New York: Mentor Books.

Tax, Sol. 1953. *Penny Capitalism: A Guatemalan Indian Economy.* Washington: U.S. Government Printing Office.

Thucydides. 1982. *The Peloponnesian War.* (The Crawley Translation). New York: Modern Library.

Tomlinson, John. 2004. Cultural Imperialism. In *The Globalization Reader,* eds. Frank Lechner and John Boli, 303–311. Malden, MA: Blackwell Publishing.

U.S. Department of State. Methanex Corp. v. United States of America. http://www.state.gov/s/l/c5818.htm (accesses May 20, 2005).

Vico, Giambattista. 1970. *The New Science of Giambattista Vico.* Translated from the third edition by Thomas Goddard Bergin and Max Harold Fisch. Ithaca, New York: Cornell University Press.

Voice of America. 2005. Bush Signs CAFTA. An editorial reflecting the views of the United States Government. August 5. http://www.voanews.com/uspolicy/2005–08–05–voa4.cfm

Wallerstein, Immanuel. 1974. *The Modern World System: Capitalist Agriculture and the Origins of the European World Economy in the Sixteenth Century.* New York: Academic Press.

Walzer, Michael. 1994. *Thick and Thin: Moral Arguments at Home and Abroad.* Notre Dame, IN: University of Notre Dame Press.

Waridel, Laure. 2002. *Coffee with Pleasure: Just Java and World Trade.* New York: Black Rose Books.

Warren, Bill. 1980. *Imperialism: Pioneer of Capitalism.* London: NLB.

Watkins, Evan. 1998. *Everyday Exchanges: Marketwork and Capitalist Common Sense.* Stanford: Stanford University Press.

Weber, Max. 1958. *The Protestant Ethic and the Spirt of Capitalism.* New York: Charles Scribner's Sons.

Weisbrot, Mark, and Dean Baker. 2002. The Relative Impact of Trade Liberalization on Developing Countries. CEPR (Center for Economic and Policy) Research working paper, June 12, 2002. http://www.cepr.net/ publications/ trade_2002_06_12.htm (accessed March 12, 2004).

Wittgenstein, Ludwig. 1958. *Philosophical Investigations.* Translated by G.E.M. Anscombe. New York: MacMillian Publishing Co., Inc.

Wolff, Richard. 1995. Markets Do Not a Class Structure Make. In *Marxism in the Postmodern Age,* ed. Antonio Callari, Stephen Cullenberg, and Carole Biewener, 394–403. New York and London: Guilford Press.

_____. 2004. The 'Efficiency' Illusion. In *A Guide to What's Wrong With Economics,* ed. Edward Fullbrook, 169–175. London: Anthem Press.

Xenophon. 1890. Ways and Means. In *The works of Xenophon.* London and New York: Macmillan and Co.

Zoellick, Robert. 2001. The WTO and New Global Trade Negotiations: What's at Stake. Speech at the Council on Foreign Relations, Washington DC, October 30. (As prepared for delivery.)

_____. 2004. Council of the Americas, Remarks of USTR Robert B. Zoellick. May 3. (As prepared for delivery.)

Index